Queen Victoria's Daughters-in-Law

Queen Victoria's Daughters-in-Law

John Van der Kiste

First published in Great Britain in 2023 by
Pen & Sword History
An imprint of
Pen & Sword Books Ltd
Yorkshire – Philadelphia

Copyright © John Van der Kiste 2023

ISBN 978 1 39900 145 8

The right of John Van der Kiste to be identified as Author of this work has been asserted by him in accordance with the Copyright, Designs and Patents Act 1988.

A CIP catalogue record for this book is available from the British Library.

All rights reserved. No part of this book may be reproduced or transmitted in any form or by any means, electronic or mechanical including photocopying, recording or by any information storage and retrieval system, without permission from the Publisher in writing.

Typeset by Mac Style
Printed in the UK by CPI Group (UK) Ltd, Croydon, CR0 4YY.

Pen & Sword Books Limited incorporates the imprints of Atlas, Archaeology, Aviation, Discovery, Family History, Fiction, History, Maritime, Military, Military Classics, Politics, Select, Transport, True Crime, Air World, Frontline Publishing, Leo Cooper, Remember When, Seaforth Publishing, The Praetorian Press, Wharncliffe Local History, Wharncliffe Transport, Wharncliffe True Crime and White Owl.

For a complete list of Pen & Sword titles please contact

PEN & SWORD BOOKS LIMITED
47 Church Street, Barnsley, South Yorkshire, S70 2AS, England
E-mail: enquiries@pen-and-sword.co.uk
Website: www.pen-and-sword.co.uk

Or

PEN AND SWORD BOOKS
1950 Lawrence Rd, Havertown, PA 19083, USA
E-mail: Uspen-and-sword@casematepublishers.com
Website: www.penandswordbooks.com

Contents

Acknowledgements	vii
Introduction	viii
Part I: The Early Victorian Years 1840–74	1
Chapter 1	3
Chapter 2	7
Chapter 3	29
Part II: The Mid-Victorian Years 1874–87	49
Chapter 1	51
Chapter 2	73
Part III: The Later Victorian Years 1887–1901	89
Chapter 1	91
Chapter 2	112
Chapter 3	122
Part IV: The Edwardian Era 1901–10	137
Chapter 1	139
Chapter 2	150
Chapter 3	163
Part V: The Georgian Era 1910–25	171
Chapter 1	173
Chapter 2	183
Chapter 3	199
Notes	206
Bibliography	215
Index	220

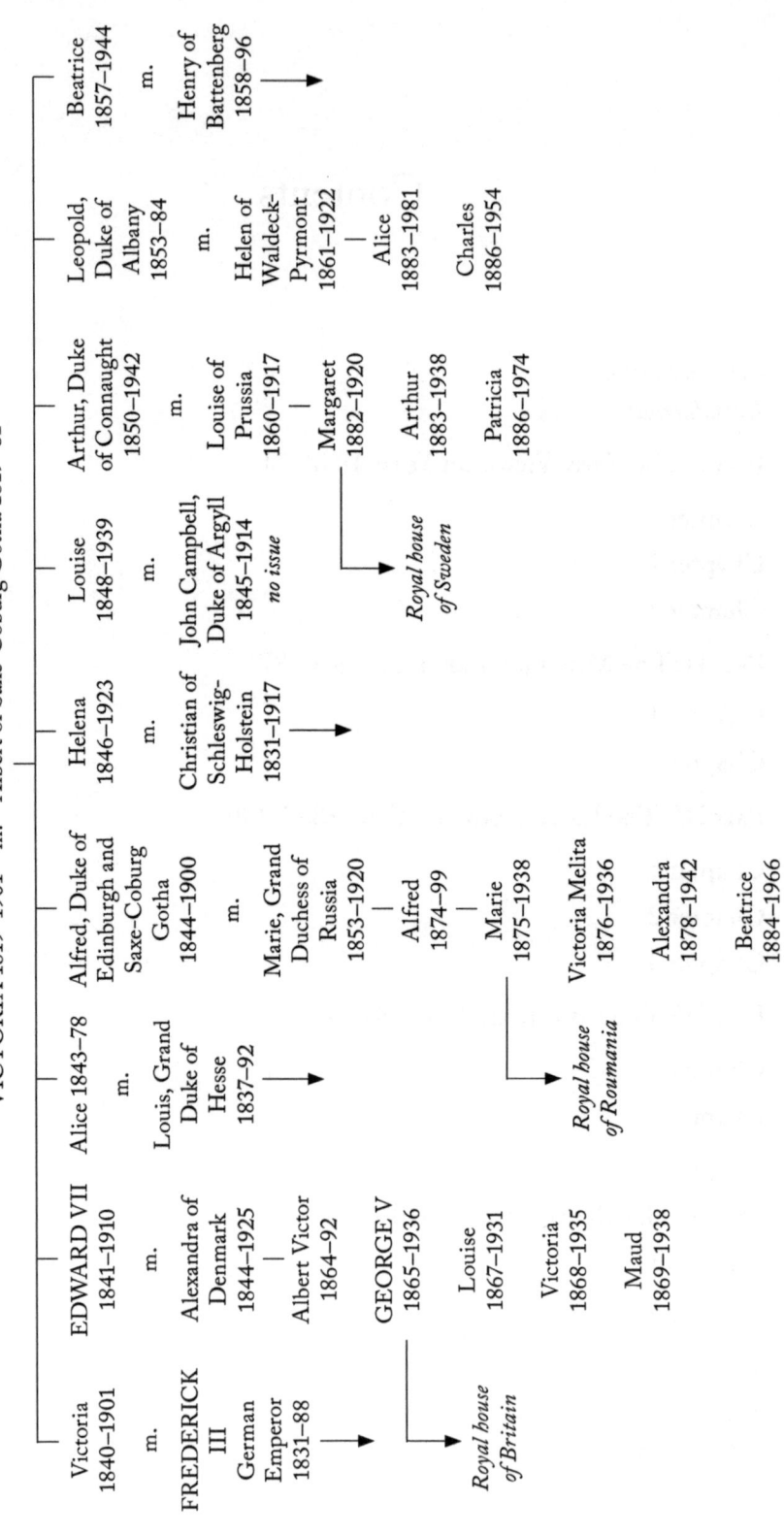

Acknowledgements

I would like to thank Her late Majesty Queen Elizabeth II for permission to quote from correspondence in the Royal Archives, Windsor; Doña Beatriz de Orleans-Borbon y Parodi Delfino, for permission to quote from previously unpublished letters from the English translation of *Ena and Bee: In defence of a royal friendship*, by Ana de Sagrera; the Royal Archives, Madrid; Catherine Uecker, University of Chicago Library; and Karen Robson, Southampton University Archives, for access to and permission to quote material from their respective collections.

My particular gratitude goes to Sue Woolmans for her sterling work in undertaking research at the Royal Archives, Windsor (to say nothing of several very interesting discussions by email on the personalities of the four royal and imperial ladies who are the subject of this book), and Julie Crocker, Senior Archivist, and Colin Parrish, at the Archives, for their help in providing access to the correspondence; Ricardo Mateos Sáinz de Medrano, for obtaining and sending me material from the Royal Archives and the John Wimbles Papers, Madrid; and to Coryne Hall, for her useful feedback and useful answers to various queries. I would also like to thank my editors at Pen & Sword, Claire Hopkins, Laura Hirst, Lori Jones, Amy Jordan, Lucy May, and Alan Murphy, for helping to see the work through to publication; Luvy Lubker, who originally suggested the subject as an idea for a forthcoming book; and my wife Kim, for her invaluable support during the three years that saw it gradually take shape.

Introduction

Queen Victoria had four sons and five daughters, and as a matriarch who always expected high standards of her children, she was equally demanding of those who married into the family. To be one of her daughters-in-law did not mean an easy life, and on occasion those who married into the family may have wondered what they had let themselves in for. All were women of determined character to a certain extent, although only the second one, born Grand Duchess Marie Alexandrovna of Russia, was known as the only member of the family whom the queen was unable to intimidate. They were likewise all sometimes exasperated by her efforts to control their lives, her constant interference in their private matters, her obstinacy and bursts of selfishness. Nevertheless, they all admired, liked, loved and respected her as a mother and sovereign, and appreciated that one has to be cruel to be kind.

In recent years, there has been a tendency towards revisionism in the biographies of some writers, and in television documentaries, to portray Queen Victoria in a harsher light as a selfish, ill-tempered, domineering control freak. It is always easy to be selective in one's research to present a more negative picture of any historical character for the sake of it, and therefore just as easy to lose a sense of proportion in exaggerating his or her faults. As a mother and sovereign, she always believed that she needed to respect the best interests of her kingdom on one hand, and the personal needs of her children and their families on the other. It was a delicate balancing act, and mistakes were inevitably made. Credit has to be given to any parent faced with often conflicting demands, particularly one who did not have the benefit of a happy childhood themselves. Hers was a lonely, difficult upbringing in a single-parent family. Her widowed mother, the Duchess of Kent, was a stranger in a strange land with a poor command of English, a woman with a strong moral compass, dominated by her secretary and comptroller John Conroy, who ruthlessly tried to manipulate her and her small daughter for his own ends, and surrounded by a family whose attitudes towards her varied between friendliness and profound suspicion. Victoria had no other family, apart from two much older half-siblings living in Germany, whom she rarely saw.

When it came to bringing up her own family, seeing them marry and have families of their own, she had no role model apart from a husband whose own early life had likewise been a sad one, largely without the presence of a mother, and who, like his mother, died unexpectedly young. No family is perfect with regard to its relationships, and that of Queen Victoria (as well as Prince Albert) was anything but perfect. She had her faults; prone to favouritism, she did not always understand high-spirited youngsters; she could be, and often was, very demanding, and on occasion remarkably tactless. Yet she was also capable of great generosity, and understood when her adult sons and their wives were in particular trouble, not necessarily of their own making.

Part I

The Early Victorian Years 1840–74

Chapter 1

On 10 February 1840 Queen Victoria married Prince Albert, second son of Ernest, Duke of Saxe-Coburg Gotha. Both were grandchildren of Francis, Duke of Saxe-Coburg-Saalfeld, whose children included Duke Ernest, King Leopold of the Belgians, and Victoria, who had married firstly Emich Charles, Prince of Leiningen, and after his death Edward, Duke of Kent and Strathearn, fourth son of King George III. The duke died suddenly of pneumonia in January 1820, leaving Victoria a widow for the second time, after only eighteen months of married life. The future queen was only aged eight months at the time.

Victoria and Albert's first child, Victoria, Princess Royal ('Vicky'), was born on 21 November 1840. When told that she was the mother of a princess, the slightly disappointed queen assured the doctor that the next would be a prince. She kept her word. Within three months she was *enceinte* for the second time, and on 9 November Albert Edward, Prince of Wales, was born. The pattern was maintained with another daughter, Alice, on 25 April 1843, and a second son, Alfred, on 6 August 1844. After two more daughters, Helena on 25 May 1846, and Louise on 18 March 1848, came Arthur, the third son, on 1 May 1850, and Leopold, the fourth, on 7 April 1853. The family of nine was completed with the birth of Beatrice on 14 April 1857.

From childhood, the four brothers all differed considerably in personality and interests. The Prince of Wales, who was always known formally as Albert Edward while Prince of Wales and more informally within the family as 'Bertie', was destined to bear the cross of his mother's resentment for many years. She had been greatly annoyed by a second pregnancy coming so quickly after the first, and by a severe labour during his birth. In his personality she saw some of the Hanoverian faults of character that she recognised in herself, saying that he was her 'caricature'. As a child he seemed apathetic, backward and slow to learn, in comparison to his remarkably quick-witted, precocious elder sister.

Although they remained close to each other throughout life, when he was small she was inclined to make fun of him for being slow and for having a stammer, which he soon outgrew. His frustration at an inability to learn to the high standards expected of him by his father and his parents' unofficial adviser, the Coburg physician Baron Christian von Stockmar, led to tantrums in the nursery and a tendency to scream, throw things around and stamp his foot until he was exhausted. At first his governess, Lady Lyttelton, a woman of remarkable understanding, was the only one who really appreciated his positive qualities. She saw that beneath his often bad-tempered exterior he could be very friendly, even charming. He was less given to lying than his elder sister who could be devious, and that unlike his father he was an outgoing personality who much preferred people to books. The queen regretted that he had inherited his antipathy towards learning and intellectual pursuits from her, saying, 'he is my caricature.'[1]

Alfred, known as 'Affie', showed signs of being much more like his father. He was a placid and industrious boy, yet at the same time a cheerful character with none of his father's predispositions to severe melancholy. Completely fearless, he could soon walk unaided and thought nothing of climbing out of windows, balancing precariously on ledges thirty feet or more above ground, leaping across streams before he could swim, or sliding down banisters. He had several lucky escapes from serious injury and was scolded for taking such unnecessary risks, but it never deterred him from doing the same thing again another day. While he always got on very well with his brothers and sisters, he was equally happy to be left to his own devices, always finding something to do like experimenting with toys and later building his own. As a quick learner who showed great aptitude for geography and the sciences, he rapidly became his father's favourite son. Albert was inclined to regret that this boy would never inherit the British crown, unless anything happened to his elder brother. However, he consoled himself with the knowledge that he was heir to the family's inheritance in Germany, the duchy of Saxe-Coburg Gotha, should Duke Ernest II and his wife Alexandrine fail to produce an heir.

During her seventh pregnancy in the spring of 1850, Queen Victoria decided that if her forthcoming child was a boy, she would name him Arthur, in honour of Arthur Wellesley, Duke of Wellington, the victor at the Battle of Waterloo. He was born on 1 May, which coincidentally was the venerable duke's eighty-first birthday, and the latter was delighted when asked by his sovereign to be the prince's godfather. It was therefore appropriate that from the cradle, young Arthur should be fascinated by anything to do with the army. The sight of a red uniform, the sound of a military band, or even just watching the changing of the guard at Buckingham Palace, always had him spellbound. 'Arta is going to be a soldier',[2] he would inform the family. A strong, healthy baby, and a well-behaved, even-tempered lad with none of the irritability or tantrums of the elder children, he had Affie's courage but not his recklessness. In his mother's eyes he was, and always remained, the least troublesome and most obedient of the nine children, and her undoubted favourite. In October 1858 she wrote to her husband, now prince consort, a memorandum in which she praised the eight-year-old boy who was 'dearer than any of the others put together, thus after you he is the dearest and most precious object to me on Earth'.[3]

Healthwise, Leopold would be the family's problem child. The queen's eighth confinement was the first to be eased by chloroform, and his birth on 7 April 1853 was trouble-free. She recovered rapidly, but he failed to thrive, suffered from weak digestion, which made him thinner than his brothers and sisters, and his cry was strangely feeble. When learning to walk he bruised easily after falling over and cried out in pain, whereas any other little boy would have shrugged it off and carried on. Soon the doctors diagnosed that he suffered from the grave and incurable condition of haemophilia, the hereditary bleeding disease that may have originated in Queen Victoria herself. To add to his woes, he was diagnosed with a mild form of epilepsy before he was one year old. Queen Victoria was always over-protective of him, much to his resentment; he longed to be treated just like his stronger brothers and disliked being given special treatment. Despite the medical diagnosis, Prince Albert seemed to hope it was no more than a passing condition that the boy would grow out of by adolescence. He did what he could to ensure that Leopold received as normal an upbringing as possible.

As frailty always prevented him from leading the active life for which he longed, he soon showed signs of being in intellect the equal of his father and eldest sister. He learned to read with ease when he was small, was rarely seen without a book in his hand, and his choice of literature was often quite advanced for such a tender age. As soon as he saw the

Italian paintings in his father's study at Osborne, he was keen to learn all about them, and soon acquired a remarkable knowledge of Renaissance art. When he was confined to the sofa after his regular accidents and injuries, his father let him use his paints and helped to guide his hand as he began creating his own pictures. He loved music, and made remarkably swift progress with his piano lessons. Between illnesses he was allowed to ride under strict supervision, join the other children with their amateur dramatic performances, and go on walks in the countryside where he enjoyed searching for geological specimens.

In the summer and autumn of 1860 the Prince of Wales was sent on a tour of North America lasting several weeks, during which he opened the railway bridge over the St Lawrence river at Montreal and laid the foundation stone of the Federal Parliament building at Ottawa. He was cheered enthusiastically wherever he went, and his parents were impressed rather more than they might have been ready to admit, that the son of whom they had expected so little had acquitted himself so well. He had been very popular, Victoria wrote to his elder sister, the Princess Royal, now Princess Frederick William of Prussia, 'and really deserved the highest praise, which should be given him all the more as he was never spared any reproof.'[4]

As the young man of almost nineteen years of age, who would be sovereign if anything should suddenly happen to Queen Victoria, it was essential that careful thought should be given to the princess who would be his wife and later queen.

Chapter 2

In 1842 Prince Christian of Schleswig-Holstein-Sonderburg-Glucksburg, a prince from a junior branch of the House of Oldenburg that had ruled Denmark since the fifteenth century, married Princess Louise of Hesse-Cassel. Between 1843 and 1858 they produced a family of three sons and three daughters. Frederick, destined to become King Frederick VIII, was the first, born in 1843, followed a year later by Alexandra ('Alix'), on 1 December 1844 in the Yellow Palace, Copenhagen, next to Amalienborg Palace, the King of Denmark's official residence. During childhood she would always be closest to the siblings who immediately followed her, brother William ('Willie') in 1845 and Dagmar ('Minnie') two years later, and when Alix and Minnie were small, they shared a draughty attic bedroom together. After a gap of six years the last two arrived, Thyra in 1853 and Waldemar in 1858.

The children were a lively, extrovert crowd, enjoying rough-and-tumble humour and practical jokes. They learned to speak English from their earliest years, partly as they had English nurses and tutors, and the princesses also became fluent in French and German. Although given careful religious instruction and remaining devout, unquestioning Christians throughout their lives, their intellectual education was somewhat sparse. The author Hans Christian Andersen was a regular guest, and it would be a special treat for the children when he told them stories at bedtime.

None of them had particularly artistic or intellectual tastes, although they inherited their mother's love of music, and the daughters would sometimes play quartets with her at two pianos. Alexandra was particularly good at needlework, and like the others she was taught to make her own clothes. She and Dagmar were taught to swim by a Swedish sportswoman, Nancy Edberg. They shared in general household chores and took their turns in waiting at table.

One of the future Queen Alexandra's earliest biographers noted discreetly that 'for such studies as were elegant or amusing she had a natural aptitude, but in those that required serious application her progress was slow.'[1] As a child she was considered the prettiest of the sisters, quick-tempered, kindhearted, inclined to be a tomboy, and unfailingly unpunctual, a trait for which she would be notorious throughout her adult life. Though not particularly clever, she was intelligent, sometimes wise beyond her years, and with a sense of tact that made her a much-valued family peacemaker when quarrels arose – which they rarely did in the remarkably united Danish royal family. She adored animals, and one day in the streets of Copenhagen she spoke angrily to a man whom she saw ill-treating his dog. At first he told her to mind her own business, but when told who he was talking to, he apologised profusely. She then told him brusquely that he ought to be ashamed of himself to invent excuses for his cruelty only after he had found out who she was.

Once every two years, the family would spend their summer holidays at Schloss Rumpenheim, near Frankfurt, the property of Princess Christian's relations, the Hesse-Cassel family. Apart from various royals, there were several other guests associated with the royal courts, including on occasion the Danish ambassador to the Diet in Frankfurt, Bernhard von Bülow and his family. Their small son, also called Bernhard, regularly played and fought with the children. In later years, the princesses would fearlessly tease the man who was to become Imperial German Chancellor for his lack of chivalry when they had been small. To this he retorted that he was handled quite roughly himself by the young princesses who always gave as good as they got. Alexandra and Dagmar, he thought, were both lively and clever, the younger one (Thyra) even more so, but 'desperately hard-headed'.[2]

By 1859, the year that the Prince of Wales celebrated his eighteenth birthday, Queen Victoria and the prince consort agreed there should be no delay in helping him to settle down with a wife and secure the royal succession. Choosing the princess who would ultimately be queen consort of Great Britain was a task that required some care. Princess Frederick William of Prussia was asked to help, and she asked the advice of her lady-in-waiting, Walburga Hohenthal. For a while, the most likely one among the possible Protestant princesses throughout Europe was Elizabeth of Wied. She was rejected as 'rather dowdy' and 'the opposite to Bertie's usual taste'. Various other young princesses from Germany, the Netherlands and Sweden were then considered.

An anonymous correspondent in *The Times* in July 1858 contributed an article including a list of 'the only ladies of royal blood who, as Protestants, are eligible for the hand of the Prince of Wales'. The seven mentioned were princesses from Prussia, Hesse, Holstein-Glucksburg, Württemberg and Saxe-Altenburg, plus a Grand Duchess of Russia. 'Without venturing upon prophecy,' it said, number five on the list was the one considered the most eligible – Princess Alexandra of Denmark.[3]

It was a bold but prescient forecast. On political grounds alone, Princess Frederick William and her mother had decided that a Danish bride would be unsuitable. Tension was increasing between Denmark and the German Confederation over the matter of the duchies of Schleswig and Holstein, and Queen Victoria and the prince consort had, unsurprisingly, always been traditionally pro-German in their sympathies. Moreover, the queen dreaded the possible influence of Princess Christian's relations, of whom she had heard so many negative remarks, and that of the young princess herself, on her eldest son.

Another factor was the close link between the Danish royal family and the Cambridges, the cousins whom she viewed with mixed feelings. Much as she liked her cousin George, Duke of Cambridge, and the dowager duchess, she strongly disapproved of the duchess's daughters, Grand Duchess Augusta of Mecklenburg-Strelitz and Princess Mary Adelaide. It was just as well that she was unaware of discussions between the duchess and Admiral van Dickum, the Danish minister in London, concerning the chances of a marriage between the British heir and the Danish princess. They had no power or influence in such matters, but it was significant that the idea had come to them at a time when it was being rejected for political reasons by the heir's parents.

When Walburga Hohenthal, who married Augustus Paget, British minster in Copenhagen, in October 1860, was invited to dine at Windsor Castle shortly afterwards and seated next to the prince consort, he told him she thought Alexandra of Denmark 'the most charming, pretty, and delightful young Princess it was possible to imagine'.[4] Only then did he and the queen begin to have a change of heart about the bride for their son whom they had previously ruled out. Princess Frederick William was approached again, and she declared that Alexandra was indeed lovely.

There was one momentary cause for alarm when it was reported that she had a small scar on her neck, which was feared to be a sign of disease but turned out to be merely the legacy of a minor childhood accident. She had seen several people who had seen her recently and gave 'such accounts of her beauty, her charm, her amiability, her frank natural manner and many excellent qualities'. In spite of this, she reiterated that any alliance with Denmark would be a grave misfortune for her as a Prussian. The normally reserved prince consort needed little if any persuasion, exclaiming that after seeing her photograph, he 'would marry her at once.'[5] Queen Victoria agreed that she was excellent; 'what a pity she is who she is!'[6]

After further discussions in April 1861, the prince consort took the Prince of Wales into his confidence, advising him that the time had come to consider the issue of his marriage. The queen was displeased with the behaviour and appearance of her eldest son, and feared that Princess Alexandra might not accept him, but nevertheless the Prince of Wales expressed an interest in meeting her. That summer he was due to spend some time at the Curragh near Dublin on military training. After that it had been arranged that he would be visiting German army manoeuvres in the Rhineland and visiting his sister, who had become Crown Princess of Prussia at the beginning of the year, who would be staying at Baden. This was conveniently near to Rumpenheim, where the princess and her family would be at the time.

A rendezvous was arranged to take place at Speyer Cathedral on 24 September. The Crown Prince and Princess of Prussia were present, as were Prince and Princess Christian and their daughter. All of them were pleased that the young people seemed favourably impressed with one another. They spent that night in the same hotel at Heidelberg, and before saying goodbye they exchanged signed photographs. In particular the crown prince and princess were prepared to put aside any political objections to the idea of such a marriage, and were very satisfied with the way the meeting had gone. The latter said that Princess Alexandra had definitely 'made an impression on Bertie, though in his own funny, undemonstrative way,' and that he told her afterwards 'he had never seen a young lady who pleased him so much'.[7]

The Prince of Wales was more non-committal, writing afterwards that the young lady of whom he had heard so much was 'charming and very pretty'.[8] To the dismay of his parents and sister he seemed unsure, not of the princess herself – whom he evidently liked – but of the mere idea of marriage. The queen was surprised by his apparent lack of enthusiasm, suspecting that he could not be in love, let alone 'capable of enthusiasm about anything in the world'.[9] While she, if not also her eldest daughter, were almost prepared to give up any idea of such a match, the prince consort was prepared to put pressure on his recalcitrant son, telling him firmly that he must not indulge in a general vague apprehension that one day he might meet someone else he would like better.[10]

A few days later, gossip that had been circulating around London society for some time at last reached the ears of the prince consort. While at camp at the Curragh a few weeks earlier, his eldest son had had a brief fling with an actress, Nellie Clifden. Most fathers at that time would have shrugged it off with barely a second thought, but the prince consort, the one paragon of virtue in a family not known for its strong collective moral compass, was horrified. He wrote an angry, despairing letter to his son and was duly assured that it was all over and finished with. Although he was already unwell, he made a special journey to Cambridge and had a long talk with him, during which he forgave him for his unseemly behaviour. It would be the last meeting they ever had under normal circumstances.

While they were out walking together, they were caught in the rain and the father was soaked to the skin. He returned to Windsor Castle, relieved but exhausted, and took to his bed not long afterwards. For years it was believed that he had caught typhoid fever, perhaps partly as a result of bad sanitation at Windsor, but more recent research has suggested it was stomach cancer, or a serious form of what was later diagnosed as Crohn's Disease. The queen was assured almost to the end by his doctors that he would recover, perhaps because they were too much in awe of her to dare suggest otherwise. Yet he had previously admitted that if he was ever to have a serious illness he would not recover. On the evening of 14 December he died, aged forty-two.

Once the queen had recovered from her initial grief, she was determined that the plans for her son's marriage would go ahead, although mourning prevented any immediate engagement. She was intending to visit Germany, mainly to make a sentimental journey to Rosenau, her husband's childhood home. Wanting to see the princess for herself, she arranged to visit her uncle Leopold, King of the Belgians, at Laeken, close to Ostend where Prince and Princess Christian would be staying with their family. She arrived at Laeken on 2 September, and met them all the following day. Everybody was rather ill at ease, but the nervous and shy princess made a good impression on the equally shy and rather less than confident queen, who presented her with a sprig of white heather that had been picked by the Prince of Wales at Balmoral as an emblem of good luck.

Meanwhile, the prince was about to make a special journey from England to Ostend, and come to join the party at Laeken. On 9 September they were all there, and King Leopold tactfully suggested they should go for a walk in the gardens, where the prince and princess should be allowed to lag behind the rest of them. They had been brought up to expect that their marriage would be an arranged one, and that their choices would be limited, especially in his case. By the time they returned, the prince had proposed and been accepted.

From his point of view, the choice of Princess Alexandra was an excellent one. Everybody around him had nothing but the highest praise for her; he had seen for himself how charming and warmhearted she was, and how much she wanted to marry him. Three days after she had accepted him, he wrote to Queen Victoria that he 'did not think it possible to love a person so much as I love her.'[11] As for the bride, she was a member of a not particularly wealthy royal family, now betrothed to the most eligible bachelor in the world.

A few days later, the family dispersed. The Prince of Wales was going to join the Crown Prince and Princess of Prussia on a Mediterranean cruise, an expedition that had been hastily arranged, partly as both the latter were very unpopular at the court of Berlin for having arranged an Anglo-Danish marriage alliance which did not suit German political interests, and they were advised that a period of absence would be in order. On 1 November Queen Victoria officially gave her consent to the engagement.[12] She had decided that Alexandra must come to stay with the family at Osborne for several weeks, and the bride-to-be arrived in England from Denmark on 5 November. In later years she would admit that as a young woman of seventeen she had been extremely frightened at the prospect, without even a lady-in-waiting of her own allowed to accompany her. Nevertheless, she put on a brave face and got on extremely well with the queen and the younger children. During this time, she formed a strong bond with Alfred, who had half-hoped that his brother might lose interest in her so that he would then be able to marry her himself. Mischievously, he persuaded her that it would be polite if she asked mama every afternoon whether she had enjoyed her forty winks.

Princess Mary Adelaide of Cambridge immediately noticed that the queen had become very fond of her, and after a visit to Osborne she saw a great change in her sovereign for the better. After nearly a year of widowhood and gloom, she was smiling again and even laughing a little. To the Crown Princess of Prussia, she wrote that she could hardly say how much she and everyone else loved her. 'She is so good, so simple, unaffected, frank, bright and cheerful, yet so quiet and gentle [...] one of those sweet creatures, who seem to come from the skies to help and bless poor mortals and lighten for a time their path!'[13] Nevertheless, the princess was refused one simple favour when she asked if she could bring one of her own Danish ladies-in-waiting with her to England once she was married. She was told firmly that it would never do for her to have someone to whom she could chatter regularly in a language her husband could not understand.

Queen Victoria may have been unenthusiastic about the Anglo-Scandinavian element, but many in Britain, both high and low, strongly disagreed. Lady Palmerston, wife of the then prime minister, spoke for many when she declared that she liked the Danish connection. 'We have had too much of Germany and Berlin and Coburgs.'[14]

In spite of the queen's disapproval, the princess returned to Denmark at her parents' insistence so she could celebrate her eighteenth birthday in her own home. She had decided that the betrothed couple were not to meet again before the wedding, which had been arranged for 10 March 1863. As that date was in the middle of Lent, some churchmen were shocked, but the queen had ruled out April because the first child of her second daughter, Alice, married to Prince Louis of Hesse and the Rhine, was expected then. She was superstitious about weddings that took place in the following month – according to an old saying, 'marry in May, and you'll rue the day'. Her objections were probably connected in part with the ceremony in May 1816 between her uncle Leopold and Princess Charlotte of Wales, a union that came to a tragic end with her death in childbirth eighteen months later. March it was going to be, despite protests from the clergy about Lent; marriage, she said firmly, was a solemn holy act, not to be 'classed with amusements'.

This was not the only stipulation that Queen Victoria made with regard to the wedding. She refused to invite any of the bride's Danish relations except for her immediate family, and as the marriage had been unfavourably received throughout much of Germany, several on the German side were similarly not invited. The exceptions included the Crown Prince and Princess of Prussia, who despite their reservations had encouraged the match all along, and the prince consort's elder brother, Ernest, Duke of Saxe-Coburg Gotha. Although he had not welcomed it, and described it as 'a thunder-clap for Germany', he entered into the family spirit of the occasion, sharing with the crown prince the duty of supporting the groom at the service. Much as the queen was enchanted with Princess Alexandra, she still considered her eldest son 'a very unpleasant element in the house', and thought that the sooner the wedding took place the better. She was *'very anxious* for the result,' she wrote to King Leopold, fearing that with regard to her hopes of future happiness, 'dear Alix is under a complete delusion'.[15]

The ceremony itself took place in the comparative privacy of St George's Chapel at Windsor Castle. Most of the public had expected that it would be either in St Paul's Cathedral or Westminster Abbey, and were disappointed that Her Majesty had chosen to stage it in what *Punch* magazine called 'an obscure Berkshire village, noted only for an old castle and non-sanatory [sic] arrangements.'[16]

Alexandra said *au revoir* to her old home at the end of February 1863 and sailed across the North Sea, then up the Thames to Gravesend on board the royal yacht *Victoria & Albert*. As she stepped aboard she was welcomed by the Mayor of Margate, and received his address of welcome, written on a scroll, with becoming dignity. Once the official committee's backs were turned, she was seen to hit her brother William on the head with it, both laughing helplessly. When the Prince of Wales stepped on to the deck to give her a hearty welcome on to English soil again, the crowds applauded ecstatically.

A couple of days later, shortly before the wedding, Queen Victoria took the bride and groom to the mausoleum at Frogmore, where her husband's remains had been interred three months previously. They stood before the tomb as she joined their hands together with the solemn words, *'He* gives you his blessing.' She attended the ceremony more as an observer than an active participant, watching from the royal closet above the chancel. Ladies of the household and royal family were asked to wear half-mourning of white, grey, mauve or purple, but the other guests were permitted any colour and jewellery that they wished.

The bride wore a dress of white satin trimmed with Honiton lace and orange blossom, while the groom was attired in his general's uniform. In the words of Charles Dickens, her face 'was the face of no ordinary bride, not simply a timid shrinking girl, but one with character distinctive of her own, prepared to act a part greatly'.[17] At luncheon in St George's Hall, Windsor Castle, after the ceremony, the former foreign secretary, the Earl of Clarendon, commented afterwards that he 'never saw in any one more grace & dignity & aplomb'. To one of her sisters-in-law, she said, 'you perhaps think that I like marrying your Brother for his position but if he was a cowboy I sh[oul]d love him just the same & w[oul]d marry no one else.'[18]

After the wedding the couple spent a week's honeymoon at Osborne. On their return to the mainland, they moved into their London residence, Marlborough House, and then spent Easter at Sandringham, the estate in Norfolk that had been given to the Prince of Wales the previous year.

Since the death of the prince consort, the few social events that were attended by royalty in public had ceased altogether. Even during his lifetime he had brought a staid influence to bear on such occasions when any representative of the royal family were present. Now the newly married Prince and Princess of Wales brought a much-needed *joie de vivre* to society life. Everyone who came face to face with her found her very attractive, charming, generous, and with a good word for all. The only people who had a mild issue with her were artists who found her an exceptionally restless sitter. The painter William Powell Frith, who had been commissioned to produce the official portrait of the bride, groom and family at the wedding ceremony, regretted she never understood 'that the keeping of her face in one position, for a few minutes only, was necessary to enable an artist to catch a resemblance of it.' After two or three attempts he took it upon himself to complain gently.[19]

Queen Victoria's unreserved approval of her new daughter-in-law was rather shortlived. She was accurate in saying that Alix understood her husband and showed plenty of character, but she was certainly not clever.

Before long she began to fear that the princess's health might not be up to the demands that her position and her husband were making of her. She was beginning to look sallow, overtired, and worst of all, seemed a little hard of hearing. As yet, hardly anybody knew that she had inherited this problem from her mother.

Bertie insisted that he was anxious to take care of his wife, but the queen thought they were too immature and irresponsible to take proper care of themselves, like two adolescents just let out of the schoolroom, free to do anything they wanted. She despaired at their 'going out every night till she will become a skeleton, and hopes there cannot be!' It was their duty, she believed, to set a good example to society, and no less important to apply themselves to their duty of providing an heir in the next generation. Instead of behaving sedately and taking care of each other at home, as she and Albert had done immediately after their wedding, both of them, she lamented, would 'soon be nothing but two puppets running about for show all day and night.'[20] It was an early example of what would be known many years later as 'the generation gap', with parents (or in this case a widowed parent) shaking their heads at the behaviour of their young and foolish offspring.

To use another term from a more modern age, Queen Victoria firmly believed in micro-management. Until she was eighteen, her movements and actions had been strictly controlled by her widowed mother, the Duchess of Kent, and her comptroller and confidant, Sir John Conroy. Although she had chafed at her lack of freedom, she would repeat this pattern with regard to her own children, and none more strictly than the eldest son, who was born to succeed her on the throne, and his wife.

She was ever-critical of her children when they were small and also as adults, and this would extend to their spouses. Although there was little she could do to prevent her married son and daughter-in-law from behaving how they wanted as long as they remained within the law, she could monitor their lives and routines to some extent. This extended to being kept secretly informed by members of their household as to such personal details as the princess's 'time of the month', thus ensuring that it would not clash with any balls or potentially strenuous activities at court as far as possible. Another problem with her eldest son and heir's wife was that the attractive and ever-conspicuous Princess of Wales was evidently much more popular with the public than she was, for all her unseen attention to state papers and other royal duties. Unlike her son and his wife, she was reluctant to acknowledge that royalty had to be seen to be loved and respected.

The queen did not have to wait long for what she discreetly referred to as 'hopes', and by midsummer the princess was expecting a child. It was only one of several important events that would affect her family in what proved to be a momentous year, for in June her favourite brother William was elected King of the Hellenes, taking the name of George I. The Greeks had deposed their unpopular and childless previous sovereign, King Otto, several months earlier, and in a plebiscite held to choose his successor, the candidate who polled far more votes than all the others put together was Queen Victoria's second son, Prince Alfred. Political considerations prevented him from accepting a throne that neither he nor his family wanted in the very least. Other potential sovereigns were considered unsuitable for some reason or else turned it down, and the Danish prince was chosen instead. The Princess of Wales admitted that the news made her very sad, for she was under no illusions as to the task that faced him in such a potentially unstable area of Europe. She prayed that God would give him strength and patience, 'to stand up to what the future may bring'.[21]

In November King Frederick VII of Denmark died, thus elevating his heir to the crown as King Christian IX. He immediately laid claim to the duchies of Schleswig and Holstein, while a rival affirmation came from Duke Frederick of Augustenburg, son of Queen Victoria's half-sister Feodora and a friend of Crown Prince Frederick William of Prussia from college days. He was supported by the crown prince and princess, and by Queen Victoria. This did not suit the now heavily-pregnant Princess of Wales, who proclaimed defiantly that the duchies were part of her father's kingdom. The crown princess recognised that her brother and his wife were 'thoroughly Danish in their sympathies'.[22] Family harmony was shattered at Windsor when the Crown Prince and Princess of Prussia and Feodora, who were all staying in England at the time, joined them. The Princess of Wales revealed a steely side to her character that nobody had yet seen. Almost at the end of her tether after persistent quarrels between them all, Queen Victoria took King Leopold's advice and forbade any further mention of Schleswig and Holstein in her presence.

The Princess of Wales expected her first child to be born in March or April 1864. As there was still much work to be done at Sandringham before they could live there, she and the prince spent Christmas at Frogmore House, former home of the late Duchess of Kent, in Windsor Park. The princess loved skating, and a frosty winter made conditions on the lake ideal. As she was about seven months pregnant, she could not take part herself and had to content herself with watching her husband and their friends from the comfort of a sledge-chair on the ice each afternoon. On 8 January she was suffering some twinges of pain, but she was determined not to be left indoors. The party returned to the house at dusk. Only then did her lady-in-waiting, the Countess of Macclesfield, herself the mother of thirteen children, realise that the time for her confinement had almost come. No nurse, baby clothes, or wet nurse were ready, as the event had not been expected for several weeks. Later that evening her first son was born. Being premature he was very small, weighing a mere 3¾lb.

Three days later, Queen Victoria reported to the Crown Princess of Prussia that he was quite healthy and thriving, and had 'a very pretty, well-shaped, round head, with very good features, a nice forehead, a very marked nose, beautiful little ears and pretty little hands.'[23] He was second in line to the throne, and his grandmother declared that the only names possible for him were Albert Victor, in honour of her and his late grandfather. His parents respected the decision, although they were displeased at not being allowed to make the choice themselves, and the prince was rather annoyed to hear that six-year-old Beatrice had told Lady Macclesfield that mama had done so already. He was christened at Windsor in March, and cried loudly throughout the ceremony at which his mother looked thin and unhappy.

There was little doubt that his mother's anxiety concerning the plight of Denmark had contributed to his early birth. Only eight days after her confinement, Prussia had sent the Danish government an ultimatum to evacuate Schleswig and Holstein within twenty-four hours. The Danes refused, and on 1 February a combined Prusso-Austrian force crossed the frontier into Schleswig. Despite its political sympathies, the British government was not prepared to go to the lengths of armed intervention in order to rescue King Christian and his domains from inevitable defeat at the hands of their stronger foes. After a war lasting only a few weeks, the heavily outnumbered Danes had been crushed, leaving most of Schleswig in German hands. Denmark was forced to relinquish her sovereignty over the duchies in July 1864, with the result that King Christian IX had reigned for only eight months before losing more than half his kingdom.

The humiliation made a bitterly upset Princess Alexandra more determined than ever to return home to her parents for a holiday, something she had intended to do in order to show them their new grandson, and also to introduce her husband to Copenhagen. Queen Victoria wanted to forbid the visit on political grounds, thinking it would be the wrong time to demonstrate such solidarity with Germany's defeated enemy and that to do so could have unfortunate consequences, but her ministers raised no objection. She conceded on condition that her son and daughter-in-law promised to travel incognito, would not allow any political discussions in their presence, include a visit to Germany in their itinerary before they returned, and send the little prince back to Balmoral on their departure from Denmark. The last condition was not made out of mere possessiveness, for the queen had her doubts that the prince and princess were fully aware of their parental responsibilities. She had been shocked to see how frail he appeared the last time she saw him.

In September mother, father and their infant son went to Denmark, and the princess was delighted to be back in her home country. Her husband soon became bored with the small, uncomfortable rooms in the Danish palaces, the monotonous food, and the boring evenings filled with nothing but small talk and tedious family games. At around the same time she realised she was pregnant again, and early on the morning of 3 June 1865 at Marlborough House she gave birth to a second son. After their experiences with their firstborn, the parents had chosen names in advance. The prince had told his mother that if it was another boy they intended to call him George, which they liked and thought was a good English name. Frederick would be the second, as it had been used regularly by his wife's Danish forebears.

Pleased as she was that the succession had been thus secured, Queen Victoria disapproved of the little prince's relaxed upbringing, and held the princess responsible. She complained that she could 'never be intimate' with Alix, who showed her 'no confidence whatsoever especially about the children'. The Crown Princess of Prussia, who was on the receiving end of many of these complaints, knew that mama was inclined to exaggerate or find fault where it probably did not exist. She also realised that she liked to exert a controlling presence, and did not appreciate that it was sometimes better to relax her iron grip a little. In spite of her criticisms, the matriarch admitted that 'nothing could be nicer or dearer than [Alix] was'.[24]

By now the princess was expecting a third child. Much to her frustration, her condition made it impossible for her to accompany her husband to St Petersburg for the wedding of her favourite sister, Dagmar, to the tsarevich, Grand Duke Alexander of Russia, in November 1866. It would have been better for his reputation and popularity if she had been allowed to go after all, for reports soon reached British society as well as her family that while he was away he had been paying too much attention to Russian beauties.

As the time for her confinement approached at Marlborough House, the princess was seriously ill. On 15 February 1867 she complained of acute pains and a chill. Her husband was attending functions at Windsor, and while he was away she stayed in bed with rheumatic fever. It took three telegrams, each worded more anxiously than the last, to make him return home. During the next few days she suffered acute pain in her leg and hip. The doctors thought it would be too risky to give her chloroform during her confinement, which ended on 20 February with the birth of a daughter. Her pains and fever did not improve, and the doctors were sure her condition could soon become serious. It was about two months before she could be wheeled to her window for a sight of the spring weather. The baby was christened Louise Victoria Alexandra Dagmar on 10 May, the first name in honour of her grandmother. Her mother attended the ceremony but was still in a wheelchair, with one leg completely stiff.

The rheumatic fever had left her permanently lame, a sad prospect for a young woman who had always enjoyed energetic activities such as dancing, riding and skating. Society ladies had already adopted her habit of wearing choker necklaces and high necklines, which she used to conceal the blemish on her neck, and now in the same way some of them copied her walk as a compliment, and it came to be known as the 'Alexandra limp'. Moreover, it exacerbated her otosclerosis, a form of deafness that could be brought on or made more acute by illness or pregnancy, and which had been inherited from her mother. As her hearing worsened, she relied more and more on a small group of close confidantes, her children, and animals. At the same time, she became heavily dependent on one or two chosen friends whose voices she could hear as they were familiar to her, and to let herself fall too much under their influence.

The worst side-effect of her deafness was the way in which it cut her off from sharing fully in the life of her husband. She had enjoyed the social round, as well as being the joint acknowledged leader of fashionable society, but as the affliction closed in on her, she found it less of a pleasure and more of a chore. It became harder for her to follow the conversations of others, inadvertently giving them the impression that she was stupid, and the result was to distance her increasingly from their ever-widening circle of friends. An ability to lip-read to some extent was only a mild consolation.

Throughout the years she was, and always remained, much more popular than her husband and her mother-in-law. When the former went to Ascot Week, he received a very unenthusiastic reception as the princess was not with him but still convalescing at home. While she may have accepted his infidelities with other married women and fashionable beauties in St Petersburg, being well aware that her family as well as the Hanoverian and Coburg dynasties had produced their share of womanizing rakes, she probably found his open neglect more difficult to bear. He did admittedly make an effort at home, especially when he had his desk moved into her sickroom so that he could write his letters and be at her bedside at the same time. Yet, at other moments, it was made gently clear to him, mainly by the doctors and the princess's ladies-in-waiting, that he was inclined to be a hindrance rather than a help in her room. Moreover, he was easily bored, and distractions in the outside world were impossible to resist. Had he spent more time at Sandringham or Marlborough House with his ailing wife, it would have boded far better for his standing at large.

It was inevitable that the home-loving princess and her energetic but not domestically minded husband would gradually drift apart, and she was not completely blameless. While Prince George was still a baby, Queen Victoria had noticed that his mother's lack of punctuality and organisation did not make her husband's home life comfortable. She observed sadly that they both regularly breakfasted alone, his crowded programme of engagements making no allowance for a wife who was rarely out of her room before eleven o'clock in the morning. All the same, despite his infidelities, and associations with some Parisian society ladies

– he had left for the Paris International Exhibition a few hours after Louise's christening – as well as with other women, the princess tolerated his wayward behaviour with dignity, saying that after all he 'always loved me the best'. Society beauties and mistresses came and went, sometimes abruptly cast aside after taking the princely lover's affections for granted, but a lawful wedded wife was forever.

Partly as a cure for her rheumatic knee, it was decided that she should spend part of the summer at a German spa. On 18 August 1867 she and the prince left for Wiesbaden, taking their three children, the complete household, and twenty-five servants. They went in the royal yacht as far as Dordrecht, then by river steamer. Suddenly she noticed a Prussian flag fluttering at the stern. The suite gently pointed out that it was required because of international agreement and custom, as was the case with the Union Jack and the Danish flag, but she still made her extreme displeasure known.

Worse was to come. The Prince of Wales was away on 19 September when a telegram arrived from King William of Prussia announcing his intention to pay her a courtesy visit at Wiesbaden any time convenient to her that evening or on the following day. Francis Knollys, a member of the entourage, took her the message directly, and she promptly dictated a refusal so blunt that he declined to transcribe it. When the prince returned that evening and found that she could not be persuaded to reconsider, he sent a tactful message to say that he himself would call upon the king, but that she was not well enough to receive visitors.

All would have been well had she not made her feelings clear by promptly travelling to Rumpenheim to attend her grandfather's funeral. The Crown Princess of Prussia, annoyed by this insult to her in-laws, begged the Prince of Wales to intercede and persuade her to see the king. Queen Louise, who hated the Prussians just as much but was prepared to observe diplomatic etiquette when necessary, was asked to try and reason with her daughter, but the Princess of Wales remained unyielding. To her, the Prussians were brigands who had unlawfully decimated her father's kingdom, and she never forgave them. The matter was only resolved when the prince sent King William a telegram inviting him to call. When he arrived, the princess realised there was no escape, behaved very civilly and the king was charm personified. Nevertheless, the whole episode had angered Queen Victoria, who wrote to Lord Derby, her prime minister, that she hoped he would stress to the heir and his wife the importance of not letting private views interfere with public duties. Everyone recognised that the prince knew his obligations, but his wife was a different matter entirely.

Despite her stiff knee, the princess had recovered well from her illness, and by the end of 1867 she was walking with two sticks. She gradually learned to glide rather than walk, and continued her skating, dancing, and even riding, as long as she moved her pommel to the other side of the saddle. Even so, it was a cross she did not bear lightly. Years later, she wrote to her daughter-in-law, the Duchess of York, that her leg was 'an awful bore and nuisance'. It made activities such as riding, running and cycling very awkward, while stairs were a particular problem, especially in company.

Plans had been made for an unofficial visit by the Prince of Wales to Ireland in April 1868, and the princess intended to accompany him. There had recently been signs of increasing activity by Fenian agitators in Britain and further afield – notably an attempt by a sympathiser on the life of Prince Alfred, created Duke of Edinburgh two years previously, while on a visit to Australia – and subsequent fears for his elder brother's safety, but the government agreed that the journey should still take place as scheduled. Although she was six months pregnant, the princess considered her place was by her husband's side rather than sitting at home worrying about any harm that might come to him. It proved a wise move, for even though the Irish were not habitually well-disposed towards the royal family, she charmed the crowds at once. She loved Ireland far more than the Scottish Highlands, and later she welcomed a plan – as did the prince – suggested by Benjamin Disraeli, and later by William Ewart Gladstone, two of her prime ministers, that they should have a permanent residence in Ireland and spend two or three months there every year. Queen Victoria set herself firmly against the scheme, and nothing came of it.

In view of the princess's prolonged convalescence, a respite from childbearing would have suited her, but by Christmas she was expecting again. On 6 July 1868 she produced a second daughter, Victoria Alexandra Olga Marie. Queen Victoria greeted the arrival of this 'mere little red lump' with little interest, writing to the Crown Princess of Prussia that this seventh granddaughter and fourteenth grandchild was 'a very uninteresting thing – for it seems to me to go on like the rabbits in Windsor Park!'[25]

The Princess's surgeon-in-attendance, Sir James Paget, suggested that her rheumatism might have been partially caused by dampness at Sandringham, and Lady Macclesfield commented on how unbearably cold it was in Norfolk every spring. The Prince of Wales realised that major alterations to the house would be needed for the family, and shortly before the birth of their second daughter he was advised that the premises would need to be demolished and rebuilt. Partly to facilitate this, it was arranged that the family would spend the winter of 1868–9 overseas, including a tour of Egypt, as well as stopping *en route* in Denmark, Berlin and Vienna.

The princess was thrilled to have the chance of showing off her children again to the rest of the family. Louise would be accompanying them for the first time, although baby Victoria was too young to travel overseas. When she asked Queen Victoria for permission to take the three elder ones, back came a reply that the boys could go, but it was extremely selfish of the princess to risk the health if not the life of her elder daughter to gratify her own foolish whim. The princess was extremely upset, and the prince wrote a firm letter pointing out that Alix had tried to meet her wishes in every way on so many occasions and was thus most hurt and pained at these accusations of selfishness and of being unreasonable. As Vicky and Alice came to England so often with their small children, which were just as strong as his, it seemed rather inconsistent 'not to accord to the one what is accorded to the others'. He won his argument, and the queen had to content herself with grumbling about the composition of their suite instead.

They left for Paris in the middle of November, and afterwards spent six weeks with King Christian and Queen Louise. After a cheerful family Christmas, on 15 January 1869 they saw their children off from Hamburg to England on the royal yacht. Though she was pleased to welcome them home, the queen wrote to express her concern that no governess had been appointed to discipline them. The prince replied, speaking on behalf of himself and his wife, that he took issue with her strictures about discipline. If children of that age were treated too severely, he said, 'they get shy, and only fear those whom they ought to love, and we should naturally wish them to be very fond of you, as they were in Denmark of dear Alix's parents.'[26]

On 26 November 1869 a third daughter was born at Marlborough House and named Maud. When the princess's pains began, the prince was away, so she telegraphed for him and he arrived shortly before the birth. She was thankful for his presence, for without him she admitted later that she would not have been able to stand the discomfort. The doctors gave her chloroform, 'but only so little that I felt everything and went off into fits of laughter into the bargain'.[27]

By this time, the British royal family had reached a height of unpopularity not seen for many years. As Gladstone had presciently observed the previous year, 'the Queen is invisible and the Prince not respected.'[28] With the Queen's continued seclusion and her son and heir's conspicuous pursuit of pleasure, the Princess of Wales was the only member of the family who never forfeited her popularity. Her husband had fallen in public estimation after being called as a witness in a divorce case, and although he asserted his total innocence where claims of adultery with the wife were concerned, his involvement did nothing to enhance the monarchy's reputation. When the princess appeared in a box at the theatre shortly afterwards she was loudly cheered, but when her husband joined her, the noise turned at once to boos and hisses.

By autumn 1870 she was expecting another child. In contrast to the previous occasions, this time she became tired and particularly depressed, with irregular bleeding that made her unsure whether she was pregnant or not. Even so, she insisted on trying to lead as normal a life as possible, taking her place by her husband's side as often as she could, perhaps so she could keep a closer eye on him. She had two unpleasant falls later in the year – one while she was skating on the ice and crashed on her bad knee, leaving her with a mouth filled with blood, followed by a fall from her carriage when attending the wedding of her sister-in-law Louise – giving further cause for concern.

On 6 April 1871 she gave birth to a third son, born six weeks prematurely, very small, and with a head that was 'quite black'. His hands and feet were very cold and his circulation poor. Within a few hours it was evident that he would not live much longer, and a clergyman was summoned with haste to baptise him Alexander John Charles Albert. He lingered overnight, the princess insisted on keeping him with her in her bed, and he died twenty-four hours after birth. She lay next to him until the evening, sobbing as she held his hand while his limbs were stiffening.

The grieving mother was not thought well enough to attend the funeral on 11 April, and could only watch the mournful procession to the church at Sandringham from her bedroom window, the Prince of Wales hand in hand with their other two sons in grey kilts, crepe scarves and black gloves. She reproached herself bitterly at being responsible for her son's death by not taking care of herself properly during the preceding months. It was to be her last experience of childbirth; there would be no more infants in the Wales nursery. The prince was discreetly warned by the doctor that there must be no more 'conjugal relations' between husband and wife as it would put her health in danger. Although some thought that his society distractions had created some distance between them, it was apparent that he remained deeply devoted to her. Six weeks later she wrote to her sister Minnie in Russia that 'no words [could] describe' what her 'angelic blessed Bertie' had been to her during the last few weeks. 'If anything could have bound us closer together, it is this, our first great sorrow.' An even greater one was nearly to befall them before the year was over.

Despite this, they rejected any suggestion from Queen Victoria that they should retire into prolonged mourning. The prince pointed out to his mother that Alix wished to resume her social duties, otherwise she would 'get into a low and morbid state which I am certain will be very injurious to her.'[29] He and the princess were anxious to resume their round of luncheons, fetes, public dinners and laying foundation stones, as it was expected of them and people would not take no for an answer. However, they allowed themselves the chance to spend several weeks that summer in Europe, so they could visit family and so that the prince could indulge himself in Homburg at the gambling tables. It was not a gesture guaranteed to reverse the monarchy's increasingly poor standing at home.

Yet fate was about to intervene. In October the prince and princess went to stay with Lord Londesborough at his house near Scarborough. Several other guests, including two servants, were taken ill soon afterwards, among them the Earl of Chesterfield and the Prince of Wales's servant Mr Blagge. On 23 November it was announced from Sandringham that the prince was suffering from an attack of typhoid fever. The princess helped the doctors to nurse him, although she had no real experience of such a situation and her partial deafness, exacerbated by stress, put her at a severe disadvantage. Her sister-in-law Alice had been staying there at the time and her presence was a mixed blessing. She had ample experience of nursing the sick and wounded during the Franco-Prussian war only a year previously, and though she proved very efficient and assertive, she was not one to suffer fools gladly – or, rather, those whom she considered less qualified than herself. Much as Lady Macclesfield in particular valued her expertise, she resented Alice's impatient and apparently dismissive attitude towards Alexandra, who in addition to her deafness and inexperience was going through the agony of seeing a seriously ill husband not far from death's door.

Alexandra's birthday fell on 1 December, but nobody was in the mood for celebration and the occasion went unnoticed. In spite of this, two days later she remembered Lady Macclesfield's birthday, and selfless as ever she presented her with a photograph and a crystal watch.

During the first few days of December the patient rallied, but in the second week of the month he had a relapse. The mood of alarm increased when both the Earl of Chesterfield and Blagge died. Meanwhile, the princess, said Lady Macclesfield, 'keeps up heroically', while most members of the family, including Queen Victoria and most of the other children, came, stayed and generally proved anything but a comfort to one another. The princess almost never left the house, except to go out and pray in the church.

On 13 December the family came close to giving up hope that he would recover. 'Poor Alix was in the greatest alarm and despair,' the ever-supportive queen noted in her journal. Almost miraculously, that evening – the eve of the tenth anniversary of the prince consort's death – the doctors reported signs of a slight improvement in his condition. Within two or three days it was evident that he would recover, albeit slowly. The children had been sent to Osborne and remained there over Christmas, while the princess and her still very weak husband stayed at Sandringham. It had been a joy to her, if not something of a luxury, for them to enjoy some completely undisturbed time with each other at home. The quiet time they spent there together, she wrote to Lady Macclesfield, resulted in what she called the happiest days of her life, 'my full reward after all my sorrow and despair. It has been our second honeymoon and we are both so happy to be left alone by ourselves.'[30]

On 27 February 1872 a special service for the heir's recovery was held in St Paul's Cathedral. The idea was not welcomed by several members of the family, least of all the queen and the princess herself, who thought it was 'making too much of *an outward show* of the most sacred and solemn feelings of one's heart.' When the queen persisted in opposing the idea, Alexandra persuaded her otherwise, on the grounds that the whole nation had been so concerned for them, and that it had 'a kind of claim to join with us now in a public and universal thanksgiving.' Blagge's death was not forgotten, and the princess presented a brass eagle lectern to be placed in the church at Sandringham in his memory, inscribed, 'When I was in trouble I called upon the Lord, and He heard me.'[31]

The severe illness of the Prince of Wales and his recovery had been followed by a turning point in the relations between his wife and Queen Victoria. The anxiety they had shared and been through at the sickbed had brought them much closer together, a state of affairs that would last for the rest of the sovereign's lifetime. In later years it was also noticed that both women shared a sense of the ridiculous, and on occasion Alexandra could make her mother-in-law laugh in a way none of her children ever could. One evening in a royal drawing room, the queen asked a lady-in-waiting to remove her shawl as she was so hot. The result was to bring 'the whole head edifice veil cap crown & all' tumbling down, leaving Her Majesty bare-headed. Far from being embarrassed, she roared with laughter until she and the princess were both in tears.[32]

Yet if anybody had expected to see the prince turn over a new leaf and become a changed man, they were to be sorely disappointed. Within a few months of his recovery he had reverted to his society life of enjoyment, often with his brother Alfred following in his footsteps.

Chapter 3

Of all Queen Victoria's sons, Alfred was probably the one who had suffered the most from the early death of their father. He had been an industrious boy, in some ways very like him in his wide-ranging interests and love of finding things out for himself. Albert had sometimes regretted that this second son would never inherit his mother's throne, but it was some comfort to consider that he would almost certainly inherit the ancestral position, that of Duke of Saxe-Coburg Gotha, as successor to the uncle who fathered several children with his mistresses but seemed destined never to beget a legitimate heir with his unfortunate wife Alexandrine.

In August 1858, at the age of fourteen, Alfred joined the navy. This entailed regular voyages around much of the world, and absences from home. He was therefore a considerable distance away from Windsor Castle on 14 December 1861 when the prince consort died. Unfortunately for Queen Victoria, he did not take after his father in leading an unblemished life. A few months later, while on naval service in Malta, he followed in his elder brother's footsteps and had a brief affair with a young woman, news of which quickly reached the ears of his angry mother. It did nothing to prevent his election as king when the Greeks were endeavouring to fill their temporarily vacant throne in 1862, although under the terms of a protocol agreed to in 1830 by the protecting powers of Britain, France and Russia, members of their ruling families were expressly excluded from accepting the Hellenic crown.

In 1866 he was created Duke of Edinburgh, Earl of Ulster and Earl of Kent. The following year he was appointed captain of the frigate HMS *Galatea*, and undertook a voyage which would result in him visiting all five continents, thus making him the most well-travelled of any of his siblings. The schedule was interrupted while he was in Australia in March 1868 when a Fenian sympathiser, James O'Farrell, attempted to assassinate him by shooting him at close range. He was wounded, sent back to England to recover and resumed his itinerary a few months later, visiting Hawaii, New Zealand, Japan and India, returning home in 1871.

His matrimonial future had already been under consideration from Queen Victoria, who was unaware that he had made his choice already. In August 1868, not long before going back to his ship, he had visited his sister Alice and her family in Germany. Among those also present at the gathering was fourteen-year-old Grand Duchess Marie, the only surviving daughter of Tsar Alexander II. Alfred was very taken with her, and soon after coming home nearly three years later he told his mother that he planned to meet the Tsar shortly and ask him for Marie's hand.

* * *

Marie Alexandrovna was born at the Alexander Palace in Tsarskoe-Selo, near St Petersburg, on 17 October (5 October O.S.) 1853, the sixth child of Grand Duke Alexander Alexandrovich, Tsarevich of Russia, and his wife, Grand Duchess Marie Alexandrovna, formerly Princess Marie of Hesse and the Rhine. She was one of eight children, the eldest of her six brothers having died at the age of twenty-one, and a sister in infancy four years before Marie herself was born. In February 1855 Alexander succeeded his father as Tsar Alexander II.

She spent her childhood in the large Romanov palaces and country estates. The Romanovs' main family residence was the Winter Palace in St Petersburg, with summer homes at Gatchina, forty miles south, and Peterhof, on the Gulf of Finland. From late summer until winter they moved to Tsarskoe-Selo. The siblings were always close to each other, and her governess noticed that the little girl was quite upset when someone reprimanded any of her brothers: 'this brings her to the state of real despair.'[1] Her parents doted on this only surviving daughter, and the tsarina would let her play with her toys nearby while she worked at her desk or welcomed visitors to the palace. It was an indulgence she rarely extended towards her sons, with whom she was more distant. As Marie was surrounded only by brothers, she became a tomboy, assertive, plain-speaking, strong-willed and independent, intelligent but not too clever for her own good, and developed a rather abrupt manner as an adult.

The eldest of her brothers, Grand Duke Nicholas, had been engaged in 1864 to Princess Dagmar of Denmark, favourite sister of the Princess of Wales, but died of spinal meningitis in Nice a year later aged twenty-two. On his deathbed, he feebly joined her hand with that of his brother Alexander. The latter, a well-built giant of a man, now became his father's heir, and in accordance with Nicholas's dying wish, accordingly married Dagmar, who took the Russian name of Marie Feodorovna. The third brother, Vladimir, was a patron of the arts while the fourth, Alexis, would become a Grand Admiral in the Russian navy. Marie's favourite brother was Serge, a disagreeable, reactionary governor of Moscow, while Paul, five years younger than Marie, was the most pleasant and popular with people outside the family.

Marie was the first Russian grand duchess to be raised by English nannies and to speak fluent English (she also became proficient in German and French). These qualifications alone were enough to make her suitable, but where Queen Victoria was concerned, a Romanov daughter-in-law would be a mixed blessing at best. Ever since the Crimean war Russia had been an enemy of England, who in turn was suspicious of the Asiatic empire's intentions over the Black Sea and central Asia, and thought the Romanovs were 'false and arrogant'. Moreover, if one of her sons married a princess or grand duchess belonging to the Greek Orthodox Church, she was sure there would be a constant procession of priests coming in and out of their residences. Yet she had long since understood that finding the right wife for her second son would be difficult, and decided that as long as he could choose one 'to suit and please him', she would not mind who she was. She knew that the choice was so narrow that they would need to find a way around any difficulties that concerned another religion.[2]

It came as some reassurance to be told that the Russian Orthodox Church, unlike the Roman Catholic faith, did not refuse to acknowledge any creed other than their own, and Lord Granville, the foreign secretary, advised her that a Russian grand duchess would be preferable to a Roman Catholic or an English subject. A daughter of George V, the former King of Hanover who had recently been dethroned after his territory was absorbed by Prussia after conquest in the Six Weeks' War in 1866, would not be readily acceptable, partly for political reasons and partly because of the fear of hereditary blindness passed down from the ex-sovereign who had lost his sight during adolescence.

After the Duke of Edinburgh had met the tsar in Germany in July 1871, the latter wrote to Queen Victoria that while he was not opposed to a union between their families, he could not impose his will in any way on Marie, and they would have to wait a year for any decision, which in any case would not be binding. Alice suggested that Marie's tender age was the main obstacle and she was too young to think of marriage yet, despite the fact that Marie's mother had been married before her seventeenth birthday. Andrew Buchanan, British Ambassador at St Petersburg, reported that the Duke of Edinburgh had made a good impression on the tsar and tsarina but seemingly not on their daughter, who still appeared very childish for her seventeen years and dreaded the idea of any marriage that would remove her from her happy childhood home.

For several months the Russian court gave such evasive answers that by May the duke and his mother were becoming insistent. A letter from the tsarina the following month merely repeated that Marie must be left free to choose for herself, and also the demand – presumably made more in hope than expectation – that once married the couple should live in Russia. The queen was adamant that this was something she could '*never* consent to'.[3] By August she was convinced that the 'Russian project' was well and truly over. She thought that the tsar and tsarina were so against parting with Marie that they would only let her marry another Russian.

After resigning himself gloomily to what seemed an end to the situation, the duke was delighted to learn after Christmas that his prospects were improving. Marie knew that she would be expected to marry before long, and her rank severely limited potential suitors. If she did not choose someone from Russia she would have to take a prince from one of the German courts, like her mother before her, or else from England, and the latter seemed preferable. In any case, her family life at home was no longer happy. Her father had openly acknowledged his mistress, Princess Catherine Dolgorouky, who had given birth to his son in 1872 and would bear him several further children. The tsarina had long accepted mild infidelity as part of the Romanov tradition, but was shocked at her husband's mistress and child being paraded so openly. The thought that her ill-health, which necessitated her spending more and more time at the Crimea, was partly responsible for the situation made her blame herself. At about the same time as the birth of the tsar's first illegitimate son, she learned that her chronic complaint was advanced tuberculosis, as she had long feared, and she had only a few years to live.

Her sons adored her, strongly resented the presence of Princess Dolgorouky, and were barely on speaking terms with their father. Marie found it hard to censure her adored father for his infidelity, much as she loved her mother. This cannot have made her home life a happy one, and at the age of twenty she knew that one day she would have to reconcile herself to the thought of marriage.

In January 1873 Count Peter Shuvalov, Tsar Alexander's confidant and head of the Russian police, arrived in London to report to Granville with assurances of the Russian Empire's peaceful intentions concerning central Asia. Soon it was apparent that he was also charged with reopening the marriage question. He spoke separately to the duke and the queen, explaining that the tsar's only objection was that he did not want his daughter to live too far away from him; an assurance that they would pay visits to Russia during their first years of marriage would suffice. On behalf of the royal family, Granville told Shuvalov that Her Majesty had already considered the scheme ended the previous year, and had been very surprised by the tsarina's vague letter of last June. The ambassador replied that the tsarina had only thought it fair not to let Prince Alfred feel he was under any firm obligation.

The Duke of Edinburgh was delighted, but the queen felt the Russians had treated them shabbily. She had further doubts on the political desirability of such an alliance, and had it not been for her son's 'very strong desire for it', she would have gladly washed her hands of the whole idea. She told the German crown princess in strict confidence – Princess Alice was not to be informed – that Affie still had his heart set on marrying Marie, as she felt she could not 'entirely refuse these (to me somewhat suspicious) *avances*'.[4]

These suspicions were soon justified. Shuvalov left England on 14 January and promised to write again within ten days, sending the Duke of Edinburgh some new photographs of the grand duchess. The next Russian communication was a telegram from Lord Loftus, requesting that arrangements for the betrothal should be suspended until Granville had received a secret letter detailing 'extraordinary rumours' about Marie. This letter appeared a couple of days later, with comments that she had had *'une affaire de coeur'* with a Russian officer, and 'regular correspondence' with another. The duke refused to believe it, but the queen warned him to be careful as the grand duchess had evidently had other affections, 'the existence of which may account for various phases in this strange affair'. Sir Henry Ponsonby, her private secretary, wryly informed Granville that 'Prince Alfred's valentine was not a pleasant one'. She might have suspected that the marriage question had been reopened simply so that an impatient father could get rid of his flighty daughter.

The duke's first reaction was to visit St Petersburg and try to find out for himself, but he thought better of it after being advised he might find the experience humiliating. This was followed by another letter from Loftus saying the grand duchess had fallen in love with the tsar's aide-de-camp, Prince Galitzin, and was willing to give up her royal position and rights to marry him. The tsar was prepared to agree if it would ensure her future happiness, but the tsarina refused to hear of it, insisting that Galitzin was sent abroad on indefinite leave. By the time the ambassador wrote to say that he suspected there may have been no genuine substance to the rumours, Queen Victoria was ready to contemplate preventing or even giving up all hope of the marriage altogether.

Nevertheless, the duke accepted an invitation to meet Grand Duchess Marie and her mother in April at Sorrento in Italy. He had the support of Granville, who pointed out that the British court could not dissociate themselves from it as they had accepted Marie in principle at the time of Shuvalov's visit. The queen insisted that there must be 'mutual attachment' between both young people, and they would have to marry within the year 'or else it must finally be put an end to'. The duke left for Italy in mid-April but his optimism was shortlived as Marie fell ill, and he was only allowed to spend a little time with her before being asked to leave. Moreover, the tsarina refused to agree to any possibility of a marriage between them. The queen put this down to 'the apparent anti-English movement in Russia' and was astonished when the German crown princess wrote to say that she had heard from a diplomat friend of Shuvalov that, in St Petersburg the court considered the forthcoming marriage as 'quite a settled thing'. The duke was prepared to put up with the tsarina's dithering as long as all ended well, much to his mother's disgust. She deplored the insolent conduct of the imperial family, complaining that her son had 'neither pride nor dignity' and seemed prepared to put up with it.

Marie had also made up her mind to marry him, and when she asked her uncle, Prince Alexander of Hesse, for his support, the tsar reluctantly gave his consent. In June he joined his wife and daughter at Ems, and invited the duke to meet them later that summer. When the latter left England for Germany he was unaware that the queen had drafted a letter to Alice detailing the problems, personal and political, that a Duchess of Edinburgh would have to face. Queen Victoria intended Alice to show it to the tsar and tsarina, but second thoughts, and perhaps the wise counsels of Ponsonby as well, prevailed and it was never sent.

On 11 July Alfred asked for Marie's hand and she accepted him. The queen and Beatrice were taking tea in the garden at Osborne House when they received his telegram to say that they were engaged, and hoped 'your blessings rest on us'. 'The murder is out!' she wrote to the crown princess, adding that she fervently hoped Marie would be sufficiently strong to alter her future husband's 'hard, selfish, uncertain character'.[5]

The crown princess was thrilled, but her delight was not shared by the German royal family. Crown Prince Frederick William gloomily considered it a poor prospect for Germany if northern Europe was about to become 'populated with anti-German marriages'. His mother Empress Augusta's acid acknowledgement of the news to Queen Victoria drew a face-saving defence from the latter that she had not really wanted such an alliance for several serious reasons, principally religious and political. 'But in spite of all difficulties, in spite of doubts and representations on both sides, it has nonetheless come to pass, and that through the decision of the young lady herself, hence I must believe that it is a dispensation of God.'[6]

She confided her anxiety to the crown princess in accepting a bride from another church into the family. This would be the first instance of such an event since the revolution of 1688 that had led to the abdication of James II, the last Catholic monarch. She was particularly annoyed that she had had no chance to meet Marie first, but she had every intention of doing so before the wedding, which she expected would take place in late October or early November. In both of these matters she would be thwarted. Because she would not travel to the Continent for anything resembling official business, one of her parents would have to bring her to England or Scotland. The affronted tsar privately dismissed his fellow-monarch as a 'silly old fool', while the tsarina's ill-health prevented her from making such a journey, though she offered to meet the queen at Cologne, only to be met with a retort that this was 'simply impertinent'. Alice tried to persuade her mother to concede, only to be told firmly that her daughter should not 'tell *me* who have been nearly 20 years longer on the throne than the Emperor of Russia & am the Doyenne of Sovereigns & who am a Reigning Sovereign which the Empress is not – what I ought to do.'[7]

As to the date of the wedding, all three parents were divided. The tsarina was convinced that a wedding in the winter would be unlucky, and preferred it to be delayed until spring next year. The tsar insisted that it had to be in January, which, as the queen observed, was still in the winter. Having disagreed on so many aspects relating to the project, the sovereigns now ceased to correspond with each other, and Victoria merely handed over all subsequent negotiations to her ministers. The tsar refused to write to her again, and she insisted she would not write to him until she received a letter from him. The tsarevich refused to take any messages, and the Prince of Wales, who got on better with him than the rest of the British royal family, said he would not ask him anything about it either. Meanwhile, Granville's telegrams to the Russian ambassador, Baron de Brunov, remained unanswered.[8]

At length the tsar had his way. He overruled the queen's insistence that the ceremony would be in England, and he and the tsarina made it clear that there could be no question of their daughter leaving Russia before the marriage. It was arranged to take place on 23 January 1874 – as the queen noted poignantly, the anniversary of her father's death – at the Grand Church of the Winter Palace. Queen Victoria did not attend, officially for reasons of security, and in fact never visited Russia in her life. She had her way in one matter, insisting that her son's wedding must be a double ceremony, with one in the Anglican faith and the other Russian Orthodox. Arthur Stanley, Dean of Westminster, was chosen to officiate at the former, and his wife, Lady Augusta, was to report to her afterwards on proceedings in the fullest detail. This would help to compensate her for not being there, as she admitted that she 'felt it very trying to be absent!'[9]

Further difficulties arose with regard to the marriage treaty, drafted by the tsar and his ministers, dealing with matters including Marie's inheritance, finances and religious observances. Gladstone read it and told the queen he thought it a most objectionable and imperiously worded document. She agreed, replying that it would have to be completely rewritten.

Tsar Alexander II was one of the world's richest monarchs, if not the richest. Between 1856 and 1881 over £20,000,000 of his personal fortune was carefully invested in London merchant banks, his annual income from the government was over £1,000,000, and his estates and frozen assets in the form of the Romanov crown jewels, accumulated over the previous 300 years, added considerably to this figure. The income at birth of a grand duke or duchess was £28,000, to which had been added Marie's dowry of £100,000 on her marriage. Although the Romanovs had never wanted for money, the queen, like her late husband, was relatively frugal by nature. It astonished her to learn that the bride's dowry was 1,000,000 roubles – about £100,000 – on which she would receive five per cent interest annually on the capital, paid half-yearly. She was also granted by the tsar, 'as a mark of his peculiar affection, and which is not to be considered as a precedent for the future,' an annual sum of 75,000 roubles – about £11,250 – for life. All these sums she was at liberty to dispose of according to her own free will and pleasure. He also assigned her a 'special marriage portion', again of 1,000,000 roubles, and she retained possession of her private capital, 600,000 roubles – about £90,000 (over £10,000,000 in 2020 values). She was reputed to be the wealthiest woman in the world at that time.[10]

In addition to these very generous financial considerations, an article in the treaty stipulated that as Duchess of Edinburgh Her Imperial Highness was 'not to be in any way hindered in the full, free, and unrestrained exercise of the religious profession of the Orthodox Church', though it was agreed that any children born to her would be raised as Protestants.[11]

The bride's magnificent trousseau was displayed in the White Hall of the Winter Palace for Russian visitors to come and admire, while British admirers had to content themselves with a detailed report in *The Graphic*. On view were silk, satin and velvet garments, Indian shawls, bonnets, gloves, 'splendid furs and lace at 1,000 roubles a yard', costing an estimated £40,000 altogether.[12]

As for the wedding of the Duke and Duchess of Edinburgh itself, it was unique among those of the queen's children in being the only one to take place outside England, and at which she was not present. At midday the imperial procession appeared. Marie wore a silver embroidered gown, while the groom wore Russian naval uniform. After the Orthodox service, everyone went to the Salle d'Alexandre for the English ceremony and the couple received the tsarina's blessings, prior to the wedding breakfast. Both parents looked pale and emotional throughout. Just before the ceremony, when the dean told the tsar that it was such a happy event for both countries, the latter told him sadly that the only sufferers were the parents, and their daughter 'has been the joy of our lives, but it must be'.[13]

The newly married couple stayed in Russia for about a month. On their way back across Europe at the beginning of March they stopped at Berlin for further visits and receptions. Four days later they landed at Gravesend and entered Windsor. Lined with troops, the town was brightly festooned with flags, flowers and banners with messages of welcome in English and Russian, and a triumphal arch. Queen Victoria greeted them at the station and embraced the daughter-in-law whom she was meeting for the first time. She found her pleasantly unaffected and civil, but not in the least pretty or graceful. All the same, she reported, the grand duchess was 'quite at ease with me and we get on very well – and she is very sensible'. On first acquaintance she did not appear too self-assured, spoke excellent English, and above all was not the least afraid of her husband 'and I hope will have the very best influence upon him.'

People did not think Marie pretty, Victoria wrote to the German crown princess a few days later, but found her frank and pleasant. She had an abrupt manner that gave the impression of haughtiness, but the queen charitably excused that on the grounds that the Romanovs tended to look upon themselves as 'greatly above all others, and therefore they have a little that manner.' In spite of this, the queen continued, the duchess 'speaks very kindly to all high or low if one names people to her. She is very anxious to devote herself to some charitable and other establishments and fond of serious books.'[14]

It was a kindly verdict with which some would soon have reason to disagree. Court life in England was less formal than in Russia, and with her inborn superiority she was loath to adapt, preferring to maintain the strict etiquette with which she had been so familiar at home. Nobody was permitted to turn their back on her, but had to conform to the principle of leaving her presence by walking backwards. Those who omitted to do so would receive the full force of her imperious stare and a lecture on the subject. It was said that one day the duke was showing her around the gardens of a country estate, and the head gardener was summoned to accept the royal compliments. He duly did so and took his leave, only to realise that there were no gates within a reasonable distance for him to retreat backwards as required. The duchess watched him to make sure he backed off properly until he was ought of her sight.[15] On another occasion she visited her neighbours at Stafford House, thirty yards from the front door of Clarence House, driving the short distance in state in her carriage, with a full complement of footmen.

Clarence House, in The Mall, had been the Duke of Edinburgh's London residence since he attained his majority, and would remain the couple's home until his death. Originally built between 1825 and 1827, it had recently had a new wing and entrance added. Most of the collections adorning the walls or filled glass cases came from his world travels. There were trophies from various shooting expeditions, and a life-size figure in Japanese armour with a grotesque grinning mask. One drawing room was arranged with Chinese antiques and curios, old weapons, bronzes, ivories, embroideries and precious jades. The duchess decorated the other with her Russian keepsakes, including *objets d'art* such as jade carvings, malachite, rock crystal, lapis lazuli, enamels mounted in gold and adorned with diamonds and precious stones from the Urals, dishes, vases, Fabergé Easter eggs and jewelled ikons, surrounded by fragrance of Russian incense, leather and cedar wood. Her emeralds, rubies, diamonds and sapphires were displayed in glass cabinets, while the diadems, tiaras, necklaces, earrings, lockets and bracelets were to be found in a glass cupboard. At Clarence House, and each of her other homes, she kept a small Orthodox chapel, its walls covered with religious pictures, and later, photographs of her mother and father on their deathbeds with an ever-burning lamp in front of them. Her retinue always included a Russian priest and two chanters.

She was not slow to make an impression on those around her as somebody who could never be ignored. Some people praised her warmly, among them Prime Minister Benjamin Disraeli, although admittedly he was more inclined than most to flatter royalty. On one of their first meetings he found her 'lively as a bird'. A few months later, he commented approvingly that she was one of those people who broke through 'all the etiquette of courtly conversation. Even the Queen joined in her vivacity, and evidently is much influenced by her.'[16]

Yet she found it difficult to settle at the British court. She detested the climate and the bland food. When she discovered with interest that the queen drank whisky, sometimes with water but usually without, she was given some to taste, but made such a face that after that she was only offered water.[17] The Edinburghs' home in London was 'gloomy', she said, and the city itself 'an impossible place, where people are mad of pleasure'. For her, there was no comparison between what she saw in England and the magnificent palaces of St Petersburg. In her eyes, Buckingham Palace and Windsor Castle could never compete with the splendours of the Winter Palace.

As for Osborne House, she paid her first visit with the duke in April. She was shown the Swiss Cottage where he and his siblings used to play, and also visited the local school. Yet she did not find the queen's island home at all relaxing, and much to her irritation, it proved a very windy day. Such conditions never suited her, as she had never been able to put two hatpins in her hats, and they blew off too easily. She remarked that as a girl she was not taught how to fasten a pin with her left hand, and did not intend to begin learning now.[18] However, a few days later the couple took a carriage drive to West Cowes with the queen and Beatrice. The streets had been decorated in their honour, the crowds were out in full force to catch a glimpse of them, and a little girl presented Marie with a posy. The queen noted in her journal that 'Affie and Marie were very cheery and she is such a charming companion.'[19]

Visits to her mother-in-law at Windsor Castle and Osborne were tedious in the extreme as she found the queen's company oppressive, and the late nights very tiring. Her second cousin, Queen Sophie of the Netherlands, had foreseen the difficulties she would face in her new country. To her friend the Countess of Derby, she had written presciently the previous year that it would 'be difficult to adapt entirely to the English ways'. A month before the wedding she returned to the theme: 'I wonder how the only and spoilt daughter of the Czar will accept her secondary position.'[20] Throughout her childhood, the Duchess of Edinburgh had enjoyed almost unlimited freedom. Now she had to accept and accustom herself to a new way of life in a foreign land where she was no longer the sovereign's only daughter but one of two daughters-in-law, with a very demanding and critical mother-in-law. Constantly on the defensive, lacking the Princess of Wales's beauty as well as her charm, and unable to inspire affection, it was inevitable that she would be respected but not necessarily liked.

Proud of her intellectual knowledge and not afraid to bask in her superiority, she thought the Princess of Wales light-minded and foolish. Having always been passionate about music, she was very disparaging about performances she saw and heard in England. Within less than a month of arriving, she wrote to her father that they often went to the Royal Albert Hall, 'all ecclesiastical and for me quite boring [...] every concert goes on for several hours – but it's worth seeing this hall.'[21] Disenchanted with Britain and life with the queen, she became increasingly homesick for Russia and was happy for any excuse to return there, no matter how briefly. British people thought her rough and masculine in her manners. Her imperious attitude towards her servants and her defiance of English convention by smoking in public made her unpopular, and she made it plain that she did not care what other people thought of her. Judged by the standards of a later age, the duchess might have been hailed as striking a blow for the rights of women to smoke openly, but defying convention was not looked on so kindly in the nineteenth century.

As Queen Victoria had feared, the Romanov connection brought various difficulties. In Russia, as daughter of the sovereign, she had had precedence over all the grand duchesses in Russia. Being an Imperial Highness in England, she bitterly resented having to give precedence to the Princess of Wales, and as the husband of a duke being only entitled to the style of Royal Highness. Her father wished her to be called imperial, not royal, 'as in all civilised countries', to which the (not yet imperial) queen indignantly retorted that she did not mind whether her daughter-in-law was called imperial or not, as long as royal came first. Then there was the issue of which title should come first – Grand Duchess of Russia, or Duchess of Edinburgh. The queen, who was not yet an empress herself, asked Sir Henry Ponsonby, who was amused by the fuss and quoted Dr Johnson to his wife: 'Who comes first, a louse or a flea?'[22]

Tsar Alexander II arrived on an eight-day visit to England on 13 May 1874, his first journey to the country since, as tsarevich, he had charmed the young, still unmarried sovereign in 1839. He and Marie were overjoyed to see each other again, and during the programme of receptions, dinners, state concerts, balls and other functions, she hardly left his side. Elaborate security was maintained throughout, but there were no serious anti-demonstrations or attempts on the tsar's life, something for which they were well prepared.

While he was in England he indicated that he was prepared to accept Queen Victoria's stipulation that the Princess of Wales should indeed precede her at court as she was the wife of the heir to the throne, but as a compromise he asked that his daughter should have precedence over her other sisters-in-law. This was something the queen would not accept, but Marie found ample compensation in other ways. As the tsar's only daughter, she had inherited the most sumptuous jewels, including some magnificent sapphires that had been collected for her since she was born. At her first drawing-room she enjoyed showing off part of her collection in front of her husband's sisters with their plainly inferior pieces. They could hardly conceal their jealousy, while the queen took their part as she looked at the duchess's pearls and diamonds with disdain, 'shrugging her shoulders like a bird whose plumage has been ruffled, her mouth drawn down at the corners in an expression which those who knew her had learned to dread.'[23] Matters were not improved for the British princesses when they realised that the duchess's annual income was in excess of over £30,000, which exceeded that of her husband, £25,000, and the parliamentary annuity for the rest of them, which was a comparatively derisory £6,000 each.

Despite the difficult relations between them both and the lack of a financial level playing field, Queen Victoria always admired this daughter-in-law's independence, strength of character and refusal to be dominated. Six months after meeting her for the first time, the latter admitted that despite their personal differences she was favourably impressed with Marie's 'wonderfully even, cheerful satisfied temper – her kind and indulgent disposition, free from bigotry and intolerance, and her serious, intelligent mind – so entirely free from everything fast – and so full of occupation and interest in everything.' All these qualities, she considered, made her 'a most agreeable companion'.[24] She had not taken long to realise that both of them had very similar characters, and that in Marie Alexandrovna she had met her match. It was recognised by those closest to her that she generally admired self-assured people around her who were prepared to stand their ground, and the Duchess of Edinburgh was not easily cowed. As she once told her mother, it was only necessary for them to give Queen Victoria 'a good fight to make her draw in her horns'.[25]

The duchess would undoubtedly have been flattered, but it did little to improve the atmosphere between them, and for some years they tended to keep their distance from each other. The queen knew that she would never extract the same measure of obedience from her Russian relative by marriage that she would have liked, and certainly received, from her own children. Significantly, the Duchess of Edinburgh's portrait was the only one of her family that she ever allowed to be hung on the wall in her private breakfast room at Windsor Castle.[26]

The duke and duchess had recently acquired their own country residence, Eastwell Park, near Ashford in Kent. Rented from the Earl of Winchelsea, it was a large, imposing, mock-Tudor mansion set in 2,500 acres that included rich woodland and rolling parks. They had planned to move there in October, but Marie was expecting and the doctors informed her that her confinement would come sooner than they had expected, so she and her husband would have to remain at Buckingham Palace. The tsarina had hoped to be at her daughter's side in time, and she left the Crimea for London on 11 October, accompanied by the tsarevich. They arrived at London shortly after breakfast on the morning of 15 October, and were just too late, for Marie had given birth to a son early that morning. She celebrated her twenty-first birthday two days later resting in bed, but recovered quickly and was back on her feet not long afterwards.

The baby was christened Alfred Alexander William Ernest Albert on 28 November in the chapel at Buckingham Palace. Queen Victoria wrote to the German Emperor William, who stood as one of the godparents and was represented by Prince Arthur, that the baby was 'a very strong, beautiful child, who will some day, I think, be like his very big Russian uncles'.[27]

Much to the horror of English society and her in-laws, the duchess had vowed that she would nurse her children herself – and not just in the privacy of her own home. Queen Victoria had resignedly accepted the fact that her own daughters had adopted what she called the 'disgusting' business of breastfeeding their children. She wrote to the crown princess that Marie also did so. As long as she remained at home, the queen said, and did not 'publish the fact to the world – by taking the baby everywhere and can do it well – which they say she does now – I have nothing to say.'[28] In spite of this pious hope, at little Alfred's christening Marie disregarded all objections by openly breastfeeding him there and then. When he threw up all over her dress, she stood up without the least embarrassment and the tsarina gently took the infant from her. While the Russian guests, who included the tsarevich and his brother, Grand Duke Alexis, regarded it as perfectly natural, the English company present could hardly believe their eyes. The mother, reported a shocked Princess of Wales to her sister at home in St Petersburg, 'ran about with her big breast hanging down in front of everyone and wiped the dress clean!!!'[29]

By this time the tsarina was unwell and coughing a great deal. Much as she was loath to take her leave of her daughter so soon, she left England the following day in order to spend the winter in Nice. Although the duchess would often make the journey to Russia to visit her ailing mother, the latter would never see England again.

One year later the eldest of the Edinburgh princesses arrived. Marie, always known as Missy, was born on 29 October 1875, not long after her parents and brother had gone to Eastwell Park, where they would spend autumn, Christmas and New Year. Clarence House was too formal and lacking in privacy, and only at Eastwell could they live like any other well-to-do family in a country house. Every autumn the duke invited a houseful of guests for large shooting parties to make full use of the facilities. Marie dreaded these get-togethers, complaining that after a day with their guns the men returned sleepy and in no mood for mentally stimulating conversation, only gossip and tales of their hunting prowess. A cultured woman who enjoyed discussing art, literature and philosophy, she much preferred the company of politicians, diplomats and artists to that of soldiers, sailors and sportsmen. Ironically, she had married a prince who was both sailor and sportsman. It never ceased to rankle her, and almost twenty years later she was telling her eldest daughter that she 'suffered so much from the selfishness of hunters in the first years in England'.[30]

Despite their differences, the duke and duchess had a common love of music. Alfred had taught himself the violin during childhood. Throughout his life he would play as a hobby at home, sometimes solo, sometimes with a pianist accompanying him, and occasionally at concerts with provincial orchestras. Marie had also been passionate about music ever since she was small, and when she was very young she had been given a piano by her father. The library at Eastwell had two pianos, and one regular guest there was the renowned pianist and composer Anton Rubenstein, who would eagerly play for his fellow Russian. As small girls, their daughters, in their dressing gowns, would secretly listen, spellbound, from the hallway. The duchess and Lady Randolph Churchill, so dissimilar in many ways yet great friends, also played together on the two pianos, and on one occasion the girls teased them by putting two tinplate toys that made the sound of frogs croaking under the piano stools.

How proficient husband and wife were as amateur musicians was sometimes disputed. The duchess's performances on the piano were often received by audiences with the same feeling of weary tolerance as her husband's violin recitals. Lady Ponsonby once commented on an evening she spent at Frogmore in January 1875 with the Edinburghs and others. After dinner, she said, Marie played the piano so badly that nobody pretended to listen, but instead turned their backs and talked. As soon as a more gifted guest sat down to perform, they all stopped talking and listened attentively. According to Lady Randolph Churchill, Rubinstein later told Marie that she 'did not play so badly for a princess.'[31] Either her playing had improved considerably in later years, or else Rubinstein was more eager to flatter than the notoriously plain-speaking Ponsonbys. Lady Churchill was one of her closest friends in England, calling her 'a warm-hearted woman of rare intelligence and exceptional character'. The duchess was in turn a fervent admirer of Lord Randolph, whom she found 'really too amusing'. After he resigned as Chancellor of the Exchequer in December 1886, much to Queen Victoria's indignation, the duchess wrote to his wife that she was 'dying to hear some more of Randolph's Windsor stories, but without the accompaniment of several pairs of eager royal household ears! Fancy if it was all reported to her [...] And that I was encouraging a minister "in disgrace".'[32]

Another of the duchess's friends was the composer Arthur Sullivan. He was a regular guest at Eastwell, and sometimes played piano duets with Marie, as well as accompanying Alfred on the violin. On an early visit in 1876 the adults decided to go for a ramble in the countryside, and when Marie discovered that Sullivan was the only one who did not have a butterfly net, she ran back to the house and fetched him one. Nevertheless, their personal relations cooled a few years later, perhaps because she had had too much of him as a person and found his over-frequent presence at Eastwell a little tiring, or else because she had enough of his comic opera style.[33]

As she was not allowed to take precedence over the Princess of Wales, relations between both were uneasy, despite their doubly close family bond. They were married to brothers who had always been close, but the princess's favourite sister was married to the duchess's brother. In spite of this, Marie could not help looking down sometimes on Alexandra as rather featherbrained, if not exactly stupid. All the same, Marie, who was never pretty but not vain, and cared nothing for her appearance apart from a passion for showing off her jewellery, was generous enough to praise Alix's good looks on more than one occasion.

The duchess had a complex relationship with the Prince of Wales. Many years later she wrote to her eldest daughter, by then Crown Princess of Roumania, that she never disliked 'Uncle Bertie' because his personality always interested and often amused her, even if she did not approve of his private life or of the company he kept.

> In my early youth, I had a great deal to suffer under him, as Papa was then his devoted slave and I did not dare move without "dear Bertie" ruling over all my movements and social entertainments. This I bitterly resented, as I never could respect his frivolous character. Having come from a strict home and not yet escaped from a highly moral education, I was greatly shocked at his "goings-on" which were well known and discussed. On the other hand, he was rather jealous of me and my riches, even I believe because of my abnormal respectability. Scenes we never had with him, for I really saw very little of him all my life. Living in London *côte à côte*, we sometime did not meet for weeks and he hardly ever came to us, perhaps once in a season for luncheon or dinner. His choice and utterly frivolous (not to say more) set never asked Papa and me and your father *au fond* disliked the set very much. Later he talked to me freely of Bertie's immoralities, but as I was never curious in my life, I did not ask much and heard them more when talked about in English society.[34]

It was Queen Victoria's two youngest children, Leopold and Beatrice, who rapidly became and remained her favourite in-laws. Leopold's all-consuming interest in education and the arts made him a man after her own heart. Because of this she was amused when he once mischievously gave her an uncomfortable moment while staying at Clarence House. One morning he came down to breakfast with a handkerchief over his mouth, explaining that he had lost a front tooth. Knowing that any accident to the haemophiliac prince that resulted in bleeding could prove serious at best, Marie anxiously asked to see the large hole in his gums. Once she had proved suitably sympathetic, he roared with laughter, admitting that the cavity was black sticking plaster and the handkerchief stains red paint.[35]

The Duchess of Edinburgh had deeply regretted leaving Russia and 'the carefree days' of her youth behind her. While she had arrived in England determined to make a success of her life in her adopted country, she was too headstrong to settle at the British Court. It had only taken her a few weeks to realise that, in spite of her best intentions, she would never be really happy in England. Soon she was complaining to her former lady-in-waiting and her mother in Russia with a long list of grievances, saying she thought London 'hideous, the air there appalling, the English food abominable, the late hours very tiring, the visits to Windsor and Osborne boring beyond belief'.[36] For someone raised in the splendours of the Winter Palace and St Petersburg, Clarence House was bound to seem dark and gloomy. The only positive comment she could make was that the English themselves were less dull than she had expected, but the people with whom she had come into contact during the first few weeks were admittedly some of the most distinguished. In anticipation of her mother coming to visit them in London, she had expensive renovations made and purchased comfortable furniture for the occasion, whenever it might arise.

On 29 August the Duke and Duchess of Edinburgh came to Balmoral for three weeks, the latter's first time north of the border. When their train drew in at Ballater Station they were welcomed not only by Queen Victoria but also a triumphal arch with the English and Russian standards above it, saying 'Welcome to Balmoral' on one sign, and the Gaelic greeting, *'Cead milleambh Failte'* ('A hundred thousand welcomes') on another. After waiting for the rain to stop they rode in an open carriage to the castle. On their journey they were welcomed by crowds of well-wishers lining part of the route, in addition to the Ballater Company of Volunteer and the Queen's Highlanders, with a piper walking in front of the vehicle as he played.

How much the duchess appreciated this enthusiastic reception is unrecorded, but the remainder of her stay in the Highlands she certainly found anything but congenial. Like several of the queen's family, she found the Scottish Highlands incredibly gloomy and dull. Walks and drives with her mother-in-law regardless of weather, which was nearly always cold and damp, and visits to neighbours and tenants, thoroughly bored her. She resented the lack of heating in the bedrooms, something that would have been totally unheard of in Russia. When she reluctantly did visit Balmoral – a summons from the queen being difficult for even her to refuse – she was frozen in her unheated bedroom and ordered that a fire should be lit for her. While she was out, Queen Victoria inspected the room and ordered a maid to throw water on the fire and open the windows.[37]

After the Edinburghs left to return south, the queen noted in her journal that the duchess 'is so pleasant even tempered, and easily pleased with everything, not at all spoilt and very unselfish. Everyone likes her.'[38] Did Marie keep her views to herself, or was the generally observant queen less perceptive than usual? One matter that had irritated her when they were at Balmoral, was that Her Majesty's Highland ghillie John Brown was abominably rude to her, forever treating his mistress 'like a small child and [seemed] to regard her with a sort of condescension'.[39] It was another view shared by several of the family, who never ceased to resent his uncouth ways and presumption. While both women could not but admire each other, they were perhaps too similar in personality, too proud and unyielding, to be altogether comfortable in one another's company. Not finding life in Britain at all congenial, the duchess was far too blunt and honest to keep up any pretence of doing so. She became increasingly homesick for Russia and always seized any chance to return there, if only for a short while.

Part II

The Mid-Victorian Years 1874–87

Chapter 1

Since coming close to losing her husband through typhoid fever in 1871 and helping to support him during his convalescence, Alexandra, Princess of Wales, had managed to find a satisfactory if not perfect balance in her family life. She appreciated that he was devoted to her and their five children, even though he was restless, easily bored and not cut out for an uneventful domestic life at home. This home environment, she knew, had to be partly a quiet sanctuary suitable for raising the youngsters, as well as a place suitable for entertaining their friends, and she ensured that it should be thus. Unlike the queen, she loved being a hands-on mother. When the babies were small, she was equally content to slip on a flannel apron and bath one of them, or change into full evening dress with all her splendid jewellery, in order to entertain the most illustrious of their guests.

The children were encouraged to mix, sometimes a little too freely for more staid observers who might share Queen Victoria's opinion that her grandsons, aged eight and seven respectively, were 'such ill-bred, ill-trained children I can't fancy them at all'.[1] Yet her exasperation was only temporary, and she readily admitted that they were often 'very amusing'. Much as the queen might have disapproved of their comparatively indulgent upbringing, she took just as keen an interest in their lives as of her other grandchildren, especially as it was inevitable that one of them would succeed his father on the throne in years to come. On the Princess of Wales, therefore, there was more pressure, a greater expectation of high standards, as the mother of a future sovereign, than on her other daughters-in-law. It was fortunate that she had sufficient charm and determination to meet the demands that the queen made of her. The latter also appreciated that, much as the wife of the heir to the throne may have had her shortcomings as a mother, inclined to be over-indulgent and lacking in discipline, she always had the children's best interests at heart, ensured that theirs was a happy home, and appreciated what a united family they always were. Alix was rarely demanding herself, but on one point she was adamant; neither of the princes was ever allowed to quarrel with his brother.

If she had a fault as a parent, it was that she had difficulty in coming to terms with the fact that they would not remain children for ever, and was reluctant to let them grow up. Even when her younger son George was a twenty-five-year-old commander of a gunboat in the West Indies, she would write to him of how she missed his 'poor dear [tear-]stained little face',[2] and her eldest daughter Louise had to celebrate her nineteenth birthday with a children's party, as that was what 'motherdear' had ordered for her.

For most of her long life Alexandra enjoyed excellent relations with her siblings, and treasured the regular summer Danish holidays when they were able to meet together once more and almost revert to a second childhood in their regular fun and games together. With her in-laws she was sometimes ill-at-ease, but never afraid to fight her corner if the occasion demanded. Because of the German plunder of her father's kingdom, as she always saw it, there were occasional difficulties with her husband's sisters who had married German princes. While she had always got on very well with the Duke of Edinburgh, she initially found the Russian-born duchess's unashamed superiority a problem.

The Princess of Wales was aware that any influence she might have on her husband was limited. Over the winter of 1874–5 Prince Albert Edward was busy making arrangements for a visit to India the following year. Initially he kept them a secret from her, as he did not wish her to accompany him. Not surprisingly, she was very annoyed when she found out. When others, not least of all the queen, tactfully pointed out to her that her duty was towards her small children who would not be able to accompany them, she insisted that her place beside her husband should come first. Her appetite for travelling to exotic places had been whetted by the family visit to Egypt, and she saw no reason why she should be deprived of a sojourn in another distant and doubtless equally exotic country. Much to her lifelong disappointment, throughout her eighty years she never had the chance to go and see India for herself.

After her husband had departed for the East, she consoled herself by inviting her parents to come and stay with her in England. Although Queen Victoria had held her daughter-in-law in high regard since the

Prince of Wales's severe illness, she made plain her disapproval of the presence in England of King Christian and Queen Louise of Denmark. When little Prince Alfred of Edinburgh was christened in November 1874, she refused to invite any of the Danish family to the chapel ceremony on the grounds that their presence would make too much of a crowd. As Sir Henry Ponsonby dryly observed, this was 'an odd way of looking at it in Windsor Castle', the spacious rooms of which had long been used to hosting vast royal gatherings from home and abroad. A little later she insisted the princess should come and visit her at Osborne House, leaving the king and queen behind in London.

The princess had no option but to obey, yet she accordingly demanded that once she had done so, she and her children should be allowed to go to Denmark and spend the winter there. With some reluctance the queen assented, but on the condition that she would return to England in time to accompany her at the state opening of Parliament in February 1875, especially as the Prince of Wales was unable to do so because he was still abroad. The princess was furious at having her visit to Denmark curtailed for what she thought was a totally unnecessary reason, and from India the prince wrote to the queen defending his wife, but the latter would not give way.

If the Princess of Wales ever became impatient with her husband's over-accommodating behaviour towards other women, she kept her feelings to herself. Being an extremely maternal woman, she not only had the dignity and the patience to rise above it, but also had compensation in the close relationship with her children. Throughout their lives the two princes (the younger, as prince and then sovereign) and three princesses (the youngest a queen consort-in-waiting) remained devoted to their parents and to each other. Albert Victor, or 'Eddy', was likeable and eager to please, but apathetic, backward and may have suffered from severe learning difficulties in an age long before such matters were understood. His brother George, or 'Georgie', was high-spirited and intelligent, though, like his parents, not in the least intellectual. Of the princesses, Louise and Victoria, or 'Toria', were very shy and tended to strike those outside their social circle as rather mournful, colourless individuals without much character; only Maud, or 'Harry', had much personality. None of them enjoyed particularly robust health, with the two younger girls particularly susceptible to eating disorders, and possibly anorexic.[3]

They failed to inherit their mother's strong constitution, and of the five children who survived to their adult years, only George reached the age of seventy. Both boys joined the royal navy and were sent to Dartmouth to begin their training in 1877 on board the cadet training ship HMS *Britannia*. Their mother found it very difficult to see them depart; to her 'it was a great wrench – but must be got through'.[4]

* * *

The Princess of Wales hoped for some time that the British royal family might one day welcome another of her closest relations into their own. There was a tentative plan to marry Queen Victoria's third son, Prince Arthur, to the Princess of Wales's sole remaining unmarried sister, Princess Thyra. It came to nothing, and in 1878 he was betrothed to Princess Louise of Prussia.

Unlike his two elder brothers, Arthur had always been and would forever remain the virtuous son of an equally spotless father. He was industrious, polite and well-liked by all, and moreover, unlike so many of his male forebears on both the Hanoverian and the Coburg side, he had apparently avoided any unfortunate entanglements with the opposite sex. His childhood interest in the army would remain a lifelong passion, and in 1866 he was enrolled at the Royal Military College at Woolwich. It was for him the start of a long and distinguished career as an army officer, which would include service during the next few years in Ireland, South Africa, Egypt, Canada and India.

Princess Louise Margaret was born on 25 July 1860 in the Marmorpalais, Potsdam, the fourth daughter of Prince Frederick Charles and Princess Marianne of Prussia. As a young man, her father had sometimes boasted of the battalion of soldiers that he was going to breed when he was married. To his disgust, his wife's first four confinements all resulted in daughters. When the third, Anna, was born in April 1858, he was so angry that he struck Marianne on the head so violently that her hearing was permanently impaired. Anna died at less than three months, but two years later Louise joined the nursery. The long-awaited son, Prince Frederick Leopold, completed the family in November 1865. It was common knowledge throughout Europe that Prince Frederick Charles and his wife were notoriously unhappy with each other. Although talk of a divorce was never realised – his brother the German Emperor William I had, allegedly, entreated them to stay together for the sake of appearances[5] – within a few years of their son's birth they were living apart.

Frederick Charles ignored his unwanted daughters, the downtrodden Marianne showed them little affection, and most of the tenderness shown to them in their young lives came from an English nurse and an English governess. Queen Victoria was always ready to consider any suitable Prussian princesses as future daughters-in-law. As early as April 1858, over two years before Louise was born, she had written to Princess Frederick William that she needed to keep a keen eye on the family, as she always thought one of the girls would be right for one of her brothers. 'You must watch over their education a little.'[6]

By 1872, the year Prince Arthur celebrated his twenty-second birthday, the queen was increasingly anxious for any princesses who would make him a good wife. It had been something of a family joke that one of the unloved Prussian sisters would ultimately become 'Mrs Arthur'. The German crown princess thought at first that one of the two elder princesses would be suitable, but as she approached maturity, the third blossomed and came to be the one. In July 1877 the crown princess wrote to her mother that Louise, now almost seventeen years old, was 'by far the nicest most sensible and nice of Marianne's girls, the only one who is intimate with our children'. She was gentle, timid and shy, seemed very ladylike in her manner and general appearance, 'but I do not think her pretty, although she has more grace and less heaviness than her elder sisters.'[7]

In February 1878 Arthur, who had been created Duke of Connaught in May 1874, came to Berlin to attend the weddings of his niece Princess Charlotte of Prussia to Prince Bernhard of Saxe-Meiningen, and of Elizabeth Anna, one of Louise's elder sisters, with Duke Frederick Augustus of Oldenburg. Meanwhile, Queen Victoria's enthusiasm for the idea of the marriage had now cooled. Her long-ingrained passion for everything and everyone German had been tempered by the ascendancy of the autocratic imperial Chancellor Otto von Bismarck, who as Prussian Minister-President had forged a new German empire after three short, victorious European wars. Moreover, she had made enquiries about Louise, and was informed that she was plain-looking with broken teeth. As Prince Frederick Charles and his wife lived apart by mutual agreement, she still thought it possible that they might divorce, and she feared her son might be tainted by association if such a scandal did happen. Arthur reassured her that she need entertain no fears that he was about to be talked into a betrothal with one of the princesses, as he had no wish to be married at present, and he quite agreed with her 'that a Prussian Princess would be unadvisable'.[8] He and his former governor, Colonel Howard Elphinstone, both thought he would be cheerfully immune to their presence.

They had reckoned without the German crown princess, an ardent advocate of the match, who had gently warned Louise that she needed to be on her best behaviour. Perhaps the duke realised that at his age it was time to settle down with a wife, and that the princess saw that this was the man who was not only thoroughly eligible but also the man she genuinely wanted. Was it love at first sight, or did they understand that they would be ideal partners and such an opportunity for them both might not occur again for a long time, if ever? Almost at once, both seemed taken with each other, and within the week he had asked for her hand. Elphinstone wrote rather guardedly to the queen that the young lady 'must have something pleasing in her character or manner, else this would never have happened.' At any rate, she would surely be 'a most dutiful daughter-in-law'.[9]

To Emperor William, the queen wrote that her son 'had formed a deep attachment' to his great-niece and had asked for permission to go and see her in the summer to ask formally for her hand. She had heard 'such good about the young lady' from everyone that she could not possibly oppose his choice. He had told her me that he was very fond of her 'and that his feelings *for her* increased every time he saw her and that he has reason to hope that this affection is returned.'[10]

After her rather protracted, not to say troubled dealings with the Danish and Russian families resulting from her first two sons' engagements, the queen was relieved by what would prove to be a comparatively trouble-free courtship. Nevertheless, her lack of enthusiasm at the news was evident in a letter she wrote in May to Sir Henry Ponsonby, saying that she did not rejoice, as so few marriages were really happy. However, it was her son's doing, and she conceded that the princess was so much praised '& said to be so good, unassuming & unspoilt, *serious minded* & *very* English we must hope for *the best* & that one so good as he is being very happy.'¹¹ Even the unpleasant Prince Frederick Charles himself informed Queen Victoria a few days later that he was 'especially gratified at Arthur's proposal [...] and I fully realise the honour of establishing a link of relationships with Your Majesty's house,' adding that Her Majesty's wishes concerning the place and date of the wedding would all be carried out.¹² Later that week Lord Odo Russell, British ambassador in Berlin, telegraphed to the queen that he had just attended a dinner at which 'the betrothal was announced by the Empress before dinner. and was received with universal joy and satisfaction.'¹³ 'I only wish I were more deserving of such kindness,' Louise wrote to her, 'but I will do my utmost always to be worthy of your Majesty's approval and regard.'¹⁴

The pre-wedding formalities were taken up with various arrangements made by Elphinstone, who was sent to Berlin shortly after the betrothal for the purpose. The more he saw of Louise, the more impressed he was, and after their first meeting he wrote to his wife that he felt they would be able to trust her unreservedly. Hers, he considered, was 'a decidedly high-minded, upright, truthful character, one that would prove strong whatever might occur, full of deep honest affection and good feeling, with tact and firmness.'¹⁵

Louise and Arthur began corresponding on a regular basis. He was impressed by her frankness in discussing subjects that other girls of her age (not yet seventeen) might have hesitated to mention, such as details about her family's behaviour and how she had felt uncomfortable after inappropriate advances and abusive behaviour from her father and grandfather. One can only guess at what might have taken place between the terrified young girl and her family, and whether it included attempts at sexual abuse as well as physical punishment for any mild transgressions. Nevertheless, she bore for life the scars of a miserable childhood, lacking confidence in herself, always frightened of doing the wrong thing and being scolded for it. When she became a mother herself she found it difficult to express her love for her children, and they grew up frightened of her. It was fortunate for everyone that she had a caring, sensitive husband who understood what she had been through and spared no effort in trying to help her adjust to a better existence as a wife than she had known as a child.

In July, on Queen Victoria's insistence, she visited England for the first time, and stayed for about ten days. The queen was very pleased with her and warmed to her immediately, though she was a little surprised when the young couple drove down to Frogmore one day without being chaperoned. It was not what she considered to be 'quite right', but her trust in their propriety was not misplaced. Arthur was one son whose behaviour had never given her any cause for alarm, and this marriage was clearly not going to bring the family any political or religious problems. She might have been ready to accept another Anglo-Danish marriage, now that the issue of the duchies that had created such ill-feeling in earlier years was long since settled, but a second Romanov attachment would certainly not have been welcome, as she had declared emphatically; 'God knows WE don't want a *second Russian* element.'[16]

Such family negotiations as were necessary took place mainly between Queen Victoria and Empress Augusta, who had long been good friends. The queen was determined as ever to get her own way regarding many of the wedding arrangements, perhaps partly as she had been obliged to concede that the ceremony for her second son would take place in Russia, as it had done in 1874, and she had never been prepared to travel such a distance, thinking it far too fatiguing for her. She restricted the number of Prussian relations who would be invited to England for the marriage and the size of their entourage, on the grounds that she did not have much room to accommodate additional people. In addition, she had decided where the bride and groom would spend their honeymoon, and what social rounds they would undertake on their return.

Fortunately for her, they were perfectly prepared to accept this degree of control. There was no danger that they would try and set themselves up as leaders of smart society in the way that the Prince and Princess of Wales had done in the early months of their marriage, much to her chagrin. Arthur explained to his future wife, with a degree of irritation, that Mama tended to 'look at everything in her own light & will not allow *anybody else* to have any views of their own.' Yet for all her faults, she was 'true to the backbone' and had always showed him 'the greatest affection & kindness'.[17] Maybe it did not take long for Louise to perceive that Arthur had always been the favourite son of a very demanding mother, and that to cooperate with her wishes and commands would surely have its advantages.

Louise had taken to her future in-laws at once. When the duke's favourite sister, Louise, heard that her husband, the Marquis of Lorne, had been appointed Governor-General of Canada and that they were due to depart almost at once, the future Duchess of Connaught wrote to her tenderly that both of them would miss her 'terribly' and were saddened that his favourite sister would not be in England for their marriage, 'but there is always a bright, sunny side in everything and so we are determined to go out and visit you there some day.'[18]

Disraeli attended the Congress of Berlin in June 1878, and one evening he sat next to Louise at dinner. He reported back to Queen Victoria that she appeared modest, calm and self-possessed, 'has an extremely interesting appearance and quite pretty [...] a beautiful complexion, a fine brow, lovely eyes, a short upper lip, and singularly beautiful hands.' As for her personality, 'she conversed freely and most naturally. All her remarks were sensible; her inquiries, as to her new home, pertinent and in good taste. I should say of a sympathizing, affectionate nature, and winning from her innocence and gentleness of manner.'[19]

Bride and groom were both destined to suffer close family bereavements in the months that led up to their wedding. Louise was back in Berlin in August a couple of months later for the marriage of her eldest sister Marie to Prince Henry of Orange-Nassau, son of King Willem II of the Netherlands. It was an effort to try and save the Dutch dynasty from extinction, and the groom was thirty-five years older than his bride. Sadly for all their efforts, Henry contracted measles and died in January 1879, leaving his widow childless and with no infant on the way. By then Arthur and his family were already in mourning after the death from diphtheria of his sister Alice, Grand Duchess of Hesse and the Rhine, on 14 December, seventeen years to the day after they had lost the prince consort. It did not help the family atmosphere that the Prince of Wales suspected Louise of repeating a story circulating around London society that Louisa, Duchess of Manchester, was his mistress and had given him several children.[20]

The wedding had been planned for 10 February 1879, the anniversary of Queen Victoria's own nuptials, but because of Alice's death it was postponed until 13 March. When someone pointed out to the duke that the number thirteen was traditionally unlucky, he answered gallantly, 'No day that gave me my wife could possibly be anything but lucky.'[21] A large array of royalty attended the ceremony at St George's Chapel, Windsor, among them King Leopold II and Queen Marie-Henriette of the Belgians, and the German Crown Prince and Princess Frederick William, who had been instrumental in helping to bring the young couple together. Among the groom's immediate family, there was one unfortunate absence. Prince Leopold had planned to attend, but while staying at Darmstadt he had injured his knee, and on medical advice he was advised to stay there until he had recovered. Lady Adela Larking, wife of an equerry to the groom, reported to the queen that as the young couple arrived at Windsor they were 'remarkably well received all along the route. The long walk from the castle to the cross road crowded with people [...] the Duchess appeared to be very little fatigued.'[22]

The honeymoon began at Claremont where the bride's father was quick to visit them, an occasion she did not welcome as he was in his characteristically bad humour and complained about almost everything. On 29 March they sailed to Calais, to begin an extensive tour of Europe with duty visits, sightseeing and various entertainments, an itinerary that began in Paris and included Spain, Gibraltar, Malta, Greece, Montenegro and Venice. They were back at Buckingham Palace by the end of the month. Bagshot Park, Surrey, had been chosen as their home. As it was still being prepared for them, and not expected to be ready until December, they settled for the next few months in the Royal Pavilion at Aldershot.

Unlike the Duchess of Edinburgh, the Duchess of Connaught was more than ready to embrace everyone and everything in her new country, particularly as she had left a family life that was never happy. Queen Victoria immediately liked her new daughter-in-law, though she could discern a strength of character in her that suggested she might find it all too easy to dominate a compliant, good-natured husband. The duchess was initially wary of the Princess of Wales, who might not be expected to welcome another Prussian princess in the family too warmly. Yet about a year after the wedding, the latter put the younger woman at ease: 'I noticed you used to consider me a most formidable personage only to be approached with fear and trembling but now we know one another I hope we shall be good friends.'[23] In spite of this, the time would come when the elder woman was not always so well disposed towards her Prussian in-law.

Once they were established at Bagshot, she was keen to immerse herself in good works on behalf of the local community, although a local clergyman was obliged to decline her offers of assistance with helping to nurse the sick, on the grounds that it was not right to expose her to the dangers of infection.[24] In spite of this, she clearly relished life in her new home. A brief visit with the duke to autumn manoeuvres in Germany in September 1880, where her father had characteristically been very unpleasant to her, was a stark reminder of the life she had been so happy to put behind her.

If the reminiscences of the duchess's sister-in-law, Princess Frederick Leopold, the former Princess Louise Sophie of Schleswig-Holstein and a lifelong Anglophile, were to be believed, the Duchess of Connaught may have become a good Englishwoman by marriage, but she 'still had the Prussian military spirit in her blood', and partly because of her husband's profession, always took a great interest in the army. Like the rest of her family, she was always very reserved, 'doubtless the result of their unduly severe bringing-up' by their father. Nevertheless, when she was made an honorary chief of her father's 8th Brandenburg Infantry Regiment, her eyes were seen to fill with tears at the honour.[25]

By late spring 1881 Louise was expecting her first child. A midwife, Mrs Brotherstone, and a more permanent nurse, Susan Chapman, were added to the Connaught household. After a very painful confinement, on 15 January 1882 the duchess gave birth to a daughter, whom they named Margaret. Her pleasure in being a mother was overshadowed first by her discovery that she was unable to breastfeed her daughter, and then about two weeks after giving birth, when she began to suffer from severe pains in the back of her leg. When it became swollen, the doctors feared that she might have blood poisoning or possibly a form of typhoid. Once she was well enough to be moved, she was taken to Windsor where she recovered to some extent. Yet the leg never healed completely, and she continued to suffer from recurring swelling and pain for the rest of her life. At first it was thought that the trouble could be traced to faulty drains at their Bagshot house. Later it emerged that her sisters, neither of whom ever really enjoyed robust health, dying at the ages of twenty-three and forty respectively, had a similar complaint.

Margaret, later 'Daisy', was christened at Windsor on 11 March. Soon afterwards, the parents left for a few weeks at Biarritz where the duchess could recuperate. Their daughter was left behind, and Mary Egerton, lady-in-waiting, reassured the queen that she was in perfect health: 'Mrs Chapman is an indefatigable walker so there is no fear of the Princess not having plenty of fresh air and exercise during the beautiful weather.'[26] Within a few months the duke was due to go on active service in Egypt. At around the same time the duchess discovered that she was expecting a second child, something that pleased neither her nor the queen.

At the end of the month, with the Prince and Princess of Wales, and the Dukes of Edinburgh and Cambridge to support her, she went to Woolwich to see off her departing husband and his fellow soldiers. It was to be the couple's first long separation. The duchess took over the effective running of their estate at Bagshot in his absence, under the guidance of Colonel Elphinstone. Fortunately the duke was only away for a few months, and arrived back in England before the confinement was due. He went to unveil a statue at Woolwich on 13 January 1883, and while he was there the duchess was delivered of their child, a healthy son whom they named Arthur after his father.

* * *

By 1880 only the youngest of Queen Victoria's sons, Prince Leopold, was still unmarried. She had never revised her opinion that he was too delicate to take a wife. Prevented through illness from pursuing an active military role, as a young man he had immersed himself in the academic world, entering Christ Church College, Oxford, studying several subjects, becoming President of the Oxford University Chess Club, and leaving with an Honorary Doctorate in Civil Law in 1876. He then travelled extensively in Europe, Canada and the United States. For a while he cherished hopes of vice-regal appointments in Canada or Victoria, Australia, but his mother refused to offer him any, although in May 1881 she conferred on him the titles he had chosen himself of Duke of Albany, Earl of Clarence and Baron Arklow.

Among the family, the Duchess of Edinburgh was particularly fond of him. They were very close in age, he being only six months older than her, and with his intellectual interests she found him more congenial company than his brothers. One wonders whether he might have been a better husband for her than his brother Alfred. He was always a favourite uncle to the young Edinburgh children and sometimes looked after them at Claremont, as in the summer of 1880 when she returned to Russia to be with her dying mother.

As a grown man he chafed under the desire of his ever-protective mother to keep him at home, and gradually understood that marriage would grant him his only hope of independence. His prospects as a chronic invalid were bound to be limited, even if he was a younger son of one of the most prestigious monarchs in the world. Queen Victoria had never really understood the full implications of haemophilia; she was aware that he had severe trouble with his joints, but nursed the hope that he would grow out of it, and sometimes she was sure he had. She seemed unwilling to accept that the bleeding was due to a hereditary condition, and thought the main problem was his epilepsy. His fits were kept a close secret within the family, but as the prince consort had hoped, the problem became less acute with maturity. Now they happened only at yearly or two-yearly intervals, usually triggered by serious episodes of bleeding, pain or severe stress, and fortunately never in public.

The names of several European princesses and English aristocratic women were linked with his as possible future brides. They included Frances 'Daisy' Maynard, later Countess of Warwick, his second cousin Princess Frederica of Hanover, Princess Stephanie of Belgium, later wife of the ill-fated Crown Prince Rudolf of Austria, and Princess Victoria of Baden, who would become a future Queen of Sweden. Queen Victoria would become almost as frustrated as he was at the continual disappointments that came his way, and at length she helped to come to the rescue.

Some twenty years earlier, Helena, Princess of Waldeck-Pyrmont, and her small daughters had visited Buckingham Palace. Since then she had had another daughter, Helen, who was now twenty. Not a word could be said against the family, who lived at Arolsen, near Darmstadt, except possibly the mother herself. According to her granddaughter Alice, later Countess of Athlone, she was 'a persistent hypochondriac' who spent most of her time in bed complaining about her poor health and demanding attention. As soon as one of her daughters approached marriageable age, or a suitable partner appeared, she soon recovered from her imaginary ailments and left her bed with remarkable speed.[27]

In the summer of 1881, while Leopold was visiting the Hesse ducal family at Darmstadt, the queen arranged for him to call upon the young princess from Waldeck on her behalf. Various delays prevented him from doing so until the autumn, and eventually he met the family at Frankfurt in November. They all got along extremely well, and after several meetings, on 17 November he proposed to Helen. One member of the family who was particularly delighted at the news was Beatrice, who had always been close to the youngest of her brothers. Immediately afterwards she wrote to both of them separately with her congratulations, telling Helen how thankful she was 'for the happiness you are giving my dear Brother.'[28] Louise was equally welcoming as she wrote to Helen the following month, telling her, 'I hope you will think of me as a sister who will always be ready to do all she can for you [...] dear Leo is so happy.'[29]

Like Leopold, Helen had always had a very enquiring mind. She enjoyed solving mathematical problems, and while she liked fiction her preferred choice of reading matter was philosophy. According to her daughter Alice, 'no one relished an argument more than she did.'[30] The queen had at first been anxious in case she might turn out to be a stereotypically remote German princess, and was relieved to be able to say in a letter to the crown princess that she was pleased Helen liked 'to go among the people'. She soon came to regard her young daughter-in-law with great respect and affection, notwithstanding her initial concerns upon hearing from the German Crown Princess that Helen was intellectually minded and unusually well-educated for a princess. Before her marriage, her father had made her superintendent of the infant schools in his principality, and in this position she devised the pupils' educational curriculum. During what would be a sadly brief life for them as a couple, Leopold proudly introduced his wife to the circle of academics he had befriended while at Oxford University.

Queen Victoria remained as superstitious as ever about a marriage in the month of May. She had decided to give the young couple Claremont House near Esher as a wedding present. Her uncle Leopold, later King of the Belgians, had married Princess Charlotte in May 1816 and settled there, and eighteen months later she died in childbirth, so April had to be the month of the ceremony. With regard to the latter she expressed herself in characteristically forthright tones, writing a couple of weeks before the ceremony to the German Crown Princess, who was unable to attend. She thought 'the idea of poor Leopold's marrying' was 'terrible' as he was 'still a complete invalid – not able to walk [...] a sad exhibition,' and feared that everyone would be shocked at the sight of him at the wedding. Her thoughts were greatly with the bride: 'I pity her but she seems only to think of him with love and affection.'[31]

The Waldeck family were slightly annoyed at the queen's insistence that the wedding should take place in England. Before they left Arolsen, Marie, Princess William of Württemberg, one of Helen's elder sisters, reminded another sibling, Queen Emma of the Netherlands, to ask their mother not to kiss Queen Victoria's hand, as she had been generous enough already and was entitled to stand on her own dignity. As the Waldecks arrived at Windsor for the wedding earlier that week, on 22 April, Leopold was on the railway station ready to greet them. Ironically, he was leaning heavily on a stick, having injured his knee badly several weeks earlier after slipping on a piece of orange peel.

The wedding took place at St George's Chapel on 27 April. Helen wore a dress that was a gift from Queen Emma. Designed in Paris, the gown was made of white satin, decorated with traditional orange blossom and myrtle and trimmed with point d'Alençon lace, with a long tulle veil held in place by a diamond headdress and a wreath of orange flowers and myrtle. She was led down the aisle by her father, George Victor, Prince of Waldeck-Pyrmont, and her brother-in-law, King Willem III of the Netherlands, with a group of eight British aristocratic women serving as her bridesmaids. After the signing of the register and the wedding luncheon, the couple drove away in an open carriage drawn by four horses with outriders and an escort of Life Guards.

That evening, the queen described her feelings in her journal. It had been very trying, she thought, to see her son 'still lame and shaky,' and she felt so much for 'dear Helen, but she showed unmistakably how devoted she is to him.'[32] A couple of days after the ceremony, she told her eldest daughter that the bride 'answered so plainly and distinctly much louder than he did – that it was heard all through the Chapel.'[33]

It was not only his lameness that had overshadowed their special day together. Helen's sister Marie was unable to join the other guests as she was nearing the end of what had been a difficult pregnancy. A couple of days before her sister's wedding she produced a stillborn daughter, and died herself later that week. The newly-married couple received the sad news at Claremont, and they stayed there for a few days seeing nobody but family.

Helen's mourning prevented her from appearing in public with Leopold that summer, and he undertook several dinners and other public engagements without her by his side, though there were inevitably times when his condition prevented him from doing so. In August he was unwell again, suffered considerable pain, and had to spend several days in bed. His wife proved a most attentive nurse, as Queen Victoria noted admiringly in a letter to her granddaughter Victoria of Hesse: 'Poor A[un]t Helen is most devoted & we can hardly get her to leave him to get out.'[34]

Soon after they settled at Claremont, the duke and duchess threw themselves wholeheartedly into local affairs. He had helped to found the Esher Church of England School, and for the rest of her life she remained actively involved in its progress. She visited at least once every term to inspect the children's standards in writing, scripture and needlework, and at the end of each academic year she presented a needlework box to the pupil who produced the best sewing. She also enjoyed exploring the local countryside, took up sculling on the Thames, and once rowed the full thirteen miles from Staines to Molesey.

Also during the summer they understood that Helen would become a mother early in the new year. They were invited as guests of the family at Balmoral that September. Helen did not feel like joining the organised countryside walks and expeditions in which she would have undoubtedly been expected to participate. The queen decided she was delicate, and sent instructions to Robert Collins, Leopold's former tutor, lifelong friend and now comptroller of the couple's household, that he must allow no heating at Claremont once they returned, as it would be much too unhealthy. Collins was one of the most devoted servants of the family; he would remain with the duchess for many years, and become tutor to their children as well.

As ever, Queen Victoria's word was law. Perhaps the superstition and a fear of history repeating itself after Princess Charlotte's death at Claremont some sixty years earlier still cast its spell over her, and she insisted that the confinement should take place at Windsor. The Princess of Waldeck, still grieving after the loss of an elder daughter in childbirth, came to help nurse her youngest daughter. This time all was well, and on 25 February 1883 a daughter was born, named Alice in honour of Leopold's still sorely-missed sister.

Although shy at heart, the Duchess of Albany was evidently a woman of determined character. Until she arrived, it had normally been the practice of members of the family to write to the queen if they had any problems. Sir Henry Ponsonby was startled when he found that the duchess refused to send any messages through an intermediary, and insisted on speaking to, or if necessary confronting, the queen face to face. After one such occasion, it was noticed, the duchess did not dine at the queen's table, but alone with the duke.[35] However, Queen Victoria always respected those members of her family who stood up to her if they had good reasons, so it can be assumed that any coolness between them was only temporary.

Having joined a large family in which there were inevitably petty jealousies and unspoken but deeply-resented beliefs of favouritism, Helen was aware that she had to tread carefully. She was perceptive enough to see at once that under many a bluff exterior lurked a heart of gold. The Prince of Wales might be given to banter and teasing, but it was never malicious. She could disapprove of him telling the family a little unkindly to call his elder son, Eddy, 'Collar and Cuffs' because of his unusually long neck and arms, yet it never lessened her gratitude to the man who showed no resentment of the fact that Queen Victoria had demonstrated the confidence in Leopold she never extended to her eldest son and heir. To the duchess and her two children, he was unfailingly generous, and she repaid his loyalty by always taking his part in any misunderstandings or difficulties he had with the queen. Some years later, he told his niece Alice how much he had always admired and respected her mother.[36]

She also displayed considerable empathy with any members of the family when they were unwell. In particular, her sister-in-law Helena experienced her sympathy during what was a difficult time for her. While some in the royal circle, especially one or two of the doctors, thought her regular bouts of illness were hypochondria, and her over-indulgence in taking laudanum verged on self-harm, the duchess realised that she was suffering from severe depression. It was partly her help and encouragement that helped Helena overcome her addiction and resume an active life, not least her active patronage of several charities, until well into her sixties.

Ella Taylor, a friend of the family, also took to the duchess immediately, noting that the more she saw of her the more she liked and admired her, 'so simple, so unaffected & good. She is clever too & full of humour &

fun.'[37] The art critic John Ruskin, a lifelong friend of the couple and a regular visitor to Claremont, wrote to a relation of his in October 1883 that she was 'really pretty when she laughs – but rather severe and alarming when she doesn't'.[38]

By the summer of 1883 the duchess was beginning to undertake engagements in public on her own, such as presenting prizes at the National Orphan Home at Ham Common. Her schedule was interrupted in June when she had a miscarriage, but she was well enough to continue the following month, and in August they went to Germany on a round of visits to relations.

Queen Victoria, and perhaps others in the family as well, had always thought it remarkable that the delicate Leopold had lived to reach the age of thirty, take a wife, and become a father. They would have been saddened, though not surprised, when they realised that he would be the shortest lived of her nine children. That autumn the duchess was expecting again. Early in the new year of 1884 the duke was afflicted with painful swelling in the joints. He made plans for them to take a short holiday together in Cannes, after another round of public engagements. Suddenly she was taken ill, and there were fears that she might have a second miscarriage. As he was still suffering, he was advised by his doctors that a short break in a better climate would be essential, and he should go on his own if necessary. The duchess was now out of danger, but the doctors warned that in her state of health it would be better for her not to travel abroad for several months.

He arrived in Cannes at the end of February, stayed with friends, and was soon very much at home. Almost at once he was making plans to buy a plot of land there on which he could build a family holiday home. One day while looking out to sea, he remarked that he 'would rather die [there] than anywhere else in the world'.[39] It would prove an oddly prescient remark.

While he was there, Louisa, Lady Knightley, went to Claremont to stay with the duchess. She had known the duke since he was a boy, had made friends with the duchess as well shortly before their wedding, and became her lady-in-waiting. On this occasion both women discussed the plans that Helen had for various good works she was hoping to do in the area. Lady Knightley found her 'very amiable, with plenty of good sound common sense and the best intentions'. She also noticed that the duchess did not seem to care much for reading, but was much more enthusiastic about her needlework.[40]

Yet tragedy was about to follow. On 27 March the duke had a fall, perhaps caused by a fit or a brief loss of consciousness, hit his knee badly, and was put to bed. Early the following morning he was found to be suffering convulsions that soon proved fatal. Helen was at Claremont with her sister-in-law Princess Helena and a group of friends when a telegram came to tell her that he had passed away. A heartbroken Queen Victoria went to visit her the next morning. 'She laid her hand on my shoulder, and kept saying: "Poor mother," and looked so sweet, young, and touching.'[41] Among the condolences from members of the immediate family was a telegram from the Duke and Duchess of Connaught, who were 'quite stunned at terrible news, God help you bear this new sorrow, poor Helen!!'[42]

The duke was buried at St George's Chapel on 12 April. His widow attended a short service in the Albert Memorial Chapel in which the coffin was to remain until the funeral the following day, then returned to her apartments at Windsor where she stayed until after the service, supported by her mother and Queen Emma. The Princess of Wales had always been particularly devoted to Leopold. It was on her arm that the queen leant during the sad ceremony, and who led her weeping back to her carriage afterwards – 'Dear Alix, so kind and helpful'.[43]

Helen had been able to see his final wish carried out. Soon after his death, she had found a letter addressed to her in which he made clear his wish to be buried in the royal vault beneath St George's Chapel and not, as the queen would have preferred, in the mausoleum she had built after the prince consort's death for his remains, and where she intended hers should rest once she was gone. Leopold had chosen St George's Chapel because he was married there, and also because 'there would always be singing over him'.[44]

Among the letters of condolence the duchess received were those from Cardinal Manning and from the Poet Laureate, Alfred, Lord Tennyson, who composed a memorial epitaph for him, and also John Ruskin, who composed an inscription for the Albany memorial tablet in Esher Church. Four months later at Claremont, in July, the widowed Duchess of Albany gave birth to a son, whom she named Charles Edward in accordance with his late father's wishes. As his sister would note in her memoirs, the little prince was not only Duke of Albany from birth, but surely the only person in the world ever to have been born a duke.[45] Queen Victoria was warned when the birth was expected, so she could be there at the actual time. According to a report on the birth left by Collins: 'On the Duchess being told it was a Boy she cried out in a heartrending manner for her beloved husband, whose dearest wish it had always been to have a son to carry on his name and title, and that the Queen deeply moved, flung herself upon the bed, and embraced and comforted her.'[46]

After the christening at Claremont in December, Queen Victoria noted when writing to Victoria of Hesse that Helen 'was greatly tried but behaved so courageously though she was nearly breaking down often, but she bore up till it was all over.'[47]

Losing her husband had come at a difficult time for Helen for yet another reason. The duke's annual grant of £25,000, which would have been payable on 1 April 1884, was withheld as he had died a mere four days previously, and from that date his widow was obliged to live on £6,000, less than a quarter of the sum.[48] Nevertheless, it was still a considerable sum of money by the standards of the time, and enabled her to maintain a staff including a lady-in-waiting, a comptroller, governess and nurse for the children, servants, housekeeper, footmen, nursery footmen, housemaids, cooks, kitchen maids, coachmen, stable boys and gardeners. Claremont House and its grounds required upkeep, but neither she nor her children ever wanted for anything except perhaps warmth, as the queen with her legendary imperviousness to cold would never allow her to install central heating there.

In England, the whole family proved readily supportive of the young mother who had been left a widow at only twenty-three, with two small children to bring up. It was ironic, although under the circumstances not surprising, that the last of Queen Victoria's daughters-in-law to join the family should have been the first to lose her husband. She had been well aware that Leopold was unlikely to live long, and the fortitude she always displayed in the face of her loss did not go unnoticed. Queen Victoria never ceased to praise her, writing to the German Crown Princess later that year how she set such a good example to everyone else, 'always a kind, sweet smile on her poor, sad face and cheerful and always thinking of others and not of herself.'[49]

Such comments may have been a veiled allusion to the queen's youngest daughter. In her late twenties Beatrice, who had seemed destined for a life of spinsterhood at home caring after Mama, astonished everyone by falling in love with and wishing to marry Prince Henry of Battenberg, whose eldest brother, Louis, had married Alice's eldest daughter, Victoria, in April 1884. The queen initially thought it was a mere passing infatuation, but Beatrice stood her ground with a determination that astonished but secretly delighted her siblings. After a brief period of coolness passed between mother and daughter, the latter had to face the realization that 'Baby' had a right to her own life as her elder sisters had done. Ever a conciliatory presence, the Princess of Wales admitted to Mama that she could well understand what a shock it must have been to her, but they must all hope that 'it [would] all be for the best, and that she will continue for many a long year to be the same help and comfort to you that she has hitherto always been.'[50]

In the final week of December 1884, the queen gave her consent to the betrothal of Beatrice and Henry, much as she could hardly bear the thought of losing her. She noted in her journal how delighted the family were, 'and poor Helen so pleased too, though it must be very trying for her.'[51] As a comparative newcomer, Helen was tactful enough to avoid taking sides too openly, while gently making it clear where her sympathies lay. Beatrice and Henry were married in July 1885, on the understanding that they would make their married home with the queen.

Helen was also among those present at the annual service at the mausoleum marking the prince consort's death in December 1884, and the queen remarked on 'her courage, her wonderful gentle, unmurmuring resignation and gratitude to God for what is left to her and her courage to struggle'.[52] Three months later, on the first sad anniversary of the Duke of Albany's death, there was an evening service at St George's Chapel, Windsor, in which the music included Chopin's Funeral March at Helen's request.

Like most mothers and children of their time and class, the duchess saw her son and daughter only at particular times, usually in the late afternoon, when Alice and Charles had their supper at a little table in their mother's sitting room. After eating, they would stay with their mother until bedtime, knitting (with Charles joining in as well), sewing or painting.

In order to encourage them at the former activity, she would wind a small bronze animal in a large ball of wool, which they could claim only once they had finished the wool. They kept their little prizes in tins decorated with pictures from *Alice in Wonderland*, given to them personally by the author, Lewis Carroll, who had been a friend of the family since long before Leopold was married. He maintained his relationship with the duchess and her children, although he found Alice a little 'unruly'. On one of their first meetings she had inadvertently made fun of his severe stammer, asking loudly and clearly why he 'waggled his mouth', and she had to be removed hurriedly by an apologetic lady-in-waiting. Helen would often read aloud to them, especially before bedtime. Keen to give them an awareness of social conditions in her choice of books, and impress on them that not everybody was born and raised in such comfortable conditions as they were, she gave them a lifelong taste for the works of Charles Dickens. Although basically republican in his sympathies, the novelist had admired his sovereign as a person, and in turn she, her daughter-in-law and several other members of royalty held his writings in high regard.

All three saw more of each other on Saturdays than any other day, when the duchess took the children for walks in the countryside. Before they attended church every week, she gave them their Sunday School lesson. She had been raised a Lutheran, adopted the Anglican faith on marriage, and throughout her life she remained a devout, even straitlaced Christian, ensuring that her children were brought up strictly. They were often invited by the queen to stay, and were therefore present during the first Christmas at Osborne of Helen's widowhood.

At family gatherings, the Duchess of Albany was in her element. It was noticed, by the lady-in-waiting Marie Mallet, that when staying at Windsor or Osborne she was always ready to prolong the entertainment of an evening after the queen had retired to bed. The duchess, Marie wrote after one such occasion, 'was such a dear and so un-stiff',[53] as she begged her to sing. Sometimes she would also turn the handle of the mechanical piano while others danced.

Chapter 2

While it might be going too far to hint at anything resembling a beauty contest between the Princess of Wales and the Duchess of Edinburgh, it was clear that the former was one of the most popular members of the royal family in the later Victorian era, and her sister-in-law one of the least-liked. The wife of the heir to the throne was blessed with good looks that remained almost unsullied into old age, as well as impeccable dress sense and charm. She also had the dubious benefit of being married to an unfaithful albeit loving husband, always too ready to mix with society beauties while his wife was at home or on holiday in Denmark, revelling in the great Scandinavian royal family gatherings that he joined with reluctance as he found them utterly tedious.

As for the woman who always considered that a grand duchess of Russia was a far greater honour than being a mere duchess in England, she was a haughty woman who also took refuge in a marriage that turned out to be less than congenial, finding more pleasure in her young children, intellectual company and in particular her music. She was too proud to be unduly concerned about what others thought of her or said behind her back about her dowdy clothes, her unladylike habit of smoking cigarettes in public, or about how jealous the princesses might be of her splendid jewellery. Plain in looks, plain-spoken and dowdily dressed, she had acquired a matronly figure comparatively early in life. Queen Victoria had noted within less than a year of her wedding that she was not pretty and graceful, and feared she would age early.[1]

While unfailingly generous to her friends, she was too brusque in manner, and too impatient with popular opinion to care about being liked by the people. Anything but vain, she had no illusions about her lack of beauty, although she was furious in 1883 when Queen Victoria commissioned her new court painter, Carl Sohn, to paint a family group of her, the duke and their two eldest children. The long sittings were an imposition, but what she disliked even more was having her 'pig-like face reproduced on canvas and handed over to posterity'. She had not minded so much being painted in previous years as 'a nice, lively, thin and fresh young lady,' but now she complained that Sohn's first sketch of her was 'monstrous'. He had been provided by the queen, she said, with 'the most atrocious photographs' ever taken of her.[2]

Having little in common with Queen Victoria apart from an indomitable personality and total absence of vanity, and also growing apart from her husband after a few years of marriage, she never felt at home in Britain, and always made the most of any opportunities to spend time in Russia or Germany with her family. In the early days of their marriage, she had also had something of a respite overseas when the duke was appointed to the command of HMS *Sultan* in 1876 and transferred to the Mediterranean Fleet. He was based in Malta, and for several months of the year the family lived at the San Antonio Palace. It was here that their second daughter was born on 25 November that year and christened on New Year's Day 1877 with the names Victoria Melita, the latter in honour of the island where she was born.

One thing that the Princess of Wales and the Duchess of Edinburgh had in common was a remarkable ability to get their own way most of the time, the former by charm, the latter by being overbearing, coupled with a refusal to let anybody stand in her way and with hardly a thought that such assertive behaviour might make her unpopular. Both were married to husbands who were not always sensitive to the needs of their wives, and they refused to play the downtrodden woman at home very well, albeit in different ways. They also fully understood the need to defend their own families at home against the disdain of Queen Victoria, who had always traditionally placed her German relatives on a pedestal and tended to give scant consideration to the national interests of any daughters-in-law from other countries.

In her first year of marriage, Alexandra had had to swallow, and never forgot, the humiliation of her father's kingdom being decimated by the first of Bismarck's carefully contrived wars of conquest that were part of his plan to establish Prussian supremacy over the other states. During the conflict that broke out in April 1877, when Tsar Alexander II declared war on Turkey, Marie had to face the possibility that England and Russia might shortly be at war against each other, a threat that would have placed her as well as her husband in the most impossible of situations. The queen was incensed against the Asiatic empire, telling her prime minister, Benjamin Disraeli, that if only she were a man, 'she would like to go & give those horrid Russians, whose word one cannot trust, such a beating!'[3] The Duke of Edinburgh was annoyed by her tactless comments that she found it 'very unfortunate' he should have married a Russian grand duchess, and he had no hesitation in showing her letters to his wife, who in turn passed on the contents of them to her father. The tsar and tsarina were equally angry at the queen's insulting remarks, dismissing them as 'worthy of a fish-wife', and regretting that her son had 'not got more character.'[4] It was an additional affront to them that for a while she would not allow Marie to come to Russia and stay with the tsarina while the tsar was away at military headquarters during the war. One small consolation for the duchess was that she had an ally in her sister-in-law. The Princess of Wales spent the spring of 1877 in Greece visiting her brother King George, and during the war that broke out not long afterwards, she was vehemently pro-Russian, favouring a territorial border adjustment between Greece and Turkey that would be to the latter's advantage.

Although an Anglo-Russian clash of arms was avoided, the duchess never ceased to worry about the well-being of her parents. The tsarina had been so ill with consumption for several years that she spent much of her time outside Russia, in more moderate climates. She was also broken-hearted, although initially uncomplaining, at Tsar Alexander II's open flaunting of his mistress, Catherine Dolgorouky, and the second family of small children born as a result of their affair. Much as the duchess loved her father, she was angry that he was so unfaithful to her mother and seemed quite shameless in doing so.

The Duke and Duchess of Edinburgh and their three children spent the summer of 1878 in the Edinburgh Palace, Coburg, and on 1 September a third daughter was born. Blonde, quiet-natured and plump, she was baptised Alexandra Louise Olga Victoria, her godparents being the reigning Duke and Duchess of Coburg. In the family, she would always be known as 'Sandra'. After their return to England, the Admiralty sent their father to sea again. Sadness would befall them just over a year later, on 13 October 1879, when the duchess gave birth to a stillborn son.

Another cause of grave anxiety that had weighed heavily on her was the fact that the tsar continually feared for his life at the hands of terrorists who had already made several unsuccessful attempts to kill him. She, too, came uncomfortably close to the experience on one such occasion on 17 February 1880, while in St Petersburg visiting him and her ailing mother.

Father and daughter were about to go in and join their guests for dinner that evening. The tsar's brother-in-law, Prince Alexander of Hesse, was one of those invited. He had been delayed by the late arrival of his train, and thus inadvertently saved their lives. Their meal was postponed by about half an hour, and as the tsar and the duchess were about to walk to the dining room, they were startled by the sound of a loud explosion. Several rooms had been severely damaged with windows broken, while the dining room was full of thick smoke, broken china and shattered glasses. Although none of the family was injured, several guards were killed and many more severely injured. In reporting the incident to Queen Victoria, Lord Dufferin, the British Ambassador to Russia, confirmed that the duchess had not been harmed, and throughout the incident 'exhibited great coolness and presence of mind.'[5]

Meanwhile, Empress Marie was unharmed but bedridden in her room in the Winter Palace. Now seriously ill and unable to talk, she could still hear the noise made by the children of her husband by Princess Catherine Dolgorouky as they played on the floor above. The tsar's insensitivity towards his wife had caused sharp differences of opinion within the family. His brothers took his side in supporting the liaison with his mistress, while his sons (apart from Alexis, a lifelong bachelor whose life according to the wags was one of 'fast women and slow ships') and their wives had nothing but sympathy for the cuckolded tsarina, and were angry with their unfeeling father. The Duchess of Edinburgh was deeply upset but found it difficult to condemn him, although it is believed that she had at least one furious quarrel with him on the subject, and she said she found it unbearable that when coming to visit her dying mother, 'Papa prohibited us from coming in unannounced.'[6] She and her siblings could barely bring themselves to discuss this state of affairs between themselves. One day, the duchess and her brother Serge were riding with their father in the park when a carriage drove past them. The tsar ordered his driver to stop, got out, said goodbye to his daughter and son, and climbed into the other vehicle, which contained Catherine and their children. Marie and Serge were so astonished that they continued their journey to Tsarskoe-Selo without exchanging either a single word or a glance at each other.[7]

The Duchess of Edinburgh left for Russia again at the end of May to be with her mother, and was in the palace nearby, although not at her bedside, when she was released from her sufferings in her sleep early on 3 June. She spent several weeks in Russia, her departure delayed by an attack of measles in July while she was staying at Tsarskoe-Selo. Meanwhile, the tsar knew that he probably did not have long to live either. Determined to provide some peace of mind for his loved one, no matter how brief, he waited for the minimum forty days' mourning as laid down by the church, then he married Catherine in a secret ceremony. The news was kept so private that not till November did Queen Victoria learn, through a letter from the German crown princess, that he had made the woman she called 'this dreadful lady' his wife. His family knew at once, and most of them were horrified. The duchess wrote sorrowfully to him that 'I pray that myself and my junior brothers, who were particularly close to Mama, would one day be able to forgive you.'[8]

For once, it was with a sense of relief that she was able to leave Russia. She and her children spent the rest of summer at Coburg, arriving in the last week of August, where the duke joined them a few days later.

The second marriage of Tsar Alexander II lasted for less than seven months. One morning in March 1881, the Edinburgh children found their mother on her knees in her bedroom at Clarence House, weeping bitterly. She had just been given the shocking but hardly unexpected news that he had met a brutal death at the hands of his own people. After attending a military review in St Petersburg, he was riding in his carriage to pay a family visit, when a bomb narrowly missed him but killed and maimed several bystanders. He stopped and walked over to see how badly they were wounded, only to be struck down by a second device. Semi-conscious and badly mutilated, he was carried back to his palace to die.

Although she feared they might fall victim to a similar outrage in the Russian capital and gave her consent with reluctance, Queen Victoria's two elder sons and their wives travelled to the Russian capital for the funeral ceremonies, which lasted for more than two weeks. When they arrived, the duchess went to the place on the street where her father had been killed, to kneel in prayer. As well as attending the obsequies under the strictest of police precautions against further attempts by the conspirators and their supporters, she and the Princess of Wales were both ideally placed to offer comfort to the new sovereigns, Tsar Alexander III and Empress Marie Feodorovna, in what promised to be an uncertain future for them. The princess insisted on staying behind for a few more days after the other English guests had departed, on the grounds that her sister needed her company for longer. When the queen objected again to her putting herself in continued danger of assassination, the Prince of Wales took his wife's side, albeit with misgivings for the same reason.

There was one moment of light relief during those days of gloom in the Russian capital. The Prince of Wales had been asked to invest Tsar Alexander III with the Order of the Garter. A small dignified ceremony was arranged to take place in the Anichkov Palace, with members of his staff carrying the insignia on velvet cushions. As they proceeded into the throne room, a loud English female voice called out very clearly, 'Oh! my dear! Do look at them! They look exactly like a row of wet-nurses carrying babies!' The tsarina and the Princess of Wales looked at each other and exploded with laughter.[9]

Queen Victoria was full of sympathy for the duchess, who had lost her mother and then her father in such sad circumstances within less than a year. 'Poor darling Marie on whom her father doted, it is almost too much to bear,' she wrote to the German Crown Princess. 'But she is very courageous.'[10] The duke asked her to extend a special invitation to stay at Balmoral that summer, and as she was now the only parent Marie had left, she may have come to view her daughter-in-law in a rather more kindly light than she had previously done. There was, however, no general truce from the Romanovs. Tsar Alexander III would never have a good word for the widow of Windsor, whom he told his family unforgivingly was 'a pampered, selfish, sentimental old woman'.[11]

Three years later, on 20 April 1884, the duchess gave birth to her last child, a fourth daughter whom she and the duke named Beatrice. She had wanted Leopold and his younger sister, Beatrice, to be the godparents of the baby, whom they had expected would be a boy. Sadly, Leopold's sudden death at Cannes had come a little less than a month before Bee was born.

* * *

By time she had reached the age of forty, the Princess of Wales was taking on an increasing number of public duties at home. Queen Victoria was grateful that she now spared her so much of 'the strain and fatigue of functions' in opening bazaars, attending concerts and visiting hospitals in her place: 'she not only never complains, but endeavours to prove that she has enjoyed what to another would be a tiresome duty.'[12] One of her particular interests was the London Hospital, Whitechapel Road, where she and her husband opened a suite of new buildings in May 1887. Its most famous and perhaps most tragic patient was Joseph Merrick, the 'Elephant Man'. Elephantiasis had turned him into a grossly disfigured monster who had suffered the degradation of being exhibited at fairs and showgrounds, until he was admitted to the hospital as a patient. The princess heard about his story and asked if she could meet him. Although the staff warned her gently on her arrival that her first sight of him would be distressing, she refused to be put off, and spent some time with him and talked to him quite naturally. For the next two years, until his death in 1890 at the age of twenty-seven, she sent him a Christmas card containing a friendly message written in her own hand. Throughout her life she had a reputation for generosity among high and low alike, cheerfully giving away money to anything and anyone whom she considered a deserving cause. As her income was not unlimited, her comptroller Sir Dighton Probyn did his best to try and maintain some control over her spontaneous kindnesses, with mixed success.

Although the Prince and Princess of Wales were personally on the best of terms with the prime ministers of Queen Victoria's reign, they always scrupulously avoided being seen to show any favour to one political party over another. This did not prevent them from being accused of once participating in, or at least supporting, agitation in favour of a new reform bill. In July 1884 a peaceful demonstration marched through central London to aid the cause, and they decided they would like to watch. The organisers were warned that Their Royal Highnesses would be watching from the house of Lord Carrington, opposite Horse Guards Parade. When the procession drew level with the house, the marchers were instructed to come to a halt and sing *God Bless the Prince of Wales*. When they did, loud applause greeted the appearance of the prince and princess on the balcony. They stood for over an hour acknowledging the hearty greetings, then the princess complained of a headache and the heat, and went back into the house. Almost at once the enthusiasm turned into boos and catcalls and she was asked to return, propped up on a pile of sofa cushions, to smile and wave until they had passed. The crowd outside the house was so large that Carrington had to ask people to make way for the royal carriage. They then formed a lane so that the princess and her daughters could drive slowly across the ground, thus earning another ovation. It went down badly with the Conservatives at Westminster, who claimed Carrington had trapped them into showing solidarity with the mob, but the prince was unrepentant and said it had been an interesting experience for them.

Matters went less smoothly for them when they visited Ireland in April 1885. A reception in Dublin was suitably loyal, and the princess was made a Doctor of Music at Trinity College, much to her delight as she remarked with a smile afterwards that her husband had become a mere Doctor of Law, 'not such a grand one as me!' There was less of this when they went the following week to Cork, a centre of Irish nationalism. On the morning they drove into the city, crowds lined the streets with a few loyalist cheers that were completely drowned out by hoots, hisses and boos from a crowd of over 2,000. Both remained calm and smiling through a mob waving black handkerchiefs and flags, and refused to cut short their programme. Nevertheless, as their equerry remarked afterwards, it was 'like a bad dream'.

The princess was wise enough to avoid involvement in any controversies, but she still had decided views of her own regarding some of the great matters of the day. She once smilingly told Henry Ponsonby, who was himself anything but a diehard Conservative, that she liked 'talking high treason sometimes and meddling in politics'. One area of foreign policy in the mid-1880s that attracted her attention was the crisis involving Egypt and the Sudan, and she was 'tired of Egyptian bother'. Egypt, a British protectorate, was responsible for suppressing Mahdist rebels in the Sudan who supported independence from their Egyptian rulers. Prime Minister Gladstone, and his Secretary of State for War, Lord Hartington, proposed non-intervention, and persuaded the Egyptian government to evacuate their garrisons in Sudan. General Charles Gordon, a former Governor-General of Sudan, was appointed to oversee the task. He believed the Mahdi must be defeated, or he might gain control of Sudan, and Egypt would surely follow. With promises of Anglo-Egyptian support, he reached Khartoum in February 1884 on a mission to expel the Mahdi. His request for reinforcements was refused, and aware they were closing in, he ordered the strengthening of fortifications around Khartoum. In April, the tribes north of the city rose in support of the Mahdi and besieged the city. As Gordon's situation worsened, the government ordered him home, but he refused, insisting he would stay. In July Gladstone reluctantly agreed to send an expedition, which took several months to organise and only entered Sudan in January 1885. Warned of the British advance, the Mahdi attacked the city wall just before midnight on the night of 25–26 January. Gordon and the entire British garrison, weakened by starvation, were slaughtered within a few hours, as were 4,000 of the city's inhabitants. The advance elements of the relief expedition arrived two days later. After the fall of the city, the surviving British and Egyptian troops withdrew from the Sudan, leaving Muhammad Ahmad in control of the entire country.

Like Queen Victoria, the rest of the royal family, and indeed most of the country at large, the princess was horrified when they learned of Gordon's death. To her, he was the greatest hero of their day, and if the army had been sent out to Africa much earlier, she was sure that they would have avoided such a debacle. Above all, she was greatly concerned for the comfort of British troops in Egypt and the Sudan. Some thirteen years earlier, her sister-in-law Helena, Princess Christian of Schleswig-Holstein, had begun a National Society for Aid to the Sick and Wounded in Time of War, of which she had become chairman. Immediately after the fall of Khartoum, the Princess of Wales started her own branch of the society, aiming to supply comforts to the sick and wounded. She was eager to send comforts to all the troops, whether sick or well, although the National Society was affiliated to the Red Cross and therefore forbidden by the terms of its constitution to do anything to help the fighting men.

Within the family, the princess remained as popular as ever. She was still implacable in her hatred for Germany, and the more German of her in-laws would never find her easy to disregard. Ponsonby was amused one night when he overheard a heated exchange at Balmoral on one occasion between her and Louis, Grand Duke of Hesse, Princess Alice's widowed husband. The subject of the war in 1864 that had deprived Denmark of the Schleswig-Holstein duchies had come up, and the grand duke insisted that it had been a Danish, not a German war, implying that her father's country had been the aggressor. She maintained firmly, '*Nein, es war Deutsch.*' They both stuck resolutely to their views, and at length he gave her 'a long explanation to which she became utterly deaf'. This rendered any further discussion pointless, thus presenting her with a victory (or so it seemed to her), at which she turned to her daughter, smiling, as if to say, 'I've settled him!'[13]

* * *

By 1883, the Duchess of Connaught had come a long way from the 'poor child' whose cause had been taken up in Berlin by Crown Princess Frederick William. Having left a country that was synonymous with her unhappy childhood, and now a mother of two small children, she had gained much in confidence and maturity, managing the affairs of her husband while he was away on campaign, and establishing a position for herself in his family. She had learnt to handle Queen Victoria's demands with a forbearance and skill that mirrored his own. Above all, she had found a kind and reliable husband who clearly loved her, and would support her in everything.

While it was an advantage for her to have married Queen Victoria's favourite child, this brought its own problems, during her lifetime and after her death. It cast a shadow over her relationship with members of the family who had been hurt by the queen's favouritism. In everyday life as well, the sovereign's favour did not exclude the Duke and Duchess of Connaught from some of the frustrations of being subject to her will. For Louise, in 1883, this was brought home most acutely in her children's nursery, where she was obliged to accept the choices and decisions of her mother-in-law.

The duke's army career was progressing favourably. In August 1883 he was appointed Commander of the Meerut Division of the Bengal Army. Louise did not consider leaving his side for a moment, and the queen agreed that her place was by her husband's side. She forbade them to take the children, on the grounds that the climate would not be right for them. When the family left Balmoral at the end of the summer, she insisted, little Margaret and Arthur would have to stay in her care.

As there was no choice in the matter, the duchess had to acquiesce. On 27 October they said goodbye to the children and left for London, deeply affected at having to leave them at such a tender age. Five days later, they left London, where friends, relatives and a detachment of Scots Guards assembled at Charing Cross to wave them farewell. They were making their way to Brindisi, where they would embark on the steamship *Cathay* for the voyage east. Any apprehension or homesickness they might have felt was soon forgotten in the efforts they were making to learn Hindustani in preparation for their new life.

The ship docked off Bombay on 21 November. As the duke and duchess came ashore, they found themselves at the heart of an unexpectedly large and cheerful public gathering, with most of the attention focused on Louise. People were keen to welcome the queen's son, but even more so her daughter-in-law. She became the first European princess to set foot in India, and great hopes rested on the effect that her presence might have, for the women of the Raj and for the greater population of Indian women. Crowds were so tightly packed in the streets that they moved as one, and the cheering became overwhelming as the coach proceeded to Government House for dinner and a celebratory firework display. Three days later, the couple left by train for Meerut.

The duke's first tour of duty lasted until 1885, and the duchess was always by his side. It was full of functions and one fascinating experience after another as she attended regimental functions, danced at balls, presented colours, and visited native princes and their wives, whose lives were so utterly different from that of a European princess. The other activities included watching hunts, camping out in the open air and riding up the Khyber Pass. The once shy duchess revelled in a chance to lead an exotic life seeing and taking part in things that she could never have imagined while living in Germany or England.

While the Connaughts had been preparing for their travels, she had always intended to take a keen interest in the lives of women she would meet in India. She made a determined effort to examine their living conditions at first hand and speak to them, and put forward recommendations for improving the treatment of the wives of ordinary soldiers, which were noted by the commander-in-chief. Keen to ameliorate welfare services, she also took an active interest in the Women's Hospital at Meerut, and her lady-in-waiting noted that her work in India was making the duchess more confident and outgoing. Her presence was also thought to be having a positive influence on Indian society.

Yet from a family point of view, the duchess's stay in India put her at a disadvantage, as it prevented her from being with her children while they were still very small and needed her as much as she needed them. When they had left Balmoral in October 1883, Margaret was still less than two years old, and Arthur only eight months. While the queen ensured that she was given regular news from Balmoral, Windsor and Osborne, wherever she was at the time, it was a poor substitute for staying at home with them, as any young mother longed to do. In fact, the queen's news, or rather reports, on her grandchildren did not make the best of reading for a young mother who was missing her small children so badly. Two-year-old Daisy, her grandmother reported in a letter in January 1884, had recognised her mama in a photograph sent from India. The child had had 'a return of extraordinary ungraciousness & wilfulness,' although adding in mitigation that she was perhaps suffering because of 'a little sluggishness of the liver'.[14]

A few weeks later, Lady Elphinstone spent two days at Windsor, and sent the duchess a long, comprehensive and much more encouraging report on the children's progress and activities. This earned her undying gratitude, writing in reply that she missed them 'terribly' and it had been a real pleasure to hear of all their little ways. 'As a rule I am told nothing except that they are very well and flourishing and which of course is the chief and most important thing, but one longs to know of all they do and say and thousands of little things.'[15]

By the end of 1884, the queen had begun to suggest to the ministers that the Duke of Connaught ought to be appointed Commander-in-Chief of the Bombay army. She was torn between wanting to see him advance in his career, and longing to have him at home again. The government thought him too inexperienced for such a prestigious army command, and it was their reluctance more than anything else that made her determined to have him promoted. As he prepared to complete his affairs in Meerut, it was with the certainty that he would return to India before long, that somehow Louise would return with him, and this time they were determined to travel as a family. On 23 May 1885 they reached Bombay and sailed for England three days later. To their disappointment, when they were welcomed home at Charing Cross Station by members of the royal family, their own children – no longer small babies – were conspicuous by their absence as they were still at home with the queen.

It had been eighteen months since their parents last saw them, and on meeting again they were almost like strangers to each other.

For Louise especially, the fight for her control of the children would continue. The government would not give the duke the Bombay army post but instead appointed him Commander of the Rawalpindi Division, the largest in India. By the late summer of 1885 she was expecting a third child. She planned to travel east with her husband and daughter in November, while it was still safe enough for her to do so. To their annoyance, Queen Victoria refused to let the duchess go, insisting that she must have her confinement in England. The appointment was delayed, and on 17 March 1886 she gave birth to a second daughter, whom they intended to name Patricia. The queen wanted her to be called Victoria, so for official purposes she was known as Princess Victoria Patricia, and soon became 'Patsy' within the family.

Six months later they went to India, arriving at Bombay on 27 September. Early in 1887 the duchess accompanied her husband on a long tour of inspection of outlying districts, seeing Aden, Karachi and Afghanistan. It may have helped to take her mind off a difficult family situation, for they had now spent three Christmas seasons away from their children. They missed the youngsters badly, and the duchess was especially lonely when her husband was busy. A letter to her mother-in-law made her feelings clear:

> I am sorry to hear darling Daisy is so shy – it seems to be in her nature and she will never get over it ... I don't think. I hope dearest Mama that you are not angry about it, she is after all only a baby – all my family are shy. Arthur makes up for his shyness by being such a chatterbox ... I hear that Daisy is now lunching every day with you.... I lead a more solitary life than before even and see less of Arthur so that the separation from the children is very hard and the brightness of life seems dim without them – I feel so terribly anxious about them.[16]

Queen Victoria had not made the situation any easier with a remarkable lack of tact, as the duke made clear in a letter to his sister Louise. In February he said to her that they had had little news from home, and were becoming 'a little exasperated' when the queen repeatedly told them about the affection their children had for 'Auntie B and Uncle Liko [Beatrice and Henry]'. It was hard enough for them to have to be separated from the children for so long, and then to be told how fond they were of other people was a little too much. 'We would give anything to bring them or have them sent out to us this autumn but I fear the opposition in high quarters "on medical grounds" will be something fearful.'[17]

At around the same time, plans were being made throughout the empire for the forthcoming jubilee to celebrate Queen Victoria's fifty years on the throne. The duchess was anxious to know about what plans were being made in London as they had heard nothing by the first few weeks of the year. In India during February, she wrote to the queen, there were to be parades of troops, a governors' ball, and special dinners as part of the celebrations. 'It is wonderful what people are doing ... and how loyal they are everybody says.'[18] A few days later, she was reporting on the telegrams of congratulation they were receiving about the anniversary, articles in the press and the general enthusiasm: 'I do wish it could have been possible for you to have had one glimpse of the rejoicings and expressions of loyalty shown to your person and to the throne.'[19]

* * *

At around this time the Duchess of Edinburgh was also spending much of her time abroad. She and the duke were both present at the coronation of Tsar Alexander III at Moscow in May 1883, a magnificent, well-organised event that came as a relief to them after the unforgettably grim ceremonies for her father's funeral. Later that year she was expecting another child, and was at Eastwell for the confinement where her youngest daughter, named Beatrice ('Bee'), was born on 20 April 1884. Years later, she regretted that she had not had even more children: 'The only real heavenly moment is the birth of the child. This cannot be compared to anything else. I think if I had even a dozen children I would have kept the same feeling.'[20]

In July 1884 they went to Ilinskoe to visit her brother Serge, who had married Queen Victoria's granddaughter Ella (Elizabeth) of Hesse and the Rhine the previous month. Queen Victoria had always taken a particular interest in the upbringing and well-being of her Hessian children, left motherless by the death of her second daughter, Alice, from diphtheria in December 1878. She was aghast when Ella had announced her intention to

Queen Victoria, the Prince Consort and their children, from a contemporary montage. Children, from left: Princess Helena; the Princess Royal; the Prince of Wales; Prince Leopold; Princess Beatrice; Princess Louise; Prince Alfred; Prince Arthur; Princess Alice.

The Prince and Princess of Wales (standing in centre), 9 March 1863, the day before their wedding. From left: Princess Louise; Princess Christian and Prince Frederick of Denmark; Princess Alice (Princess Louis of Hesse); Crown Prince Frederick William of Prussia; Princess Dagmar of Denmark; Victoria, Princess Royal (Crown Princess Frederick William of Prussia); Prince Louis of Hesse; Princess Helena; Prince Christian and Prince William of Denmark.

Alexandra, Princess of Wales, shortly before her marriage.

The Duke and Duchess of Edinburgh with Tsar Alexander II and his son the Tsarevich, later Tsar Alexander III, c.1874.

The Princess of Wales with her children, c.1873. Left to right: Princesses Victoria, Maud, Louise (front); Princes Albert Victor and George.

Queen Victoria, the Duchess of Edinburgh and Princess Beatrice, 1877.

Princess Victoria Melita, Prince Alfred, Princess Alexandra (front), Princess Marie of Edinburgh, 1880.

The Prince and Princess of Wales at Osborne, 1880, Children, left to right: Princesses Maud, Louise, Victoria (front), Princes Albert Victor and George.

The Princess of Wales with her sons Prince Albert Victor and George.

Prince Leopold, Duke of Albany, and Princess Helen of Waldeck-Pyrmont at the time of their engagement, 1880.

Queen Victoria with the Prince and Princess of Wales, 1887.

The Prince and Princess of Wales and family at Marlborough House, 1889. Standing, left to right: Prince Albert Victor; Princesses Maud and Louise. Seated: Prince George, Princess Victoria.

The Duke (seated centre) and Duchess of Edinburgh (standing, back left) and family, 1890. Seated, left to right: Prince Alfred; Princess Beatrice (back); Princess Alexandra; Princess Marie; standing; Prince Ernest of Hesse; Prince Max of Baden; Princess Victoria Melita; Prince George of Wales.

The Duke and Duchess of Connaught and family, 1892. Children, left to right: Prince Arthur; Princesses Margaret and Patricia.

The Duchess of Albany and her children, Charles and Alice, 1898.

The Duchess of Saxe-Coburg and daughters, c.1898. From left to right: Marie, Crown Princess of Roumania; Victoria Melita, Grand Duchess of Hesse; Alexandra, Hereditary Princess of Hohenlohe-Langenburg.

The Duchess of Albany (centre) and her family, c.1907, Standing, left to right: the Duchess of Saxe-Coburg holding her son, Johann Leopold; Charles, Duke of Saxe-Coburg. Seated, left to right: Alice, Countess of Athlone, with Lady May Cambridge on knee; Alexander, Count of Athlone.

The Duke and Duchess of Connaught and their family, 1906. Standing, left to right: Princess Patricia; Prince Arthur; Prince Gustav Adolf of Sweden. Seated: Princess Margaret of Sweden, holding her baby son, Prince Gustav Adolf.

The Duke and Duchess of Connaught, 1907, with Princess Patricia and Prince Arthur.

Queen Alexandra, Queen Mary, the Duke and Duchess of York and King George V on the balcony, Buckingham Palace, after the Yorks' wedding, 26 April 1923.

Queen Alexandra's funeral procession, 27 November 1925, including King Haakon VII of Norway, King Christian X of Denmark, Crown Prince Carol of Roumania, King Albert of the Belgians, and the Duke of York.

marry into the Romanovs and did her best to try and make her reconsider, warning her carefully to think about the severe Russian climate and the unsettled state of the Asiatic empire. The duchess of Edinburgh was furious, telling a friend that any prospect of such a marriage was probably going to fall through 'under the deplorable influence of the Queen,' for whom she had no words strong enough. She believed that the matriarch had set herself firmly against the scheme because her brother Serge 'had the greatest of all misfortunes, he was Russian and she had enough of one Russian in the family (meaning me of course).'[21]

Since his birth, Alfred, Duke of Edinburgh had been heir to the duchy of Saxe-Coburg and Gotha. As the future duchess, Marie was pleased to have a reason for basing herself on the European mainland, particularly at Germany where she felt much more at home. She had a palace built for the family in Coburg, known appropriately as the Edinburgh Palace, across the central square from the Ehrenburg Palace, the reigning duke's official residence, next to the town's opera hall. The couple had always been avid collectors, the former having not only been the first member of royalty to develop a passion for philately but also notable for bringing a large number of mementoes back from his foreign travels during his cruise on HMS *Galatea* before he was married, and the latter surrounding herself with icons and assorted curios from her homeland to recreate her own personal 'little Russia' wherever she settled. Many such pieces adorned her quarters at the Edinburgh Palace.

As another reminder of her homeland, she enjoyed organising entertainment and hospitality in the Russian fashion. In January 1886, the duke was appointed Commander-in-Chief of the British Mediterranean Fleet, based in Malta. In October the family sailed south aboard HMY *Osborne*, and on arriving at the capital, Valletta, they were received with salutes from the forts surrounding the capital. They moved into San Antonio, the governor's summer palace, where Ducky had been born. The duchess sometimes found island life dull, but it had its advantages over living in England, away from the cold, damp weather during the winter months, the fact that she no longer had to compete with her in-laws for precedence, and the lack of worry about unexpected visits or sudden summons from Queen Victoria and her advisers. She proved an excellent hostess, and enjoyed arranging parties to entertain the naval officers and their wives.

Part III

The Later Victorian Years 1887–1901

Chapter 1

During the summer of 1887, nearly all of Queen Victoria's family from all the corners of Europe were reunited at home. They returned briefly to London to take part together in the festivities for her jubilee, marking the fiftieth anniversary of her accession. They included religious ceremonies, military inspections, naval reviews and receptions, and many members of royalty from all corners of Europe came to participate. A specially commissioned group portrait of every member of the family present at Windsor was painted by the Danish court artist, Lauritz Tuxen, showing her in the drawing room of the castle surrounded by her children, children-in-law and their families.

One of the main events during those few days was a thanksgiving service at Westminster Abbey in June. For the ceremonial procession through the streets of London in the gilded state landau drawn by six cream-coloured horses, the queen had decided that she would not wear her crown and robes of state, but instead her usual black mourning dress with a white bonnet, as a symbol of her motherhood of the nation and the empire. Her family thought this would be less than appropriate, and decided to ask the Princess of Wales, whom they deemed the special favourite among them, to try and persuade her otherwise. The queen would not be talked out of her decision, and Alix emerged from the discussion, complaining that she 'was never so snubbed' in all her life.[1]

Three months earlier, the Duke of Edinburgh had relinquished his command of the Mediterranean Fleet, and the family moved to Coburg. Their main residence was the Edinburgh Palace where the duchess held court. Her husband, occupied with his naval affairs, was away most of the time. Responsibility for the education of their five children fell upon the duchess, who remained as ever the strictest but most devoted of mothers. Returning to London that summer with their children, they invited Grand Duke and Duchess Serge from Russia to come and stay with them at Clarence House. The Duke of Connaught was not officially entitled to home leave yet as his command was still relatively new, but it was unthinkable that he and the duchess should be absent from the celebrations. A special bill had to be passed in Parliament to facilitate their return to England for the purpose. On 24 May, the queen's birthday, they sailed from Bombay and arrived home just in time. They had not expected to be seeing the children so soon, and they had inevitably changed rapidly since they had last seen them.

The Duchess of Connaught had recently had a recurrence of the swelling in her leg. As the time came for the duke to return to Bombay, she was not well enough to return with him. He took her to Aix for a cure, then returned to London to prepare for his departure, sailing from Brindisi on 22 August. It was the first time they had been apart since his active service in Egypt five years earlier, and both felt the parting very keenly. Her happiness, she told him, 'depends on *you* & *only you!*'[2] They had one consolation, in that when autumn came and Louise was pronounced well enough to leave, all three children went with her, accompanied by Sir Howard and Lady Elphinstone, on the strict understanding that they would be returned to their grandmother in the spring. The family arrived off Bombay on 14 November for a happy reunion with the duke, who hurried on board the ship as soon as it had anchored.

Within weeks the duke and duchess were at last able to enjoy their first family Christmas with all three children. The Elphinstones kept Queen Victoria informed, describing the couple's routine, his military duties, the time she was spending with the youngsters, and their love of being outside in the open air. At length the time came for the children to return home to their grandmother. Queen Victoria always trusted the Elphinstones, perhaps rather more than her own family. Sir Howard advised her that at least one of the Connaught children should be allowed to stay in India, writing in February 1888 to explain the position from the duke and duchess's point of view to the queen. Because of the duchess's position, he pointed out, it was impossible for her to 'make intimate friendships' while they were out there. If one of their children could be sent out to keep her company, it would be most desirable, and also give the duchess 'both that occupation and interest which is so essential. The presence of the children out here has already produced a marked effect upon the duchess and made her so much more bright and cheerful than Sir Howard has ever seen her.'[3] He also assured her that he had made enquiries about the climate, and saw no reason why it would harm their younger daughter, who was healthy and active. The queen assented, and when the two elder children returned to England in March with the Elphinstones, Patsy stayed with her parents.

That summer, Patsy had occasional trouble with her eyes, but otherwise enjoyed good health. Queen Victoria thought it might make life easier for the duchess if she had an additional lady-in-waiting come to India and assist her. 'I am very grateful for your most kind thought,' she replied, 'but I fear it would be a great difficulty to have an extra person out now, and I get on perfectly well without a lady in waiting and have hardly ever to ask one of the ladies of the staff to come.'[4]

Added to her difficulties was news from England that Daisy, now aged six, had been unwell. Beatrice also reported to her that young Arthur, then five years old, was 'slow and wanting', and that both children were allegedly very disobedient. Recognising that they needed their mother, she was impatient to return home or alternatively persuade her mother-in-law to allow them out to India so they could be reunited.

In the autumn of 1888 their aunt Louise went to Balmoral to spend some quality time with the youngsters. She felt quite indignant on behalf of her brother and sister-in-law, and reported to them in strict confidentiality on the situation regarding them and the evidently much-favoured children of Beatrice and Henry. The parents had not been happy about leaving their children with the queen as they were 'quite sure that the Battenberg children would be made no. 1'. They were annoyed at pressure being put on them, and knew that the queen was not in favour of their coming out to join their parents in India during the winter 'and quite looks on it as a condescension on her part'. Neither his mother nor his youngest sister, he went on, 'understand children and I fear ours have rather high spirits.' Little Arthur was occasionally naughty, as all small boys are, but he was also intelligent and thoughtful, and the duke thought it was absurd to expect him to be obedient all the time when he was only five years of age.[5]

Such issues would fortunately not remain a concern for long. The duke and duchess sorely missed the two elder children, and their wish was granted when they were sent out to join them at the end of November. 'It was a day of unimagined, delightful joy and thankfulness when we welcomed them back,' Louise wrote to Queen Victoria on their arrival.

'They have both grown and improved in every way – Arthur has grown the most and he is such a big boy now and so good and affectionate and obedient and his manners have so much improved too. Daisy is, and was *always* so good – I cannot tell you dear Mama what happiness is it to have them back with us again and they seemed delighted to see us.'[6]

By this time, various other family members had also made plans to visit them. Louise's sister, Elizabeth, and her husband, Frederick Augustus of Oldenburg, had written in September that they would be coming before long. To the duchess, it was 'the *best* news we have had for a long long time and I feel delighted.' She also hoped that the queen would allow Beatrice, Henry and their children to come and join them as well: 'I know dearest Mama that it is a very bold thing my asking you this but as I know you are anxious for dear Beatrice to see this country … it would, of course … be simply delightful for us – a bit of home as it were.'[7] Beatrice and Henry were unable to come, mainly as his father was very ill, and died a few weeks later. However, Louise's sister and brother-in-law arrived in December with their cousins the Count and Countess of Hohenau and stayed until April, leaving the duchess feeling rather flat after their departure.

Now that the children were growing older and the duchess's health was giving some cause for concern, the duke strongly believed that a home command for him would be more suitable for them all. He relinquished command of the Bombay army, to take effect in mid-May 1890, and the children stayed with friends for a few days before taking the ship home to England. Meanwhile, their parents set off for one last eastern adventure on the P&O liner *Kaiser-i-Hind*. They visited Ceylon, Malaya, Hong Kong, China and Japan, an itinerary that gave Louise the distinction of having travelled across the world. She enjoyed Japan the most, even though it was in Tokyo that the party experienced their first earthquake, albeit a mild tremor. They also visited a traditional theatre and were welcomed by the imperial family. Emperor Meiji invested Louise with the Order of the Imperial Crown, making her the only foreign lady apart from the Russian tsarina to be thus honoured. Everywhere she went she was fascinated by the scenery and buildings, and she found Japan and the Japanese more sympathetic than China and its citizens. She and the duke celebrated his fortieth birthday in a hotel in Majanoshta, and their tour of the country lasted until 8 May, when they set off on the steamer *Abyssinia*, bound for Canada, then an overland crossing and the journey home via

Liverpool. As their train pulled into Windsor, six weeks and half a world away, Queen Victoria and the children were there to greet them.

During the next decade, which corresponded with the last ten years of the queen's long life, the Duke and Duchess of Connaught were content to rebuild their lives in England, with representational duties and family occasions. For Louise these years were marked by poor health, necessitating long visits to the European spas at Aix and Dresden. Sometimes she took one or other of the children, sometimes she went alone, but she and her husband always found the separation a hard one. Having been her brother's favourite sister, she relished the opportunity to pay a visit to his family home, Glienecke Castle, near Potsdam, in the summer of 1890.

Prince Frederick Charles had died in June 1885, the summer after Prince Arthur's first spell in India. As Queen Victoria noted, there was 'something so indescribably sad in such a death when the nearest can only be relieved by the departure of one, to whom she had been bound by the nearest ties and who hated him.'[8] In fact, Louise would be the last survivor but one of a not very long-lived family. Her eldest sister, Marie ('Mia'), who had been left a widow so soon after her first marriage but taken Prince Albert of Saxe-Altenburg as her second husband, died on 20 June 1888 of puerperal fever, two days after the birth of a daughter. The other, Elizabeth, who had visited them in Bombay, passed away suddenly in August 1895 after a short illness. She had suffered from a similar leg swelling problem, possibly a form of rheumatoid arthritis, to Louise. Of the siblings only Prince Frederick Leopold, the youngest and the sole brother, still remained, the only one to live beyond the age of sixty.

Unlike several of her in-laws, including those who had married into the queen's family, Louise particularly enjoyed their regular visits to Balmoral. The cold rooms and the remote atmosphere of the Scottish Highlands evidently did not grate unduly on her, for she enjoyed outdoor life and was particularly keen on fishing. Her sister-in-law Princess Frederick Leopold, a lifelong Anglophile, came from Germany to join them on one such occasion. She loved their drives through the countryside, but could never enter into her enthusiasm for the rod and line, much preferring bicycle rides with her little niece Patsy.

* * *

In March 1888 the Prince and Princess of Wales celebrated their silver wedding. To the annoyance of the princess, the more formal celebrations were curtailed because of mourning for the death of William I, German Emperor, who had died at the age of ninety on the day before the anniversary. She had never ceased to regard him as the personification of Prussian might, and one of the enemies of her father's family. All of them were deeply moved by the plight of the new emperor, Frederick III, the queen's beloved son-in-law. The previous year he had been stricken with cancer of the larynx, and was now unable to speak above a whisper after having had a tracheotomy. When he ascended the throne, it was evident that he could only survive for a matter of weeks.

In Alexandra's words his son, now Crown Prince William, was 'mad & a conceited ass'.[9] While Queen Victoria was always ready to make allowances for the prince who was her eldest grandchild, he had few friends and admirers among the rest of the family in England. When he made a speech comparing the German Reich with an army corps that had lost its commander in the field and whose first officer had been severely wounded, his English relations as well as his mother and dying father were outraged. Queen Victoria reported it to the Duchess of Connaught in India, and she was as furious as the rest of them. 'I can hardly tell you how indignant,' she replied, 'I may say angry, I have felt when reading Willy's speech – the want of heart, tact, obedience & sense wh[ich] it shows are quite appalling – it is the *most* foolish and unfeeling speech I have ever read.'[10]

Alexandra was just as moved by the rest of her in-laws by the plight of Emperor Frederick. When he died on 15 June after a reign of ninety-nine days, she put her detestation of Prussia on one side, and for the sake of the widowed empress, she accompanied her husband to the funeral in Berlin. She greatly pitied her sister-in-law, 'all her plans and ambitions crushed and nothing left but remembrance of the past'.[11]

For the Duchess of Connaught, these two deaths of close relatives within five days came as a heavy blow. She was full of sympathy for those most closely affected:

> Poor dearest Vicky, her grief must be quite unthinkably overwhelming ... it is so terrible being so far away – it makes all sadness so very much greater ... I had a letter only this mail from my poor brother-

in-law talking all of my sister's confinement – poor dearest sister, and now she has been taken from us, from him and her poor little children ... it makes my heart break to think of it ... I hope it will not be long before we return home ... one longs to get home – it is a hard banishment ... pray forgive my speaking so openly – of course where my duty takes me then I go.[12]

A week later, she was thanking Queen Victoria for her 'dear and loving words of sympathy,' heartbroken at the thought that she would never see Mia or Fritz again, and thankful that 'sweet Patsy is our little sunshine in all this trying sorrowful time.'[13] She was still incensed by the unfilial demeanour of her nephew, now Emperor William II, who seemed determined to regard his liberal father's brief reign as best forgotten and to heap every indignity possible on his mother. 'Willy – one thing I cannot forgive, and that is that he considers his dear noble father is wiped out – that is an outrage I cannot get over ... I know how strongly you feel, as I do myself in this display of Willy's behaviour.'[14]

That same day she wrote the widowed empress, now known as Empress Frederick, a heartfelt letter:

It is difficult for me to know how to tell you how deeply touched I was that you thought of me and wrote me such a kind letter ... It has been such a terrible shock to me and came so unexpected that I felt quite overwhelmed by so much sorry and sadness. Our thoughts are automatically with you dearest Vicky – no words can say how deeply we mourn with you for him who was so good, so brave, so able, so wise and grand.[15]

* * *

While Alexandra could be thankful that her sons were nothing like the new young German Emperor William, she soon had to face the fact that her firstborn, 'Eddy', was less than perfect. A dear, good and dutiful son he may have been, but as a future king he gave his elders increasing cause for concern. He had many of the faults of his father, with few of his positive qualities, lacking concentration and being too fond of amusement.

This might not have mattered so much had it not been for the fact that the next few years were to be unhappy ones for her, caused to some extent by her husband's folly. In September 1890 the Prince of Wales attended a house party at Tranby Croft, Yorkshire, where a fellow guest, Sir Arthur Gordon-Cumming, was accused of cheating at baccarat. In the following summer, the latter brought a lawsuit for slander and the prince was called as a witness. Although he was innocent of any wrongdoing, his close involvement in what would be remembered as 'the great baccarat scandal' caused him and the royal family some embarrassment, although his mother and wife stood loyally by him, no matter what their private feelings on the business. His public standing fell further that same year when he was asked by the unscrupulous Frances, Lady Brooke (the former Frances Maynard who had once been considered as a wife for Prince Leopold), to retrieve some compromising correspondence from Lord Charles Beresford, a former lover of hers and a close friend of the prince. The matter was eventually settled, but again not without much annoyance and embarrassment to those involved, and at some cost to the heir to the throne's good name. As ever, the Princess of Wales supported him steadfastly, but like her mother-in-law, she must have wondered despairingly whether he would ever learn to keep well clear of such dubious entanglements.

As ever, she had the consolation of her family life, especially as they became grandparents in May 1891 with the birth of a daughter, Alexandra, to their eldest daughter, Louise, who had married Alexander, Duke of Fife, in July 1889. (Their first child had been a stillborn son in June 1890). The princess was thrilled with this addition to the family, who 'squeaked like a little sucking-pig'[16] when she held her in her arms for the first time.

Yet this was one ray of hope on the horizon for her. The difficulties regarding the future of her eldest son were another matter entirely. His life of dissipation and readiness to fall in love with any woman, whether suitable or not, worried his parents greatly. At length it was decided that he must either be sent on a colonial or continental tour, where he might be safeguarded from the temptations of the opposite sex, or else married to that most eligible of distant cousins, Princess Victoria Mary, daughter of Francis, Duke of Teck, and the former Princess Mary of Cambridge, a cousin of Queen Victoria.

Once his future had been agreed on by the elder generation, the princess left for a short holiday in Denmark, proposing to return to England in a few days. After hearing disturbing rumours about the Beresford affair, she cancelled her return to England and instead left for Livadia, in the Crimea, where the tsar and tsarina were celebrating their silver wedding. The Prince of Wales was left at home to spend his fiftieth birthday on his own, an occasion overshadowed not just by his wife's absence abroad (something of a reversal where the family was concerned), but also by a fire at Sandringham a few days earlier that had damaged several rooms and a collection of priceless Goya tapestries. Worse was to come, with Prince George becoming unwell and taking to his bed with typhoid a few days later. The princess came home a little earlier than anticipated, but after a few days of mounting anxiety, their second son was on the road to recovery.

In the first week of December the ever-pressing problem of Prince Albert Victor was solved. He was invited to a house party at Luton Hoo in Bedfordshire, as had Princess May of Teck. Although he had been warned to be on his best behaviour, make her acquaintance and get to know her a little better, in his eagerness to please he proposed to her almost at once. Mindful of where her duty to crown and family lay, she accepted him, though few if any really close to them had any illusions that it was a love match.

It looked like a happy ending to what had been a difficult year for husband and wife, with their son's wedding arranged to take place on 27 February 1892, but tragedy was about to strike. On 4 January Princess May and her parents went to Sandringham to join in the celebrations for Prince Albert Victor's twenty-eighth birthday four days later. Despite feeling under the weather, he accompanied his father and other male guests on shoot on 7 January but returned early, complaining of a severe headache. Next day, his birthday, he was too ill to rise from his bed and influenza was diagnosed. Despite the efforts of the doctors, he swiftly deteriorated. His parents, brother, fiancée and sisters all gathered around his bed in the tiny sickroom, watching grief-stricken as he died on the morning of 14 January.

Queen Victoria's heart went out to them. Later that week she wrote to the Empress Frederick that her son was 'broken down, and poor dear Alix, though bearing up wonderfully, does nothing but cry, Bertie says.'[17]

She told her mother-in-law that she would never recover from the shock of his death. Several days and sleepless nights watching over him, as he became delirious and gradually sank into his final sleep, left their mark on her. The worst moment for her was to come when she watched his coffin being carried out of Sandringham Church as he left his home for ever. She had wanted him to be laid to rest there and the Prince of Wales agreed, but the queen told them that he had to be buried at Windsor, where the funeral took place on 20 January.

Four months later, in May 1892, Prince George was created Duke of York. Even before his brother was buried, there had been whispers in the family that after a suitable interval he would become betrothed to Princess May, who, as the Prince and Princess of Wales had said, became a widow almost before she had become a wife. Precedent for such an arrangement had existed less than thirty years earlier when Princess Dagmar of Denmark, having watched Tsarevich Nicholas die of tuberculosis, became betrothed after a decent interval to the future Tsar Alexander III. In May 1893 the duke proposed to May and was accepted. Though she would have been reluctant to admit it to anyone else, the Princess of Wales was not alone in knowing in her heart of hearts that the lively, industrious George would make a far more satisfactory husband (and king) than 'poor dear Eddy'. With eagerness she welcomed her future daughter-in-law into the family, writing with affection, but also a slightly ominous note, which unconsciously echoed something of her own mother-in-law's desire for control, though in a far more diplomatic manner. She said she knew that both of them would always understand each other, 'and I hope my sweet May will always come straight to me for everything.'[18]

The wedding took place at the Chapel Royal on 6 July. Nicholas, Tsarevich of Russia, who was among the guests and whose marked physical resemblance to his first cousin the bridegroom resulted in some confusion among at least one or two of the others present, noted that his aunt Alix 'looked rather sad in church – one can quite understand why'.[19] Another of his aunts, the Duchess of Edinburgh, was also there, but found little to praise. Writing to Missy three days before the wedding, she observed – as others suspected – that the couple seemed 'rather depressed and not a bit in love,' and he hardly spoke to her at all. When they went to Marlborough House to see the presents, it was 'simply too wonderful, but rather disgusting for my taste.'[20]

Three years later it would be the turn of Princess Maud, the youngest of the Wales siblings, to marry her cousin Prince Charles of Denmark, the future King Haakon VII of Norway. Meanwhile, Princess Victoria, or 'poor Toria', was destined to remain the unhappy, increasingly embittered spinster at home, constantly at her mother's beck and call.

* * *

Apart from short spells on Malta because of the Duke of Edinburgh's Mediterranean command, by the mid-1880s he and the duchess were spending more of their time at Coburg, preparing themselves for the day when he succeeded to his German inheritance. While they were there, they stayed at the Edinburgh Palace in the main square near the official residence of the dukes of Coburg. Like her mother-in-law, the duchess took grave exception to the conduct of Ernest II, a notorious libertine and womaniser, the opposite of his virtuous, late younger brother, Albert, and she was anxious to keep her distance from him. Her relations between Queen Victoria had thawed a little by this time. When the queen took her regular spring holiday on the Riviera in March 1888, staying at the Villa Palmieri in Florence, the duke and duchess were there as well for a few days at the end of the month. They met briefly, accompanied by Olga, Queen of Württemberg, the duchess's aunt and last surviving daughter of Tsar Nicholas I. It proved to be the last time she saw her niece, as she died four years later.

As a mother, the duchess was always quite demanding where the children were concerned, and she made it clear that she expected the highest standards from them. Her husband was rarely at home, and had little say in their upbringing. Their son Alfred was a likeable enough but indolent youth, adored and idolised... and idolised by his sisters, but lacking in motivation and personality. She was frequently impatient with him, found him a grave disappointment and rarely spoke to him. Of their sisters, the outgoing Missy and the rather more reserved Ducky were relatively strong and resilient characters, but Sandra, who always followed and looked up to them, was rather shy and, in her eldest sister's words, inclined to be 'always fearful of reproach'. Bee, the youngest by six years, was inclined to be slightly spoilt, and as a lively child with pronounced artistic interests, very much their mother's daughter.

The duchess firmly believed that princesses must marry young. Once they reached the age of twenty, she maintained, they were inclined to think too much for themselves and develop too many ideas of their own. Moreover, an unmarried princess had 'no position at all'. As they had travelled and moved around so much in their young lives, the princesses' education had been disrupted with having so many different teachers, and with having to speak different languages. Missy and Ducky studied together, but the latter with her excellent memory was a quicker, better learner than her elder sister. Sandra, the slowest at learning and the least proficient linguist, always studied on her own, while Bee showed signs of being bright, quick-witted, and potentially perhaps the cleverest of them all.

Unlike her daughters, the duchess loved to speak French. She always spoke to them in English, and never taught them Russian, as she said she had no desire to see or hear her beloved language mutilated. The Princess of Wales felt a special affection for her husband's nieces. She expressed her regrets to her second son George that his cousins had to be 'entirely brought up as Germans', speaking English with a strong German accent.[21]

In August 1890 the Duke of Edinburgh took up what would be the last command of his career, a three-year period of office as Commander-in-Chief at Devonport. They settled in the official residence, Admiralty House, close to that of the General-in-Command, Sir Richard Harrison. His daughters were the same age as Missy and Ducky, and became their close companions on their walks, games of croquet and sailing trips. It was the first time that they had had contact with girls who were not princesses.

The duchess never enjoyed living at Admiralty House, her husband's official residence, and only made occasional visits there with the children. A contemporary in Plymouth, Hilda Picken, thought that the duchess gave the impression 'she had come down in the social scale, having married a mere duke, and being obliged to come into contact with the likes of us.' The contrast between her daughters' cheerful faces and her 'glowering looks' was 'quite remarkable'.[22] A few weeks in the West Country at least had the effect of making her appreciate the capital rather more. 'London seems to me a real paradise after Devonport and Clarence House a grand palace after our terribly small lodgings there,' she wrote to her eldest daughter after one such visit.[23]

By this time, husband and wife had little in common other than a shared interest in music and their family. Always reserved, taciturn, and ill-tempered by nature, he was now drinking more heavily. Others found him increasingly rude, touchy, wilful, unscrupulous, improvident, and unfaithful. He and the duchess were now living separate lives more and more, both grateful that his various duties and social engagements allowed them to keep their mutual distance. For a long time, she kept her marital troubles a secret from her children. Only some years later did she admit to their eldest daughter, Marie, who had long since become an adult and had gradually found out that all had not been well for a long time, that she felt she was never anything more than his 'legitimate mistress'.

All four sisters and their brother joined each other at Coburg for the winter of 1890, where they were together for the last time. Separation loomed as Alfred, now sixteen, was about to begin his military studies. The family was about to be broken up, as the parents were now considering the matter of husbands for their elder daughters. The duke had hoped that Marie would marry her cousin George of Wales, whom he greatly liked and admired. Of this the duchess was well aware. She knew that both her mother-in-law and her husband would approve of such a match, but she recalled her loneliness and her heartaches, and knew too well what life was like for the wife of a sailor. As her nephew was likewise making the navy his career, she was convinced that such a match would not be right for her daughter. While she was fond of him, she did not want Missy to suffer in the same way. Moreover, she had no desire for any daughter of hers to marry into the English royal family. Nor was she particularly enthusiastic about choosing a husband for her daughter from the ranks of her own Romanov relations. Her own father's infidelities had left a lasting scar, and when her cousin Grand Duke George Michaelovich expressed an interest in her hand, the duchess made it clear that this could never come about.

Without discussing the matter with her husband, she helped to arrange a match with Ferdinand, Crown Prince of Roumania, a pleasant, likeable youth, but without much personality. She took the initiative in asking the German emperor to help plan the marital future of her eldest daughter. Flattered to be asked to help in any matchmaking that concerned his cousins, William II was delighted to assist. Around the time of the autumn manoeuvres, he spoke to King Carol I of Roumania who told him confidentially that his nephew and heir, Ferdinand, was in love with his wife's lady-in-waiting, Helena Vacarescu, much to his irritation. The king had sent the romantically minded queen, who had unwisely encouraged them, away to her mother's home and the lady-in-waiting into exile, while the prince was warned sternly that such a liaison was incompatible with his status as heir to the Roumanian throne.

Following his manoeuvres with the German Army, the emperor planned a grand banquet in Wilhelmshöhe Castle at which Missy was seated next to Ferdinand, attired in the uniform of a Prussian Commander of the Guards. After spending Christmas at Rosenau, a villa on a hill with excellent views of the surrounding countryside around Coburg, Missy was invited to visit the Berlin court for the first time, and went to stay at the home of her cousin 'Charly', Charlotte, Hereditary Princess of Saxe-Meiningen and the emperor's eldest sister. Meanwhile, the emperor advised him not to waste time, as George was also in love with her, and reminded him that George was next in line to the British throne after his father, the Prince of Wales. In March, the duchess invited her relations to Munich, and Ferdinand was among those invited. Missy found him very shy, and he seemed to be laughing more than ever, as if to mask his timidity. Despite these problems, it was not long before a betrothal between both young people took place. The triumphant duchess had to be first to tell the emperor, neither consulting her husband nor allowing her daughter time to consider what she was doing.

Her telegram announcing the news formally caused Duke Alfred such embarrassment that he briefly considered withholding his consent, but as heir of the duchy of Coburg, he had to submit to the desires of his nephew the German emperor. He confided in tears to his mother that he had wanted a better future for Missy than this pleasant but colourless young man, who might be heir to a throne but of a rather unstable kingdom at that. As for Queen Victoria, it was said that the union between Marie and Ferdinand of Roumania was the only marriage among her descendants that was 'pulled-off without consent'. At a grand banquet organised in May, the emperor celebrated the engagement at Potsdam, but the Duke of Edinburgh was conspicuous by his absence. The bride and groom were married eight months later, on 10 January 1893, in Sigmaringen Castle, the seat of the princes of Hohenzollern-Sigmaringen and the home of Ferdinand's father, Leopold.

The Duke of Edinburgh's appointment at Devonport came to an end in June 1893 on the expiry of his term as Commander-in Chief and promotion to Admiral of the Fleet. A few weeks later his uncle Ernest, Duke of Saxe-Coburg Gotha, caught a chill while hunting and died on 22 August, aged seventy-five. With his passing, and no legitimate heir to succeed him, his nephew and niece were now duke and duchess of the German ancestral home. She was pleased not only for herself but also her husband, believing that for him it was 'a real God-send and I cannot thank Providence enough!' At a time when he was retired and did not know what to do with himself, he now had a 'a new activity, and a new, fine position, with plenty to do and at the head of a charming country and master of such beautiful possessions.'[24]

The duke saw matters very differently. He was already saddened at having to leave the naval career he had so loved, and unlike her, he did not look forward to his new role. Since infancy he had been trained to rule in the duchy, but did not come into his ducal inheritance with any great enthusiasm. His life there, he feared, would be extremely dull, with very few duties to speak of apart from trying to make some order out of the chaotic state of the finances that his uncle had left him, and only the compensations of good hunting and a well-stocked wine cellar to occupy his time. The duchess foresaw that there would be plenty of work for him to do, and that it would probably occupy him from morning until night.

At first he took it seriously, and seemed contented, but before long the *'grand ennui'* returned. He still maintained Clarence House as his home in Britain, and enjoyed returning to England from time to time so he could enjoy the company of his brother officers from service days and reminisce about old times. Having never been particularly close to his five children when they were small, perhaps he found the gap impossible to bridge now that they were adults. While they had all been brought up to look up to him as their father, there is nothing to suggest that there was ever a close relationship between them, and they always found this slightly remote man something of a stranger.

Their mother had remained and would ever be the major parental presence in the home. Unlike him, she thoroughly enjoyed their new role. She had never felt at home in England, and now in Germany she was answerable to nobody. As her eldest daughter put it so succinctly in her memoir some forty years later, the duchess revelled in her new-found independence at Coburg, where she was 'sole arbiter of her own fate, no tribunal sat over her, weighing all she did or left undone. There she was her own mistress; it was a small kingdom perhaps, but her will was undiscussed, she took her orders from no one, and could live as she wished.'[25]

The Empress Frederick wrote to her daughter Sophie, Crown Princess of the Hellenes, of the sympathy she felt for her brother, Alfred, now that he had to give up 'dear London for good', and instead devote himself to new duties in his German home. Perhaps she had not foreseen that he never intended to sever his ties completely with his old life in England. 'But he will do it all so well, and Aunt Marie will love being No. 1, and reigning Duchess, I am sure.'[26] It came as no surprise when in January 1894 the new Duke of Saxe-Coburg decreed that in future his wife should be styled Her Imperial and Royal Highness, thus settling a score that had rankled with her for twenty years.

The woman who was more than happy to style herself Duchess of Saxe-Coburg Gotha instead of Duchess of Edinburgh had always liked Germany, although she never cared for the previous duke, and relished the prospect of living in what had now become her and her husband's new ducal estate. They now moved to Schloss Ehrenburg, their official residence, but preferred their summer house at Rosenau. Ironically, this gave her something else in common with Queen Victoria, both having always loved this part of Germany, albeit for different reasons. The duke and duchess also had two residences in Gotha, where they had to live part of the year, the castles at Friedenstein and Reinhardsbrunn. The estates surrounding both provided the duke and his sporting friends with ample hunting grounds. The duchess took on responsibility for refurnishing the castles with more modern items, and with supporting various local charities, including the opening of a home for the mentally handicapped. She also made a point of supporting and visiting the opera and the theatre in Coburg and Gotha.

Despite her husband's love of music, fine arts and collecting, especially postage stamps, his interests had narrowed with age, and an indulgent lifestyle that contributed to indifferent health had made him elderly before his time. Described by one contemporary author as a man 'with an abominable temper [and] the most glaring want of tact,'[27] he was increasingly impatient with his wife's devotion to reading, theatre and serious conversation, constantly grumbled 'and made everybody uncomfortable and nervous'.[28] She never ceased to blame his inability to get on with others on his 'thoroughly English education'.[29] Perhaps he had taken after his father, not only in his enquiring mind and breadth of interests during boyhood, but also in personality. During his youth and in fact much of his adult life, the prince consort had been subject to bouts of intense depression, but had the consolation, such as it was, of hard work to keep his ever-active mind occupied. The latter was a pleasure not granted in his last years to the son, who had little purposeful activity to fill his waking hours.

When autumn came the duchess and her daughters left for Roumania to be with the crown princess, who was expecting her first child. The first part of her marriage, far from being happy, was marked by loneliness. While her sisters accompanied the duchess to Russia and were being fêted there, Marie, confined to the palace, unhappily overcame the first months of her pregnancy and her lack of independence. She was delighted to have her sisters around her. To the disgust of their mother, when her grandson was born in October, her youngest daughter Bee, only nine years old, inevitably came to learn something of the facts of life. It was a lesson that had been kept from the innocent and inexperienced young mother in Bucharest until she had discovered a few months earlier that she was *enceinte*. The baby, a prince named Carol after the sovereign, would eventually succeed to the throne and cause his widowed mother no end of heartache during her last few years.

Eight months after the duke and duchess came into their inheritance, their second daughter was married. By now the duchess seemed to have become reconciled once more to the idea of her marrying into the Romanovs, especially as she suspected that Ducky was in love with one of her bachelor cousins. This time she did not get her own way, as the matchmaking instincts of Queen Victoria prevailed. She had made up her mind that Princess Victoria Melita would make a suitable wife of her first cousin Ernest, who had succeeded his father as Grand Duke of Hesse and the Rhine in March 1892. 'Ernie' and 'Ducky', who coincidentally shared the same birthday, being born exactly eight years apart, gave the somewhat deceptive impression of enjoying each other's company on family visits and sharing similar interests. Other younger, more perceptive relations suspected that they were not really in love with each other, and that the young Grand Duke of Hesse seemed less anxious to propose to his cousin than he was for his grandmother to be present at their wedding.

The duchess was angry that matters seemed to have been taken out of her hands. Ernie and his grandmother, she wrote to Missy, 'will want to have it all their own way, as a revenge for your engagement,' with 'Granny' indicating precisely when and where the engagement was going to take place the following year.

The engagement took place in January 1894. During the next few weeks the Duchess fretted about what she called the bridegroom's 'constant Anglomania'. She had to have a long talk with him in private, explaining in full her grievances against their English relations and in particular his grandmother, 'why we could not really like them and how often they had been nasty and spiteful to me'. She was not convinced that Ernie had completely believed her, but she insisted that 'he must not always be dragging Ducky to England in perpetual adoration of granny,' otherwise she feared there would be 'conflicts' before long.[30]

The wedding itself took place at Coburg on 19 April. The queen had done her best to arrange for the ceremony to take place in England, as well as naming the date, but on both matters the duke and duchess overruled her. Nevertheless, the queen ensured she would be there, making her first visit to Germany since she had come to see the mortally ill Emperor Frederick there six years earlier. The gallery of royalty from England, Germany and Russia was the grandest seen in Europe since her jubilee a year before that, and did not escape the notice of a photographer who managed to capture the family in a couple of large group pictures.

Two of the guests at the wedding, and their possible marital future, seemed to be attracting almost as much attention as that of the bride and groom themselves. The grand duke's youngest surviving sister, Alix, was known to be very fond of Nicholas, Tsarevich of Russia, but hesitant about converting to the Orthodox religion. She had initially turned Nicholas down, and only after tactful pressure from Emperor William II did she agree to take his hand in marriage the second time he asked her. Some thought that she might have been glad to leave her childhood home at the court of Darmstadt because of her aversion to her cousin Princess Victoria Melita, and the fact that she would be taking precedence over her once she was grand duchess, because her ever-forthright Aunt Marie, Duchess of Saxe-Coburg, would be 'playing the dictator round Darmstadt'.[31]

It was expected that they would have a reasonable time to adjust to the responsibilities of being heir and heiress to the Russian throne, for Tsar Alexander III was only in his late forties. To everyone's horror, he became seriously ill that autumn and by November he was clearly dying. The Duke and Duchess of Coburg left for Livadia at once, joining the family gathered around the deathbed at the tsar's summer palace of Livadia and finding him sitting up in an armchair, still bravely and painfully signing documents almost to the end while his failing strength still allowed. 'Thank God I've arrived in time to see you once more,'[32] the Duchess tactlessly told her brother as she came in.

Also heeding the family summons were the Prince and Princess of Wales, who had only reached Vienna when they received a telegram to tell them that he was dead. When they joined the grieving family, presided over with extreme reluctance by the stunned new Tsar Nicholas II, the princess's first meeting with her now widowed sister as dowager empress was one of 'unspeakable agony'. For the second time in fourteen years they stayed in Russia for the funeral ceremonies of the sovereign, and this time they remained for the wedding immediately afterwards of the young sovereign and his bride, who thus became Empress Alexandra.

During his thirteen-year reign, through sheer force of personality, the huge, bear-like Alexander III had kept his often-fractious family united, and his empire at peace. Ironically he, like his father, had constantly lived with the threat of assassination, yet he was fated to die from ill-health at a comparatively early age. His sister feared all too correctly that her shy, insecure nephew would cut a sorry figure after his larger-than-life father.

With regard to her own family, the duchess had two more daughters for whom husbands would need to be found. As in the case of their eldest, she brushed aside the objections of her husband, and helped to arrange a match for Sandra. At a shooting party organised by the Duke of Saxe-Coburg the previous year she had been introduced to Prince Ernest of Hohenlohe-Langenburg, the only son of Prince Herman VI and his wife, Princess Leopoldine of Baden. Aged thirty-three, a diplomat who was familiar with the courts of London and St Petersburg, he had studied at the universities of Bonn and Baden and then joined the army, in which he was promoted to captain. He could claim distant kinship to his future wife, being her second cousin as a grandson of Feodora, the half-sister of Queen Victoria, though the latter had her doubts about such a marriage.

The duchess was the first person to see that this was no ordinary flirtation, but was rapidly becoming a true love match. She told Prince Herman that her daughter was much too young, and really needed to see one or two other eligible princes before she made up her mind. Yet the young couple would not be dissuaded. In September 1895, just after her seventeenth birthday, their engagement was announced. The duke had initially had his reservations, but soon changed his mind, especially on seeing that they were clearly so happy together. For once, he was just as annoyed as his wife when Queen Victoria, apparently put out because there had been talk of a match between Ernest and another of her granddaughters, Princess Helena Victoria ('Thora') of Schleswig-Holstein, acknowledged their telegram with what was said to be 'a nasty and rude reply'.[33]

That Ernest was not what was called 'a brilliant *parti*' did not concern the duchess unduly. There were reservations, shared to some extent by Crown Princess Marie of Roumania and her father as they did not consider him sufficiently bright, and also because Sandra, on marrying a Serene Highness, would be reduced to an inferior rank in the *Almanach de Gotha*.

Never one to flatter her daughters for the sake of it, the duchess said it did not matter as Sandra 'was the least interesting of her four daughters'. Since childhood she had also been noted for her regular minor illnesses, or what the duchess referred to scathingly as her 'bobos'. Impatience with perpetually recurring and apparently trivial complaints was another matter on which the duchess and Queen Victoria were totally united, although the former was cautious about being seen as unsympathetic, and she did express concern about the severe colds and coughs they always had in winter. She would regularly call in the doctors, but Sandra always submitted herself to the professionals' attention with a readiness that others found alarming, if not simply unashamed attention-seeking. In spite of this, she did concede that this third daughter of hers had a talent for organising parties and such functions as the Christmas bazaars at Coburg.

The wedding was celebrated on 20 April 1896 in the chapel of Ehrenburg Palace. Sandra and Ernie spent their honeymoon at Langenburg Castle, near Hesse, which was to be their home. That same day, her youngest sister, Beatrice, 'Baby Bee', celebrated her twelfth birthday.

One month later, the duke and duchess and their five children were in Russia again for the coronation of Tsar Nicholas II and Empress Alexandra in May 1896. The duke had initially suggested that Bee, the youngest, ought to stay at home as the lengthy Russian ceremonies at Moscow would be far too tedious for a child of such tender years, but the duchess disagreed and all four of the girls joined them. The little girl would always be grateful to her mother for having won the argument, noting in later years that she had only been there as a result of her mother's insistence as she prophetically declared that it would be 'the last time!' Sadly, it would long be remembered not only as the last of its kind, but also as the festival that would be deeply tarnished by the tragedy at Khodynka Field, when over a thousand loyal and enthusiastic spectators were crushed to death in a stampede for free gifts.

As the duke and duchess were now technically a German head of state and consort, the queen was obliged to choose somebody else from her family to represent her at the coronation, and the senior members available for this duty were the Duke and Duchess of Connaught. Having never forgotten the magnificent if not ostentatious collection of jewels with which the Duchess of Edinburgh had covered herself at court receptions, the queen decided to lend the Duchess of Connaught some of her finest items so she would not be outshone by the Romanov grand duchesses in their own country. She and the duke regarded the queen's gesture with mixed feelings, wondering if they would be expected to provide the necessary insurance cover to the value of £30,000.[34]

Chapter 2

In June 1897 all the surviving family were present in London for what would be the last great celebration of Queen Victoria's reign, a procession and thanksgiving service to commemorate her sixty years on the throne at the diamond jubilee. The Princess of Wales had her own idea as to how the anniversary ought to be celebrated. She wrote to the Lord Mayor of London, suggesting that a fund should be opened to provide a dinner for the poorest in the city slums, and enclosing a substantial personal donation. Her motives may have been generous but her timing was unfortunate, coming in the wake of several other appeals of a similar nature. This particular project might not have proceeded any further but for the intervention of Thomas Lipton, a millionaire tea merchant, who promptly came to the rescue by writing a cheque to cover the amount she had been hoping to raise. Some critics thought it blatant self-advertisement on his part, especially as he was awarded a knighthood in the next honours list.

Two of the family guests invited were prevented from attending. The Crown Prince of Roumania was seriously ill with typhoid and possible pneumonia, and for a time his life was in the balance as the crown princess helped to nurse him slowly back to health. While the Duke of Saxe-Coburg was glad to go to London and take part in the festivities, the duchess was singularly unmoved by the queen's milestone of sixty years on the throne. She went with some reluctance, and vented her irritation with everything and everyone in a series of letters to her eldest daughter (who was distraught at being unable to accept her invitation and leave Bucharest). She complained about the stuffy atmosphere in central London after the fresh Rosenau breezes, the 'most unaffected and unnatural' English acting that she saw at the theatre, and how dull it had been at a large garden party at Windsor that she was obliged to attend. For her, it was a relief to return to Germany afterwards. At the end of July she and her youngest daughter, Beatrice, came to Roumania to keep

Missy company, as well as share the vigil at her sick husband's bedside while he was on the slow road to recovery.

The greatest sadness to befall Queen Victoria's children during the previous two years had been the sudden and totally unexpected loss of Henry of Battenberg. Chafing after several years of inactivity if not sheer boredom at home, in November 1895 he begged to be allowed to go and fight on behalf of queen and empire in the Ashanti War in Africa. Soon after arriving there he contracted malaria and was sent home to recover, but died on the journey back in January 1896.

During the first few bleak months of her widowhood, Beatrice found solace in the company and solicitude of the Duchess of Albany, who had also lost her husband unexpectedly young. Only four years apart, the sisters-in-law had bonded firmly at once, and remained a source of comfort to each other for the rest of the duchess's life. In October 1897 Beatrice wrote to John Taylor Smith, Anglican bishop of Sierra Leone and honorary chaplain to Queen Victoria, praising Helen as 'a good excellent woman', remarking that they were 'very intimate together and she has been so loving and full of sympathy with me in my sorrow.'[1]

Although always a tireless patron of charities, the Duchess of Albany kept very much to herself during this time, above all providing a good home for her two children at Claremont. In December 1897 Arthur Benson, a housemaster at Eton College, was invited to stay for a while, partly as 'the little Duke', Albany, had been entered for his house three years previously. He got on very well with the duchess, and found her 'most sensible and wise' in her intention that her son should be treated at school like everyone else. She evidently placed great store on keeping youngsters of that age fully occupied, and thought they should not be allowed to 'loaf'. He came away at the end of his few days there feeling refreshed by the simplicity of their family life, and thought his hostess 'big and solid, with a kind, plump, easy-going face, very genial and friendly smile and absolutely simple.'

In the months that followed the jubilee celebrations, there were several more deaths which, though perhaps not unexpected, all brought sadness on a personal level. The Duchess of Teck died suddenly in October 1897, from complications following what should have been a routine operation. Early the following year the heir to the throne and his wife paid what was to be their last visit to the elderly and ailing William Gladstone, who had retired as prime minister in 1894, and his wife at Hawarden. He was touched at the kindness the couple had always shown him, all the more so in view of the queen's everlasting hostility. When he passed away in May 1898, the princess wrote his widow a long and graceful letter, calling him 'one of the most beautiful upright and disinterested characters that has ever adorned the pages of history'.[2]

The greatest sadness to befall the princess at this time came when her own mother, Queen Louise of Denmark, died in September 1898 at the age of eighty-one. She had been warned that the matriarch was seriously ill and unlikely to recover, and was able to reach Bernstorff Palace to join the bedside vigil as the end approached, as well as provide some company for the bereft widower King Christian.

As the Prince of Wales became older, his appetite for affairs with other women declined. The last such important relationship of his life was with Alice, wife of George Keppel, twenty-six years his junior. She had a happy family life, was intelligent and discreet, and never gave others the impression of self-seeking ambition. Almost everyone else liked and respected her. Among the few who did not was the Princess of Wales, who tended to resent her presence. Nevertheless, she still appreciated that Alice played a vital role in keeping the prince entertained, good-tempered, and preventing boredom from getting the better of him.

* * *

During the first few weeks of 1899 the Duke and Duchess of Connaught and their daughters visited Egypt and had a short audience *en route* with the pope. The queen and her household were rather startled by the efforts Louise was prepared to make in identifying herself with her husband's world and sharing in the military aspects as far as reasonably possible. It was reported that she insisted on riding over the battlefield at Omdurman in spite of protests from the duke – who might have been expected to give her a measure of support instead – and from Field-Marshal Herbert Kitchener, commander of the Egyptian army. With the sight and smell of dead men and horses all around them, the experience was one at which some men would have quailed. According to the Queen's lady-in-waiting, Marie Mallet, it was an appalling sight, 'quite unfit for any man to witness, much less a woman. Thousands of vultures and the hottest sun have done but little to thin the ranks of these terrible corpses.'³ The Duchess of Connaught must have been quite fearless, or very brave, to subject herself to such an ordeal.

Just as his two eldest brothers had had enduring friendships with other married women, even the Duke of Connaught's name was about to be linked with others, although it appears quite respectably. Some years before, he had briefly met Leonie Jerome, whose elder sister, Jennie, became Mrs Randolph Churchill and the mother of Winston, the future prime minister. Leonie had married Sir John Leslie, an Irish baronet, in 1884, and had four children. In 1895 the septuagenarian George, Duke of Cambridge, retired as Commander-in-Chief of the army, and the Duke of Connaught had long hoped to be appointed as his successor. Much to his disappointment, Lord Wolseley, who had been seen as the only other serious contender for the post, was chosen instead. It was at around this time that he was introduced, perhaps for the first time – and possibly while the duchess was away in Europe on one of her cures – to Leonie Leslie.

Was Louise pleased or upset when she discovered that what had been a casual acquaintance was ripening into what appeared to be an enduring relationship? Evidence suggests that the former was the case, and if the memoirs of Lady Leslie's granddaughter are correct, she accepted it gladly. For Lady Leslie, it seems, became the first person in British society to become a close friend of the Connaughts, who were generally regarded as a rather reserved couple, even 'somewhat forbidding'.⁴ It was said that she 'ruled the Duchess and ran the Duke,' and the relationship became 'the happiest of triangles – or perhaps, thinking of Jack Leslie, of quadrangles'. The duchess went as far as to tell a younger member of the family that she and the duke 'never had any *fun* until we met Leonie'.⁵ The latter, and maybe to a lesser extent her husband, helped to bring a gaiety into a royal household that had perhaps been too heavily overburdened with official duties and regular separations, and encouraged them to be themselves for once.

Moreover, the duchess undoubtedly appreciated that the companionship of another woman was vital for her husband, especially as perpetual ill-health meant that she was away from his side much of the time and the nature of his royal duties meant they were bound to lead partly separate lives. A shy woman who lacked self-esteem and suffered from persistent ailments she had become a loving wife, but perhaps found it hard to be the helpful companion to her husband that she wished she could, aware that she did not compare well with Queen Victoria's elder daughters-in-law. Unlike the Princess of Wales, she was no beauty; unlike the Duchess of Edinburgh, she never had the strength of character to hold her own against her husband's family, who were generally welcoming but not always uncritical towards her, or indeed to each other. She may have secretly reproached herself, or felt a little guilty, for not being in sufficiently robust health to be at his side, and probably thought that what appeared to be a perfectly respectable platonic friendship would go some way to ease the situation.

Far from resenting the presence of another woman, she was said 'to blossom in this warm atmosphere'. She even went so far as to admit that Lady Leslie 'could hand you a key to unlock your own shell'. It was a curious relationship, but never gave rise to any whiff of scandal. If the duke was in love with Leonie, he was not the only one; it was said that 'half London was'.[6] While the Princess of Wales had good reason to resent her husband's personal relationship with certain married ladies, it seems that no annoyance, embarrassment or scandal ever besmirched the Connaught-Leslie connection. Leonie filled a vacuum, and she had the grace never to try and exploit any advantages for personal gain that might have presented themselves to a close associate of royalty. The duke and duchess respected her and knew that any advice they sought from her would be sound and selflessly given.

* * *

When the Boer War broke out in October 1899, the Princess of Wales was as ever greatly concerned with the welfare of the wounded and sick. She selected and sent twelve nursing sisters out to South Africa, and from this developed the body later known as Queen Alexandra's Imperial Nursing Service. The conflict made Britain extremely unpopular throughout the rest of Europe, where sympathies were almost overwhelmingly on the side of the Boers.

Because of the rampant Anglophobia in France, the Prince of Wales reluctantly cancelled what had become his regular holiday on the Riviera, and in April 1900 he accompanied his wife on her family visit to Copenhagen, which was for him a less congenial environment. While their train was standing in the station at Brussels, a fifteen-year-old youth, Jean-Baptiste Sipido, brandishing a revolver, leapt onto the footboard of the royal compartment and fired two shots through the window. The bullets passed through the carriage between the prince and princess, but nobody was hurt. When he was arrested, he admitted that he wanted to kill the prince, whom he thought would be an easy target and, as the queen's son and heir, must be partly responsible for the deaths of hundreds of people during the war in Africa. Much to his would-be victim's annoyance, he was tried but acquitted because of his age and allowed to go free.

Like the rest of the household, Marie Mallet was very fond of the Princess of Wales, and seriously concerned about her well-being, particularly her apprehensions about what lay ahead for her and her husband. In March 1899 she thought that 'her restlessness is alarming and her one idea is to be constantly travelling, she looks ill, so do her daughters, and I hear she dreads the possibility of reigning.'[7] At the time Queen Victoria was almost eighty years old and still in good health, but everyone in the family was aware that, with the passage of time, her time would draw to a close before long.

* * *

Widowed at only twenty-three years of age, the Duchess of Albany remained dressed 'in deepest black' for a long time. It was several years after her husband's death before her children could remember her putting aside her mourning to appear in a pale grey summer dress instead.

Having had a Lutheran upbringing in Germany, but with the benefit of a liberal-minded pastor, as a wife and prematurely widowed mother it was easy enough for her to become a good, faithful Anglican. She remained 'a bit of a Covenanter' with very strong views on morality, and was at pains to instil a strong religious faith into her children. Her daughter Alice maintained that she could be a strict disciplinarian, 'sometimes too domineering in her anxiety to bring us very ordinary little urchins up as perfect beings.' Yet she was an accomplished storyteller, and on their Saturday walks she would always have some exciting tales with which to keep them entertained.[8] Brought up in a harmonious family atmosphere, it had not taken her long to see that beneath the surface, her in-laws had often been bitterly divided over petty differences and often inclined to argue vociferously. She had always been determined not to get involved, and particularly after Leopold died she was resolved to find her own path and remain out of the public eye as far as possible.

Much of the rest of her life was devoted unfailingly to her children, and in later years her grandchildren, as well as her favourite charities. At the time of her betrothal, her mother-in-law to be had been anxious lest she might not readily adopt the British royal principle of visiting the poor and sick. Any such fears were soon to prove unfounded, and to her relief she would learn that, on the contrary, Helen liked 'to go among the people'.[9] It was her good fortune that as a personality she was naturally gregarious, outgoing and curious about everything. She was never afflicted with the desperate shyness that bedevilled some of her royal contemporaries.

One domestic explosion briefly disturbed the harmony at Claremont. In July 1886 the duchess wrote to Queen Victoria to ask for her assistance with a problem. Little Alice's nurse, Eliza Creak, a spinster, had suddenly turned on her one day in the nursery in front of the children, complaining that she was being 'badly used, & that she had no position in the house, that *all* were unkind & never thought of her feelings, & that if I showed I would not give her her due position, others could not do so either.'[10]

What had provoked this began as a trivial dispute over who, mistress or nurse, should have invited two retired nurses to visit the household. One of them had looked after Leopold and the other after Helen in their younger days, and it came as the climax to six months of steadily deteriorating relations between them. Until then, they had been good friends. On the queen's recommendation, Helen told the nurse that she was overworked, and they had decided she ought to take a period of leave from the family to allow her nerves to settle. Miss Creak's sister, Mrs Wilson, who had been a nurse before her marriage, would provide temporary cover, and the queen suggested that the duchess should recall Miss Smith to help her. Eliza took the news calmly at first, though the duchess thought that she might use little Charles's state of health – he was teething and rather feverish – to manipulate the situation and avoid being sent away. This much the duchess had managed to tell the queen in a second letter before going to the nursery where another painful scene took place. Eliza began to cry and play on the boy's health, refusing to go away until he 'had those teeth'. She insisted she had always done her duty by the children, and would do anything she could for them, for their sakes and for that of the memory of their father. The duchess said, 'very gently & not for me upon which she said *no*.'[11] It was an odd thing for her to say to a young widow, still grieving for her husband who had died so young. A theory exists that Miss Creak harboured something of a crush for the duke and it found fulfilment in her care for his children, at the same time somehow firing a sense of resentment against his widow.

The duchess assumed that after a month Eliza Creak would return refreshed, and they could continue happily as before. It was left to the more far-seeing queen, who had seen similar situations over the years, to suggest that a permanent break was the only solution. Helen and the children were about to leave for their annual Scottish holiday at Birkhall, and she expected that Eliza would be joining them. However, it was her replacement, Victoria Nicholls, who came instead, and she proved to be the right person for the job. Miss Creak was awarded a pension of £15 per year, and it was the end of her association with the family.

The duchess continued to devote her time generously to good works. The charities that claimed her attention included the Hospitals Joint Appeal, the Hospital for Epilepsy, the Waterloo Hospital for Women and Children, and the Needlework Guild. The one for which she would always be remembered most, however, concerned the welfare of the so-called cattle market girls of Deptford. In the days before the advent of refrigeration, all cattle from South America arrived alive at London, where they were slaughtered. From the age of sixteen, girls were employed at a wage of 2*s* (two shillings) a day to clean out the guts by hand and make products such as sausage skins.

She did not content herself with sending a representative from her staff or a friend on a fact-finding mission, but also visited the market in person to see the more unpleasant aspects of their labours, not shrinking away or turning her eyes when it came to walking through the blood, filth and repellent conditions in order to discover just what the girls were subjected to every working day. Greatly perturbed by what she found, she made a point of going to speak to the government ministers concerned. Such work was stopped forthwith, and machinery was installed to complete the grim tasks. For the benefit of the girls who were consequently put out of work, she founded a new charity in 1894 named the Deptford Fund, to provide them with alternative employment. Five years later she launched the Albany Institute, a community venue that would in time become a combined community and performance centre, with the theatre venue becoming the Albany Empire.

Every summer from the period after the death of her husband to that of Queen Victoria, the duchess and her children would spend some of their time in Scotland, close to the Balmoral estate. The queen lent them Birkhall, a shooting lodge near Ballater on the river Muick. Little Princess Alice remembered these days as some of the most carefree of their life together, with a sloping garden full of fruit and sweet peas, and a chain bridge over the river where she and Charles used to play. The duchess was very fond of picnics, so when weather permitted they went for long drives, or long walks when they were older. As there were only horse-drawn vehicles, Birkhall was a stopping-place for the deer stalkers to drop in for a generous tea consisting of scones, cakes and jam.

Each spring, the Albanys would holiday in Cannes, at the Villa Nevada, where the duke had died. The villa had been given to the duchess as his next of kin. Queen Victoria had visited on several occasions, and placed a memorial there to her son. The duchess's views on the matter were never recorded, but her daughter Alice called these 'various tokens of her taste in decoration, some of which were quite unsuitable and spoilt the appearance of the place.' With her 'passion' for 'relics', she had ordered the building in the garden of 'a large and singularly repulsive marble bench seat surmounted by the inscription "Not lost but gone before"' in his memory. The Albanys, she confessed, 'took a scandalous pleasure in destroying it.'[12] One would like to assume that they had the tact to wait until grandma was no longer around to see its destruction.

Although their views on sculpture and memorials might have diverged, Queen Victoria always retained great admiration and affection for the widowed Duchess of Albany and her children. It inadvertently provoked some occasional jealousy among other members of the family. Once the queen had to ask her eldest daughter whether she could use her peacemaking skills to ask the Duchess of Connaught to be a little kinder to 'dear Helen'. It was a request with which her own family would have agreed. 'Louischen' may have been glad to escape from her unhappy early life and the barracks-like environment in Prussia and settle in England, but she remained her father's daughter. Within her own home, she was said to adopt an almost militaristic sense of discipline that sometimes left her small daughters trembling in sheer terror. If this was the case, perhaps they were a little relieved when their parents spent so much time abroad and they could be looked after by their grandmother. Some of Louise's in-laws would also see from time to time the seam of iron beneath the apparently amenable surface.

Chapter 3

For the Duchess of Saxe-Coburg, the end of the nineteenth century would be marked by three close family deaths within two years. The unfortunate, in one case ultimately tragic, problems of her elder children would have one positive result in that they at last brought her closer to the mother-in-law with whom she had had such a difficult relationship for some years.

The behaviour of young Alfred, her wayward only son, had long been a cause of concern. Separated from the sisters whom he had idolised, he had been sent to join the army in Berlin, and devoted himself less to his military career than to a dissolute life of women, drink, and, before long, venereal infection. Aware that he was destroying his health, his mother sent him to go and stay with the Crown Princess of Roumania when he was twenty-one in the hope that she could instil some commonsense or at least a more respectable way of life. Rumours that he had contracted a marriage in 1898 with a young Irishwoman of noble birth and had a daughter are unsupported by evidence, and it is apparent that they never even met each other. However, although Missy was at least teetotal, she was no paragon of virtue herself. Marrying a gentle but colourless husband had led her into the path of temptation with several lovers, until her mother had to warn her sternly against leading a 'disorderly life'.

The duke and duchess's marriage had never been one made in heaven. Alfred cared nothing for his wife's literary or theatrical interests, while his naval and sporting passions had never given her any pleasure. With her outgoing nature and love of conversation, she found him increasingly taciturn, moody and unapproachable as his health deteriorated through excessive drinking and smoking. She preferred life when he was away from her, telling their eldest daughter if only she had any idea how easy and comfortable life was without him.

Nevertheless, in January 1899 the silver wedding of this ill-starred couple was celebrated with a large family gathering at Schloss Friedenstein, the official ducal residence in Gotha, to which their Russian, British and German relatives were invited. There was one notable absentee from the festivities – the son and heir. The official reason for his not appearing was that he was seriously ill with tuberculosis. Only those who were closest to the duke knew that the despairing young Alfred, convinced that he had no future in any shape or form, had shot and seriously wounded himself. For a few days he was cared for at Friedenstein, but largely on his mother's orders and despite the doctors' insistence that he was too weak to travel, he was sent to Meran, in the Italian Alps, to convalesce. The journey proved too arduous for him and he died on 6 February, attended only by a doctor and servant. He was laid to rest at a funeral in which his normally undemonstrative mother sank to her knees, sobbing uncontrollably in front of the coffin when it arrived for internment. Ironically, the ceremony took place on 10 February, which would have been the anniversary of Queen Victoria's own marriage in 1840.

Though very few people were aware, the duke was already unwell with the first signs of what proved to be cancer of the larynx, the disease that had claimed the life of his brother-in-law, Emperor Frederick III, also a heavy smoker, at a similar age. He had left Alfred's convalescence to his wife's initiative, but on learning from the doctors that he should have remained immobile and that the journey would be dangerous, he was furious with her, holding her partly responsible for his son's death through neglect. With less than eighteen months to live, he would, from then on, have very little contact with his family.

As the Duke of Saxe-Coburg and his now deceased only son had no male heir between them, the succession to the duchy devolved on Queen Victoria's third son. It was a poisoned chalice that he had no intention of accepting. The Duke and Duchess of Connaught were thoroughly English, and he was just as fond of his army career as his brother Alfred had been of his life in the navy. The duchess had no desire to return to the Germany, where she had spent such an unhappy childhood, and although her husband was on better terms with Emperor William than any of his siblings, he probably had no desire to be in any kind of subordinate position below the *enfant terrible* of mainland Europe, which, as a German head of state in the empire, he would be in effect. At the time of their nephew Alfred's tragic death they were in Egypt, where the duke was due to lay the foundation stone of the Assuan Dam a week later.

If the Connaughts refused to accept the Coburg succession, it would fall to the Albanys, or more precisely young Charles, as the heir of Queen Victoria's deceased fourth son. It was a prospect the Duchess of Albany viewed with great alarm. In March, Collins wrote to Queen Victoria, pleading the case of her daughter-in-law:

> who feels very strongly that, if her son was once recognised as the next in succession, it would be almost a necessity for him to finish his education in Germany, and practically to live there; that under such circumstances his position without a Father to look after him ... would be a very difficult one. The Duchess as a woman could do little to help him. She said that she would have no fear of any difficulty with the Duke of Coburg, but did not feel equally comfortable at the prospect of being ... with collision with the German Emperor.[1]

Reluctantly, the Duke of Connaught bowed to the dictates of duty at first. On 9 April a declaration was read out to the Diet at Gotha in which he declared that he and his House were prepared to 'fulfil our duties towards our ancestral Duchies',[2] therefore accepting his designation as heir to his elder brother.

However, Queen Victoria knew that Arthur emphatically did not want to become Duke of Coburg, and did not intend his son Arthur to do so either. Within a couple of weeks, the Connaughts were making their attitude increasingly clear. The Duchess of Saxe-Coburg reported afterwards to Missy that the family visit 'went off well,' although her account of her in-laws' various attitudes suggested rather the opposite. She found the Duchess of Connaught 'not a bit amiable and very cold', causing difficulties and refusing to see how important it was that her son should be educated in Germany if he was going to succeed to the position one day. 'She has become so intolerably English that she can only see this case in an English light and thinks her son's career in England will be a brilliant one.' At length, Louise was almost persuaded that young Arthur would have an excellent career as one of a new generation of sovereigns, 'with a charming country and a big fortune of one's own'. However, Marie's son-in-law Ernest and her husband's secretary were both quite annoyed with Louise's obstinacy, though Marie suspected that Louise might have second thoughts. She hardly had any opportunity to speak to Arthur, although he seemed to be much more approachable than his wife, as he spent most of his time talking to his brother Alfred while he was there.

One day, Arthur went to meet Emperor William, who 'was not very gracious' and told him that he ought to enter the German service at once, or else people would not accept him as future Duke of Coburg. Marie dismissed this as 'nonsense', but was convinced that Arthur needed to come and settle in the duchy as soon as possible: 'He is a nice, quiet boy, seemed to enjoy his stay, but does not look strong and is really very lame. I think it is all nonsense to imagine that he will ever be capable of serving and for him, it seems a real Godsend to become once Duke of Coburg.' In spite of this, and much to the Duchess of Saxe-Coburg's anger, everyone left without having come to any decisions whatsoever. The Duchess of Connaught left behind the least agreeable impression. From what she saw of them, Marie liked the princesses, 'Daisy quite pretty and grown up, Patsy amusing and lively, but … mortally frightened of their Mama.'[3]

Arthur was adamant that he and his family would not uproot themselves and they intended to stay in England. He was even more determined not to be ordered around by his Hohenzollern nephew. From the moment that William tried to tell him what to do, any idea that the Connaughts would meekly submit to the Coburg succession died, and with it the fate of the Duchess of Albany – or rather her son – was sealed. No matter what the rest of the family might say, Queen Victoria gave the Connaughts her unstinting support. From Coburg, her daughter-in-law, still grieving for her only son, was furious with Louise, telling the Crown Princess of Roumania that 'Aunt Louischen was simply detestable and as one says *plus Catholique que le Pape* being so disgustingly English that Germany does not exist for her any more but she seems even to dislike it!'[4] Despite the Duchess of Connaught's deeply ingrained antipathy for the country of her birth, the thought of her adolescent son being trained as the next duke of the ancestral duchy was plausible enough – to others, if not the duchess herself – in view of his Hohenzollern blood. Earlier that month, Collins had discussed the matter with Queen Victoria in person. He told her that the Duke of Saxe-Coburg was very angry at his brother renouncing the succession for himself and his son, that the Duchess of Albany would not consent to Charles leaving Eton and could not afford a separate establishment.[5]

However, with Queen Victoria firmly in the Connaughts' camp, to use a military metaphor, there was no way the Duchess of Albany and her son could avoid their destiny being carved out for them. Her elder sister, Emma, Queen Mother of the Netherlands, was full of sympathy for her plight and the way in which she was apparently being bullied: 'I find it dreadful that the Connaughts are resigning their duties to Coburg and that they thus fall on Charlie's shoulders.'[6] It was a view evidently shared by some of Helen's in-laws, particularly the Prince of Wales. He was full of admiration for the way that she had managed as a single parent, having lost her husband after such a brief married life and thrown herself so tirelessly into her charitable work.

The Dowager Duchess of Albany shared the distaste of most of the family for the German Emperor and his desire to micromanage everything to do with his relations within the German Empire. She knew that her son could not escape his duty, but she did not want him to leave his home or education in England and have to make his permanent home at Coburg until he was an adult. According to a report by Collins at this time, she decided that 'she must for at least 2 or 3 years be with him … to do all in her power to bring him up as a German and to make him look on Germany as his country.'[7] It would be a wrench for her leaving England, as well as a financial worry. 'I must incur considerable expense in making a home for Charlie and Alice and myself elsewhere and I am afraid it will end in my having to spend some of the savings I have put by for my children,' she wrote to Queen Victoria. 'So you see, dear Mama, I have every reason for being rather anxious and worried, and I hope you will make some allowances for me under all circumstances.'[8]

The queen thought her daughter-in-law's anxiety was unnecessary. She assumed that Charles could stay at Eton for the next two or three years, and need not live in Germany after that. Whether this would apply to him as heir or as reigning duke, should Duke Alfred die within the next couple of years, she did not make clear. She probably expected that her son, now in his mid-fifties, would still live for several years, and might not have anticipated that the German Emperor, and public opinion throughout the German Empire, would not take kindly to such an idea.[9] Emperor William made his views plain; the heir to the duchy of Coburg, he declared, had to be a German and must live in Germany. He had not insisted on this during the lifetime of the late Duke Ernest, and accepted that the Duke of Edinburgh still had his own naval career in England until shortly before his uncle's death. Yet times had changed since then, and such a state of affairs would no longer be acceptable.

The Duke of Connaught understood that he had no choice but to decline the Coburg succession for himself and his son, a decision that made his son and his wife thoroughly relieved. Lengthy discussions with other senior members of the royal family, including the German emperor, followed his decision, and on 30 June his renunciation of the succession was read out to the Coburg Diet. Three days later, a bill was adopted confirming the Duke of Albany as the new heir. Along with his sister Alice and his widowed mother, he had to move to Germany in order to satisfy nationalist opinion. With heavy hearts, the Duchess of Albany and her children bowed to what was expected of them: 'I gave in about Eton and agreed to take Charlie in August to Coburg.'[10] It was nevertheless stipulated by the Diet that should the young Duke of Albany die without leaving a male heir himself, the rights and place in the succession of the Duke of Connaught and his descendants 'would revive'.

When the Duchess of Albany and her children arrived at Reinhardsbrunn, they were rather disconcerted to meet the bibulous Duke of Saxe-Coburg quaffing champagne, while everyone else was partaking more decorously of afternoon tea. Almost at once, he made it clear to them that he wanted young Charles to come and live with him and his family, though he could not offer his sister-in-law and little niece a permanent home as well. She declined his offer, aware that he was one relative to whose influence she did not wish to expose her doubtless impressionable schoolboy son. The duchess was furious with her sister-in-law, who, she told the Crown Princess of Roumania, was 'frightfully obstinate and tactless and wrote down every kind of outrageous condition,' if her son was to succeed as duke. Helen, she said, wanted to establish herself at Coburg with him, and thought the present duke and duchess should provide a separate establishment for herself and her son there. The idea was quite unacceptable, she said, 'as she would make herself impossible ... I foresee terrible battles, as she is as obstinate as a mule and as calculating as an old Jew, just trying to get out of us as many financial advantages as she possibly can.'[11]

King William of Württemberg, a distant relation, came to their rescue by providing mother and both children with a suite of rooms in the palace at Stuttgart. It proved unnecessary, as Helen decided she would settle at Dresden instead. The Duchess of Coburg was relieved, as she had 'made herself very disagreeable' and the plan would keep her away from Coburg. She was equally angry with the Connaughts for renouncing their place in the first instance, blaming 'Aunt Louischen' above all, convinced that it was because of her personal hatred of Emperor William that she could not bear the idea of her son being in Germany.

While realising that Charles could succeed to the duchy at any time, they would find the waiting time considerably shorter than they might have anticipated. His sudden departure from Eton gave the duchess some problems regarding the rest of his education. The Empress Frederick recommended a school at Frankfurt which, according to the duchess's daughter in terms that would sound quite unacceptable in a later age, 'was supposed to be very modern but was mainly attended by the sons of rich Jews.' This did not meet with Helen's approval any more than 'a horrid scruffy place near Reinhardsbrunn' – again, in Princess Alice's blunt phraseology – that had been recommended by Duke Alfred.[12] It was noticeable that the Empress Frederick, whom Alice accused of 'continually meddling', never shared the anti-Semitic prejudices of some of the younger generation, and ironic that in later life Charles would pay a heavy price for his association with Adolf Hitler, which would alienate him from nearly all his royal relatives in England. At length, Emperor William arranged for his young cousin to attend the Leichterfelde military cadet school, the German equivalent of Sandhurst, and he was also provided with a German tutor.

While he was there, Emperor William placed nearby Villa Ingenheim at the disposal of Helen and her children. They enjoyed the garden with its lilacs and shrubs, as well as the grounds that ran down to the river Havel, where they rowed in a boat she had had sent out from Claremont. Less pleasant, particularly where Alice was concerned, was the inexpensive but ugly German furniture, and above all a horse butcher's shop opposite them, with its often pungent smell.

* * *

Still grieving over the pathetic fate of her only son, the Duchess of Saxe-Coburg was as ever deeply worried by the situation of her elder daughters, and feared that both marriages were doomed. While Ernie and Ducky were staying with her at Gotha in the spring of 1898, she realised that he got on his wife's nerves and 'she simply cannot stand him sometimes ... I am sometimes in despair about that couple, how on earth is it to go on?'[13]

Meanwhile, in Roumania Missy was temporarily in disgrace and had been sent back to her parental home at Friedenstein, Coburg. Her marriage to Crown Prince Ferdinand had been very much an arranged affair, and was proving to be no happier than that of her mother. In the autumn of 1897 she had become pregnant by one of her lovers, generally assumed to be Zizi Cantacuzino, a Roumanian officer who had been appointed to her service by King Carol during the crown prince's serious illness. What became of the child remained a well-kept secret. Marie evidently did not learn from her indiscretion, and two years later the same thing happened again. In a quarrel with King Carol, she claimed that Grand Duke Boris of Russia was the father, although this may have been her way of shielding Cantacuzino, who would be easier to punish than a close relative of the tsar.

The affair was apparently reported by Elizabeth Saxton Winter. An English governess who had previously worked in a similar capacity for the royal family of the Netherlands, she was now in charge of the nursery at Bucharest, presumably on the grounds that not to have done so could have laid her open to accusations of aiding and abetting the crown princess's affair, and being disloyal to the king, who was after all her employer. Yet the news proved impossible to contain within royal circles, and rapidly spread throughout Europe. Although the duchess realised that her eldest daughter had behaved scandalously, she defended her, writing angrily to Winter that because of her actions, 'you undo a whole life of honest and successful labour in Holland and your name will bear the stamp of infamy and intrigue, never to be wiped out during your whole life.'[14] At one stage she was convinced that the only solution was for Missy to threaten to leave Roumania for good and take her son Carol with her, renouncing if possible his name in the succession. Prince Leopold, Nando's father, told King Carol that his son had accepted the fact of his wife's affair but blamed himself for having been so careless and weak in the first place. Nando and Missy both insisted that he and not Cantacuzino was the father of her expected child. Leopold urged the king to permit a reconciliation, which the couple both desperately wanted, vowing that they would behave more carefully in future.

A further source of stress to the duchess had been her husband's debts. Part of her fortune had gone to pay off Duke Ernest's arrears, in addition to her regular lavish expenditure on the upkeep and furnishing of Clarence House, and by this time their finances were in such a parlous state that she was worried their creditors would threaten to repossess the Edinburgh Palace. He appealed to Queen Victoria for assistance, and she contributed £95,000 towards their debts, enabling Marie to purchase the residence from her husband.[15]

The four sisters were reunited for Christmas with their mother in the duchy at the end of what had been a very difficult year for them, and on 6 January 1900 Marie gave birth to a second daughter. Named Marie after her mother and grandmother, but known as 'Mignon', she would later become Queen of Yugoslavia. Crown Prince Ferdinand and the Roumanian ministers came to Gotha, where a birth certificate was issued, naming him as the father of the newborn child. He then returned to Bucharest, followed by a letter from the duchess insisting that she was not going to let her daughter be treated like a nobody. If he wanted his wife to return to Roumania and did not wish to be rid of her completely, Miss Winter would have to go, otherwise she would seek a divorce for her daughter. Realising that the duchess would be satisfied with nothing less and that she would not hesitate to do what she called 'the greatest damage' to the Roumanian royal family by involving her relations in Russia and England, King Carol and Queen Elisabeth appointed a new governess, Miss Anne Ffoliott, and in April Miss Winter departed. At last a line was drawn under the unhappy, protracted business.

By this time the Duke of Saxe-Coburg was living in a little cottage in the grounds at Rosenau. The duchess was worried by Ducky's depression and a difficult second pregnancy, which culminated in the birth of a stillborn son in May. She was also upset that the irascible duke did not want to see much of his family, and was alarmed at being told so little about his state of health, which she now feared was much worse than any of them had supposed. In the middle of June she received a letter from him saying he was not well enough to join her in London later that month, but he was improving and hoped to be well again in about three weeks. Like Queen Victoria, she was sure his entourage were trying to keep the true state of affairs from them all and withholding bad news, or else underestimating the seriousness of his condition. Neither of the women were aware that for some weeks he had been unable to swallow and could only be fed by a tube.

Full of sympathy for the duchess who had lost her son in such tragic circumstances, was upset by her two elder daughters' difficulties, and was unsure of her husband's state of health, the queen invited her and her youngest daughter, Beatrice, at sixteen the only unmarried child still at home, to come and stay in England. They arrived in June, spending a few days at Clarence House, and in London the duchess was among those who joined the Prince and Princess of Wales at the opening of the Wallace Collection at Hertford House. Later that week she and her daughter joined the queen at Windsor.

Having celebrated her eighty-first birthday a month earlier, the matriarch who had held the family together for so long was suddenly ageing. She seemed to be far more accommodating, even gentler to those around her than formerly, and the duchess immediately noticed an improvement in her general attitude towards others. After they had enjoyed a carriage drive together, broaching difficult family matters during the journey, she wrote to Missy from Clarence House that did not think she had 'ever seen her so nice with me before.'[16] The sudden warmth between both women, united in sadness, continued throughout her stay, and the following month she continued in a similar vein: 'Granny' was 'very dear and kind and has "taken to me greatly" this time to me and seemed really pleased to see me.'[17]

The duchess then went to spend a few days at Darmstadt with the Grand Duchess of Hesse, who seemed to be on the verge of a nervous breakdown. Yet it was not until she returned to Windsor in July that she learned from the queen and others just how ill her husband was. 'I was terribly distressed when I heard the truth about Papa,' she wrote to Crown Princess Marie. 'He must have suffered terribly and we knew nothing about it.'[18] Later that week they returned to Coburg, and only then did they see for themselves the true state of affairs. There was nothing to be done, they realised, but to try and make his last few days as comfortable as possible. On 27 July he arrived at the Rosenau, and Marie told Queen Victoria that he 'speaks with difficulty, but walks about, dreadful trial.'[19] The duchess and their three younger daughters were with him on the evening of 30 July, while Missy was on her way from Roumania to join them. They spent a peaceful evening sitting in the garden at Rosenau, then he retired at his usual hour, and died peacefully in his sleep, within less than a week of what would have been his fifty-sixth birthday.

At Osborne the queen received the news in tears early next morning, noting in her journal that it was 'so merciful' that after fighting such a debilitating illness he had passed away without any struggle, but heartrending for them all the same: 'Poor darling Marie who knew of no real danger, when she left, such a short while ago, without a fear. It is too terrible also for the poor daughters, who adored their Father! I was greatly upset, — one sorrow, one trial, one anxiety, following on another.'[20]

Her youngest daughter, Beatrice, who had never been quite the same since unexpectedly losing her husband, Henry, four years earlier to fever after being invalided home from Africa and succumbing on the journey, was likewise filled with compassion for the family. She wrote to the Bishop of Ripon that they could not 'bear to think of the desolation in that house at Coburg, my dear sister-in-law still mourning the death of her only son ... But she is so good and brave, I know she will bear with resignation, this further crushing blow.'[21]

In Coburg a magnificent funeral on 4 August was presided over by the German emperor and attended by most of the imperial princes. At forty-six years old, Marie was Dowager Duchess of Saxe-Coburg and Gotha, while her nephew Charles, who had only celebrated his sixteenth birthday eleven days earlier, became the new duke. As a widow, she stayed for a while in England. One of her immediate tasks was to oversee the removal of her possessions from Clarence House, which was now to become the official London residence of the Duke and Duchess of Connaught.

During Charles's minority, the regency and guardianship devolved on his uncle, Ernest of Hohenlohe-Langenburg, for nearly five years. There had been a suggestion that the Duchess of Albany should assume the role as she was his closest relation, and that she had declined the responsibility of being regent. It was, however, unlikely that the German emperor would have allowed a woman, and one who had spent almost thirty years of her life in England, to be appointed.

Duke Alfred's death had inevitably cast a shadow over the whole family. Despite their occasional differences, the Prince of Wales had always been devoted to him, and the black mood that descended on him and the princess deepened after he returned from the funeral at Coburg and a visit to the Empress Frederick at her home near Kronberg. Just after losing his favourite brother, he had seen with his own eyes that his favourite sister was seriously ill with cancer of the spine, in great pain for much of the time, and not expected to survive much longer.

The Duke of Connaught had suffered from a severe bout of influenza earlier that year, followed by bad attacks of asthma. To compound his disappointment at being passed over for the position of commander-in-chief in succession to his second cousin George, Duke of Cambridge, he was refused an active command in the war in South Africa. The duchess felt particularly for him in his depression at these setbacks. She was likewise enduring trouble with her leg and the constant remedies that alleviated the pain without curing it. A letter from the duke to Queen Victoria that July mentioned that at last he could reassure her how 'her leg is going on very satisfactorily', but how frustrating it had been for her to remain in bed for so long.[22] Yet the duchess could never forget that none of her sisters had reached the age of forty. In an unusually morbid frame of mind, she began making plans for her own funeral.[23]

Later that year, accompanied by Beatrice, the Duchess of Saxe-Coburg visited the various German courts to give thanks personally for the affectionate condolences shown to her on her husband's death. Emperor William was naturally pleased with her decision to stay at Coburg, rather than return in her widowhood to England, where she had never felt at home. Shortly before Christmas she and Beatrice also went to Kronberg, so they could be with the Empress Frederick. The latter had been very close in recent years to her brother Alfred, and deeply mourned his passing. Having always been passionately English, she could not understand how her sister-in-law, having the chance to live in London, preferred to remain in Germany now she was no longer a reigning Duchess. From her home at Friedrichshof, near Bonn, the empress wrote to her daughter Sophie, Crown Princess of Greece, telling her about the 'sad meeting' with her sister-in-law, whom she had not seen since young Alfred's death and who was 'very nice and kind ... though she hates showing her feelings in general, she did not conceal from me how much she suffered.'[24] Marie was equally upset, telling Crown Princess Marie about 'poor, wretched Aunt Vicky' and how upset she was 'by her *Jammerbild* [picture of misery]'.[25] Although the family feared that she might predecease her mother, the empress survived until the following summer, scarcely able to leave her bed except on fine days when she could be taken outside in the garden in a wheelchair.

The duchess then went to spend Christmas at Darmstadt with Ducky, recalling sadly how her husband had always loved the festive season. 'I cannot, cannot realise that he is gone. I always think that he is absent and coming back soon.'[26] Though their marriage had not been happy for several years, it was apparent from her letters how much she missed her husband. For all his faults, she evidently cherished his memory and missed him badly.

After Christmas she made what she sensed would probably be her last visit to Queen Victoria, the mother-in-law with whom she had discovered a new understanding just in time. She also needed to go and make arrangements in person for the removal of her last remaining possessions at Clarence House, including the little blue and gold chapel with its Russian icons. On her journey from Darmstadt to London she took her daughter Beatrice and granddaughter Elizabeth, five-year-old daughter of the increasingly unhappy marriage of the Grand Duke and Duchess of Hesse.

It was increasingly clear to those around her that Queen Victoria's health was failing. In addition to the frailty of old age, she was grieving the deaths of her son Alfred and grandson Christian Victor, son of Helena and Christian of Schleswig-Holstein (the latter from fever while serving with the army in South Africa), and also by news of defeats in the Boer War. A feeling that she had been less than fair to her Russian daughter-in-law over the years troubled her, and anxious to make amends, she was eager to invite her and her daughters to come and stay at Osborne House.

Aware that the end of an era was approaching, the duchess came willingly. She was suffering badly from headaches and neuralgia, and complained of working from morning till night at Clarence House in order to sort her old home out with the Duke and Duchess of Connaught 'always in and out'. As ever, she found Osborne House miserable with the prevailing family gloom, and thought it a wretchedly inhospitable place to stay in during the depths of winter as it was chilly and draughty, battered by howling winds that perpetually shook the windows.[27] The atmosphere preyed on her nerves, and as she told her eldest daughter, her patience with the queen's daughters was limited: 'they all lost their heads and did not know what to do, those foolish, childish Aunts.'[28]

She joined Queen Victoria each day on a short carriage drive in the grounds of Osborne, until the middle of January when the latter was no longer well enough to go outside. On 16 January the duchess took her place in the carriage as usual, while her mother-in-law was placed in her seat, and they waited for the rain to stop and the fog to clear. When there was no break in the cloud, the queen was carried back to her bedroom and never left it again. She suffered a couple of strokes, became progressively more enfeebled, and all members of her family in England and Europe were warned that she was slipping away. The Empress Frederick longed to be there as well, but she was too ill to travel from Germany and join the growing throng of concerned relations at Osborne. The Duchess of Albany, accompanied by Charles and Alice, left Germany as soon as she could, and arrived a couple of days too late.

Early in the evening of 22 January 1901, surrounded by her other children, children-in-law and several of her grandchildren, the sovereign who had given her name to an age entered her final rest. The Princess of Wales knelt beside her, holding her hand at the end. 'We all still kissed her hand and then she passed away quietly,' the Duchess of Saxe-Coburg wrote to her eldest daughter. 'She looked quite fine and very peaceful, not one feature was distorted or changed. In fact she died of no illness but simple old age and gradual sinking.'[29]

Part IV

The Edwardian Era 1901–10

Chapter 1

On the death of Queen Victoria, her son and heir assumed the name King Edward VII. She had hoped that he would reign as King Albert Edward, but he had always preferred the more English Edward, a name that had been borne by six of his predecessors in Plantagenet and Tudor days. Alexandra was now queen consort, though it was a title she did not intend to use. As Viscount Esher, Permanent Secretary to the Office of Works, and one of the most respected of royal confidantes, would note, 'she means to be "the Queen"'.[1]

Nevertheless, for the first few days she remained in some awe of the recently deceased matriarch, of whom she had always been so fond. Sir Frederick Ponsonby, who had been Queen Victoria's assistant private secretary and now served her eldest son in a similar capacity, was sure that the new monarch and his consort both 'hated' coming to the throne, even though they had long been prepared for the inevitable. 'The Princess of Wales refuses to be called Queen as she says that at present there can only be one Queen and she wishes to remain Princess of Wales until after the funeral.'[2]

For all the family, there was an air of unreality hanging over them as they struggled to accustom themselves to life without the matriarch who had been the cornerstone of their existence, as well as the kingdom's, since long before any of them were born. In the immediate aftermath of the queen's death, and indeed for several weeks afterwards, the king was tired, hoarse, and short-tempered with everybody, while his sisters seemed rudderless and irritable.

The no-nonsense Duchess of Saxe-Coburg found the general lack of organization astonishing: 'No, the English people, one must say, are "a rum lot".' Nobody, she told Crown Princess Marie of Roumania, had even thought to order a coffin, and Emperor William had to do so as the new king needed to go to London for his proclamation. Long-ingrained habits die hard, and she was equally amazed at hearing some people continuing to refer to him as Prince of Wales. She and her sister-in-law Louise, Duchess of Argyll, 'could not stand it any longer so we sent for the Master of the Household and explained to him that it was highly improper and that he must give orders to the household to call their new Majesties by their proper and due names.' It also irked her that the new queen, 'out of false sentimentality', expressed a wish that she was not to be called thus as long as she was still at Osborne. She thought it 'too naïf for words! ... One would really think one was living among a pack of babies.' Her sisters-in-law, she added, were either much upset and crying, quarrelling with the Duchess of Argyll – who was looking 'absolutely poisonous' at times – or 'terrible busybodies and absorbed by small things'. The only one who was keeping her head and did not seem to irritate her was the Duchess of Albany – who had put on weight and was 'twice the size' – even though there had recently been problems between both ladies with regard to the Coburg succession. Yet at least the level-headed Helen was acting more calmly than the queen's daughters, as she had 'a very mild disposition and even lets her children be with the others.'[3]

Queen Victoria's funeral took place at Windsor on 2 February. As befitted her status as the pre-eminent monarch of her time, it was attended not only by members of her immediate and extended family, but also royal representatives from every corner of Europe, as well as from south-east Asia, with even Vajiravudh, Crown Prince of Siam and later King Rama VI, among those present. Once she had been laid to rest at the mausoleum, the Duchess of Saxe-Coburg and her youngest daughter, Beatrice, returned to Germany, as did the Duchess of Albany and her children. The Duke of Connaught went back to his post in Dublin as general in command of the forces in Ireland a few days later, while the duchess stayed at Windsor which she found 'horribly sad' after her mother-in-law's passing. Her sisters-in-law, she said, seemed to have lost their heads and were unusually fractious. Beatrice, whose life had revolved around her ever-demanding mother even more since her husband Henry's unexpected death from fever in Africa five years previously, as well as their four small children, was not only more lost than ever but also preoccupied to the point of obsession with some items of glassware that she was expecting the Connaughts to give her.[4]

* * *

Queen Victoria had presided over what was on the surface a fairly united family. There had been disputes from time to time between the brothers, sisters and their spouses, notably when the Prussian wars of the 1860s had taken their toll with divided loyalties to different German states or other countries on the European mainland, and again some years later with petty personal differences in character between the younger daughters. Yet a sense of solidarity had been maintained under the woman who ruled over them all and whose word was nearly always law. Now she was gone, the situation was suddenly changed. King Edward had always been much closer to the brother and two sisters closest to him in age – two of whom were now dead, while the eldest was dying and had only six months to live – than to the younger siblings with whom he had never had much in common. While Queen Alexandra was invariably kind and charming to those who knew her, for political and personal reasons she had never been particularly close to them either. Although the Duchess of Saxe-Coburg was closely related by marriage to the Dowager Empress of Russia, there had never been a great deal of love lost between them, while she had had little opportunity to establish a close relationship with the Duchesses of Connaught and Albany. It was inevitable that her husband's accession to the throne would see a loosening of the bonds.

Throughout her thirty-seven years as Princess of Wales, Queen Alexandra had always been very popular and would remain so. While her husband's affairs and such matters as the Tranby Croft baccarat scandal had brought him criticism, if not open censure, she had never forfeited the love or respect of the nation. Some might regard her as stupid, not making due allowances for her deafness, an ever-increasing burden that she managed to come to terms with to some extent through lip-reading.

She never claimed to be an intellectual, and although, for family reasons, she would always champion the rights of Denmark and Greece, she knew better than to lay herself open to charges of meddling in politics. King Edward did not allow her to see the contents of his official boxes, a restriction to which she never objected, even though he allowed their son and heir, George, Duke of York and soon-to-be Prince of Wales, to do so as he was the king-in-waiting. Devoted to her children, dogs and horses, and a tireless patron of charities, she was, and would long remain, everybody's favourite member of the royal family, the one who, in the eyes of the public, never put a foot wrong throughout a long life. Some even opined that 'it was she who kept the throne for her husband'.[5] At times she could still be unworldly to an eccentric degree. Although her niece Patsy of Connaught was now an adult, and almost six feet tall, on one of her birthdays a footman delivered to her presents suitable for a child of ten, with the verbal message, 'To darling little Patsy from her silly old Aunt Alix.' As Patsy commented, when in the company of her aunt, 'you suddenly had the sensation that in every way time stood still.'[6]

The reign of King Edward would see a subtle change from the Victorian age of respectability and remoteness to a more free and easy morality. King Edward VII was no hypocrite, and would never claim to be a paragon of virtue. It remained for Queen Alexandra to preserve the respectability of the previous century without detracting from a more modern, decorative air, proving in the words of her biographer, Georgina Battiscombe, that 'royalty could be both glamorous and good,'[7] a delicate balance that she managed to strike to perfection. Once she was queen, she could be obstinate. Now she was answerable to nobody, except her husband, and would insist on her own way whenever possible. She remained as unpunctual as ever, and if others tried to hurry her along as the king had important engagements and a full timetable, her response was invariably one of 'keep him waiting, it will do him good'.[8]

At first she refused to consider moving from Marlborough House, which had always been her main married home in London, to Buckingham Palace and Windsor Castle. Only when other members of the family supported the king did she reluctantly accept that she had a duty to conform to what was expected of the sovereign and his consort. When they went to Windsor, she wanted to live in the state apartments, but the king insisted that they must occupy Queen Victoria's old rooms, and in this she had to acquiesce. After a visit to Copenhagen in the spring, she returned home, and as she wrote to the dying Empress Frederick, she regretted that during her absence the king 'has had all your Mother's rooms dismantled and all her precious things removed.'[9]

Despite the weight of their new responsibilities, King Edward and Queen Alexandra were doting grandparents who were more than happy to take charge of the York children when their son and daughter-in-law, the Duke and Duchess, went on an eight-month tour of Australia, South Africa and Canada from March to November 1901. For the youngsters, whose parents had always been strict and left them for the most part to the not-so-tender mercies of unsympathetic domestic staff, there would be an idyllic few months in which they were delightfully spoilt. Queen Alexandra had always had a habit of treating her children as children, even when they were grown up – albeit in the most pleasant way possible – and with her grandchildren she was in her element.

Looking after the three princes, aged between one and seven years, and the four-year-old princess, gave the queen some respite in what was an otherwise very demanding year. There was the pressure of adjusting to the position of first lady of the land, a responsibility that admittedly laid less heavily on her shoulders than the commensurate role on her husband did on his. Both of them were saddened by the sufferings of the Empress Frederick, who at one stage the previous year had been thought likely to predecease their mother. Queen Alexandra paid her a short visit in April while returning from a family visit to Copenhagen and was very distressed by her agonies.

When the empress died on 5 August, the queen's hatred of Germany and contempt for Emperor William II did not prevent her from accompanying the king to the funeral a few days later. The sadness of the occasion was exacerbated when the emperor briefly, and unwisely, threatened to bar his uncle and aunt from coming to attend the ceremony. Once he had relented and allowed them to be present after all, he could not resist the temptation of exploiting it as an opportunity to show off the military might of his empire through grand parades of the Prussian infantry at every turn. The king, who found the weather unbearably hot in the tight uniform that he was obliged to wear, found such ostentation at this particularly sad time for the family uncalled for. The Duke and Duchess of Connaught and their son were also present at the funeral, the emperor having raised no objection to the presence of the English uncle who had always been his favourite, as was the young Duke of Saxe-Coburg.

No less worrying was the physical state of the king himself. Having finally inherited the crown in his sixtieth year and not in the best of health, he proved himself a conscientious worker who would spare himself nothing in his acute attention to detail in reading his official papers and discussing matters of state with his ministers. It was not surprising that he subsequently became more irritable and short-tempered. He was smoking more heavily than ever, despite his chronic bronchitis, drinking more than was wise on the grounds that he needed it as a stimulant, and above all eating so much that his clothes no longer fitted properly.

The coronation had been scheduled for 26 June 1902, a delay of seventeen months since the king's accession, which was occasioned by the conclusion of the Boer war in Africa and the signing of a peace treaty at Vereeniging at the end of the previous month. From the beginning of June he was clearly unwell, but angrily rejected any suggestion that the ceremony should be postponed, only submitting to the inevitable when his doctors told him that he had no alternative but to undergo a major operation for an abdominal abscess. Following several weeks of convalescence, it was a slimmer, impatient, yet more relaxed sovereign and his consort who were duly crowned in a ceremony – slightly curtailed in order not to overtax him – at Westminster Abbey on 9 August.

* * *

In July 1901 reporters in the British and American press suggested that the Duchess of Albany was going to accompany King Edward VII on his visit to Scotland, and that it would be made the occasion for the announcement of her betrothal.[10] The man in question was a widower, and a senior British politician, namely Archibald Primrose, Earl of Rosebery, a former leader of the Liberal Party and prime minister from 1894 to 1895. There had been a precedent of sorts when one of the king's younger sisters, Princess Louise, had married John Douglas Campbell, Marquis of Lorne, later Duke of Argyll, and for a while a Liberal Unionist Member of Parliament. Nevertheless, Lord Rosebery was not destined to become a member of the royal family, and the Dowager Duchess of Albany remained a widow for her remaining twenty years.

Although she was still living in Germany so she could offer support to Charles, she returned to England during the coronation season in the summer of 1902. In the procession to the abbey she took her place in the fourth carriage, with her sister-in-law Louise, now Duchess of Argyll, and the Crown Prince and Princess of Roumania. During the festivities she planted an oak tree on Esher Green to celebrate the occasion, and placed part of the estate at Claremont at the disposal of the residents of Esher. The highlight of the functions there in coronation week was a dinner for the aged, a tea for young persons, fireworks and a large bonfire.

Not long after Charles had succeeded to the duchy, Helen was staying in England and one day met Lady Knightley at Buckingham Palace for tea. Both ladies discussed how the family were managing, and Helen commented on how the change had 'affected the Duke unfavourably.' He had been obliged to pretend he liked being a German while the opposite was the case, and 'now he has got over that'. She was impressed with Ernest as regent, hoping he 'would be able to clean out the sink of corruption Coburg had become under Duke Ernest and which Duke Alfred had not succeeded in remedying.' Above all, the German emperor was kind to her, she seemed very happy and was most proud of her daughter as well.[11]

Emperor William II had taken a leading role in his young nephew's education and military training along Prussian lines, and invited him regularly to the imperial court at Berlin, where some spoke of him as 'the seventh son of the Emperor'. He joined the cadet school at Potsdam, and was given training in the Prussian interior ministry and in royal asset management. Later he went to Geneva, where he learned French, and to the state ministry in Gotha, where he was introduced to administrative procedures in the duchy. In May 1903 his scholastic days reached their final stage when he went to study law and political science at the University of Bonn.

By this time the duchess had decided that her son, now in his nineteenth year, could manage happily without her nearby, and in April 1903 she and Alice departed Germany with some relief as they moved back to their more congenial old home at Claremont. This would not be the case for long, for in November 1903 Alice was betrothed to Prince Alexander of Teck, the youngest of three brothers of the new Princess of Wales. They were married in February 1904 in St George's Chapel, where her parents had done likewise just over twenty years earlier. For the next few years Helen would always be glad to welcome them back to Claremont, particularly during Alice's three pregnancies. Between 1906 and 1910 her two sons and daughter would all be born in the house where Alice had grown up and had never ceased to love. Meanwhile, she returned with vigour to her charitable enterprises, regularly presiding over her Deptford Fund meetings, in addition to a regular schedule of opening new hospitals, training homes and similar institutions.

* * *

Queen Victoria had been predeceased by her second and fourth sons. During the reign of King Edward VII, the position of his only surviving younger brother and sister-in-law underwent a marked change. In the queen's lifetime the Duke of Connaught's career had flourished, and he had an assured position at Court. He hardly ever gave her a day's worry or cause for dissatisfaction, and in an ill-considered display of favouritism, she had sometimes told others that she always loved him more than her other children.

It was perhaps only to be expected that after her death there would be a certain coolness between the brothers, and mild, accumulated resentment on the part of the elder. Moreover, the king was probably more annoyed than he was prepared to reveal by the duke's refusal to bow to the dictates of family duty and accept the Coburg succession in 1899, no matter how reluctant he (Prince Arthur) might have been to do so. To the sovereign, it was nothing short of a dereliction of duty, regardless of the fact that he had Queen Victoria's full approval for standing back and allowing the young Duke of Albany to accept what some might have foreseen would become a poisoned chalice in the years ahead. With her well-known hostility for political, if not personal, reasons to most Germans, there was little empathy between Queen Alexandra and the Duchess of Connaught, even though the latter had felt herself thoroughly English ever since the first days of her marriage, escaping from a home environment and country never amenable to her. When the king and queen, accompanied by several members of the royal family, attended Ascot Races on 20 June 1902, a few days before the coronation should have taken place, the duchess felt that she had been snubbed, perhaps because she was not expected. After receiving 'such looks,' she wrote sadly to Leonie, 'I felt inclined to sink into the ground & was miserable all day – & longed to speak to you, who care for me a bit – & you would not come! So all was spoilt – the Queen treated me as if I was air!!'[12] She was known for her sensitivity and a tendency to take offence where none was intended, but Queen Alexandra always had a tendency to be chilly to those with whom she had had long-standing differences.

Even the close friendship between the Connaughts and the Leslies was partly responsible for another problem between both brothers. Exactly what happened is open to doubt, but it is apparent that around the end of 1901, or a little later, King Edward made some allusion to Leonie to the duke that contained an unpleasant innuendo. Refusing to let it bother him, the duke mentioned it briefly to Leonie, adding that those who lived in glass houses should not throw stones.[13]

Yet the correspondence between Lady Leonie and the duchess, which continued to the end of the latter's life, testifies to the fact that the bond of friendship remained as strong as ever, and the duchess clearly relished having someone outside the family circle in whom she could confide. In November 1902 Sir Jack and Leonie were invited to join the duke and duchess on an official tour of Egypt and India – an enjoyable few weeks for them all. Such a state of affairs was bound to cause occasional problems, and about a year later the latter feared that there was some kind of a crisis looming. The duchess feared that Leonie might be close to 'folding up her tent', bringing everything to an amicable conclusion, and severing her connections with them. Suffering from severe neuralgia, feeling depressed and out of sorts, the duke thought the same, and confided to his wife that the prospect made him utterly miserable. Whatever misunderstandings or doubts there may have been were soon smoothed over, and matters continued as before.

One problem that gave the couple no little annoyance was an effort to sell a letter written by the duchess to Sarah Chapman, the child's nurse, when she left their household after eight years in 1890. Mrs Chapman evidently had an eye on profiting from the collectors' market, and had apparently done the same with an item of Queen Victoria's correspondence (for £21) a few years previously. The duke told Sir Francis Knollys, the king's private secretary, that the duchess had been ordered by the queen to write a farewell letter in much more familiar terms than she had ever used before, and he was instructed to give her a pension. 'She had not behaved well latterly & bullied the children so we were glad to get rid of her under any conditions.'[14]

There were allegations of not only bullying but also drunkenness on the part of the nurse, yet it was never established who was trying to sell the letter. However, Mrs Chapman could not have been responsible, for she had died in 1898 at the age of fifty-four, having nursed her elderly father for some time and collapsed with a stroke only a month after his death.

Relations between the sovereign and his wife, and his brother and sister-in-law, remained difficult at best. In May 1904, when they were all expected to attend a function in London, the duchess confided to Lady

Leslie: 'I only hope H[is] M[ajesty] will be in good temper & civil – I suppose if the weather keeps fairly fine & his horse wins he will be – but she [Queen Alexandra] so very little genial (?) to me & *shares* the *general* feeling of disliking me that it is all very uphill work & very unpleasant - & H.M. only *occasionally* tries to make an effort to be nice!!'[15]

How happy the marriage and home life of the Duchess of Connaught really was is similarly open to question. If there ever were any severe issues between the couple, it remained behind closed doors. Although his relationship with Leonie Leslie remained free from scandal, Louise could hardly have been blamed if she felt sidelined and no longer her husband's adequate partner for life. Her letters tended to give a cheerless picture of life in the Edwardian era, even a longing for the how matters had been during her mother-in-law's reign. One change that saddened her was King Edward VII's handing over of Queen Victoria's beloved family home on the Isle of Wight to the nation. In September 1904 she wrote to Leonie Leslie of 'a dismal day' in spite of splendid weather. 'We visited Osborne H^{se}, it was my first return to it, since the Queen's death, her rooms are left much as they were, & *full* of all sorts of memories, the rest of the house being transformed into a sort of hotel for invalid officers does give one a strange and sad impression – in fact, I was glad to leave it.'[16]

Occasional remarks from the letters of the Duchess of Saxe-Coburg suggested that all may not have been well between husband and wife, and if that was the case, the Duchess of Connaught may have been the one to blame. In July 1905 the duke was one of her guests at the Rosenau, and she found him very grateful for her company and attention. Ducky was also present, and afterwards admitted that she felt quite ashamed to think she had been very critical of him not long before, perhaps because of his renouncing the Coburg succession: 'she readily understood that he was not feeling happy at home, he let it out, poor man.'[17]

* * *

For the remaining years of King Edward VII's short reign, Queen Alexandra's life continued much as before, except that she no longer lived in the shadow of the formidable mother-in-law of whom she had always been very fond, if somewhat in awe. She continued to dote on her grandchildren, especially when she was looking after them for a few months while George and Mary, who had been created Prince and Princess of Wales in November 1901, undertook a tour of British India over the winter of 1905–6. It was, however, to be a time of sadness for her, when she lost her 87-year-old father, King Christian IX, in January 1906.

She and her sister Minnie, Dowager Empress of Russia, had always remained very close. Keen to retain their family links to each other and the country of their birth, in 1907 they jointly purchased Hvidøre, a villa near Copenhagen, as a private retreat. It remained an early autumn residence where they generally stayed together each year from September to November, until the outbreak of war in Europe seven years later prevented them from returning.

Her generosity to all remained as strong as ever. One day in 1908 she suddenly arrived at the door of St Luke's House, Bayswater, a home for terminally ill children. A couple of days earlier she had received a letter from Martha Massy, a factory girl in the final stages of consumption, who was eager to see her before she died. Without any warning the queen decided she would go and visit her. The servant girl who answered the doorbell recognised her at once and was just as amazed as the matron in her office. Martha, lying in her bed, was overcome to receive a large bouquet of flowers cut specially from the gardens at Sandringham, as were the other patients in the ward who were each presented with roses and a kind word.[18]

Throughout most of her life, the queen had enjoyed painting and photography in her spare time, sometimes combining both crafts by annotating her albums with painstaking, hand-drawn decorations as well as short anecdotes, and collages of professional photographic prints layered over her own watercolour paintings. Her first love, however, was using her Kodak camera to photograph family, friends, pets, views at home and on holiday abroad, and important events such as naval reviews in which she was involved. Some of her work was shown in various exhibitions, and in December 1908 she published a selection, *Queen Alexandra's Christmas Gift Book: Photographs from my Camera,* with the profits going to various charities.

Chapter 2

After the death of Alfred, Duke of Saxe-Coburg, his widow continued to spend part of each year in the duchy. She generally divided the rest of her time between a villa in Tegernsee, near Munich, and enjoyed wintering in the more hospitable climate of Château de Fabron, a property near Nice that they had inherited after the death of Duke Ernest. Once she had got over the sadness of her husband and mother-in-law passing away within six months of each other, she relished a sense of freedom, at last beholden to nobody. Her one remaining unmarried daughter, Beatrice, was her companion for much of the time until she, too, came to choose herself a husband.

The duchess was never lonely. In addition to her youngest daughter, during the first few years of the decade she enjoyed entertaining members of her family from Russia, notably her brothers Grand Dukes Serge and Paul. Serge and his wife, Ella, an elder sister of Empress Alexandra, were childless, and were the recognised carers of their nephew Dmitri and niece Marie, the children of Paul, who had been left a widower when his wife, Alexandra, died in childbirth in 1891, less than a week after Dmitri was born. Marie, who had been born the previous year, loved visiting Tegernsee, which she never ceased to find fascinating. Despite the duchess's brusque ways – those who did not know her found quite intimidating on initial acquaintance, Marie noted in her memoirs – underneath the forbidding exterior she was a high-spirited woman with an ironic but endearing sense of humour, too honest to conceal her opinions, always saying exactly what she thought. There was always lively banter when her brothers were around, for although they teased her gently about her grand airs, they clearly had a great deal of respect for her. Years later, she could still picture her aunt sitting in a large armchair, 'an interminable piece of knitting in her hands, looking over her big spectacles at the bustling and plotting of the people who moved around her; seeing everything, judging everything with a kind of serene mockery.'[1]

Another relation to whom the duchess had always remained close was the grand matriarch of the Romanov family, her brother's widow, Dowager Empress Marie Feodorovna. The latter had been familiar with the south of France for many years, albeit for one of the saddest of reasons. It was where her first fiancé, Grand Duke Nicholas, tsarevich and eldest brother of Duchess Marie, had died in 1865, soon after their betrothal. Some thirty years later she wanted to commemorate her visit to Nice by enlarging the Orthodox Church. As there was not enough land to so do, she asked Tsar Nicholas II to convert the Villa Bermond into a cathedral. This was accordingly done, and in April 1903 the duchess laid the foundation stone. Nine years later the cathedral of St Nicholas, one of the finest examples of Orthodox architecture outside Russia, was consecrated.

Yet it seemed that the duchess's daughters would always cause her anxiety. The marriages of the three elder ones were little happier than her own. Crown Princess Marie of Roumania and Princess Alexandra of Hohenlohe-Langenburg both had affairs outside their marriages. The former had returned to Bucharest, but only after her mother had insisted that Saxton Winter should be dismissed. King Carol thought she had done an excellent job with the other children and wanted to keep her, but reluctantly had to inform her that, in view of recent events, there could be no alternative to her departure. He admitted to a member of the family that he could not hold on to her, as the crown princess 'and especially her mother, who is in every way an insane and violent woman, would hear nothing of it.'[2] He was hardly justified in describing the Duchess of Saxe-Coburg thus, for while she had a very firm sense of right and wrong and readily admitted that her daughter had behaved badly (albeit in circumstances that could have been thought extenuating), to the end she always remained a strongly supportive mother.

Meanwhile, the ill-starred marriage of Ernest, Grand Duke of Hesse and the Rhine, and Princess Victoria Melita ended in divorce in December 1901, much to the consternation of several in the family. In Russia the tsarina and her sister, Grand Duchess Serge, were particularly angry with the sister-in-law whom they had never really liked, while the German Empress Augusta Victoria also regarded it as a disgrace and a stain on the family's honour. Several of them laid much of the blame at the door of the Duchess of Coburg, who 'must have raised her daughters very badly'.³ She had never really been reconciled to her second daughter's marriage, and had long been annoyed with Missy for her persistently wayward behaviour, telling her that she and her sister were both only too ready to get rid of their husbands. 'Flirt, amuse yourself, but don't loose [sic] your heart, men are not worth it.'⁴

A few weeks later the newly divorced grand duchess was staying with her mother in Nice. Her persistent depression and simmering anger alarmed everyone around her, and she insisted that all her belongings had to remain untouched in the marital home at Darmstadt, even though she had left the premises. One day she gave her mother a fright after what the latter called 'a shameful fit of unbounded fury' against Lilian Wilson, her daughter Elizabeth's nurse, apparently about a letter from Darmstadt referring to her jewels. When she started screaming, all the servants rushed upstairs to see what was going on. They found her slapping Wilson, tearing at her hair, and then trying to seize a large lamp to throw at her head. Wilson managed to remove it from the room before any harm was done. Frightened maids ran into the duchess's room to fetch her, and the duchess found her daughter crying bitterly 'but the first fury over'. Everyone who had watched the scene was pale and trembling at the thought that the enraged former grand duchess might have injured or even killed Wilson.⁵

Yet she did at length find happiness with one of her Romanov cousins, Grand Duke Cyril. At around the same time Beatrice made the acquaintance of another Russian cousin, Grand Duke Michael, the only surviving brother of Tsar Nicholas II. They met each other on several occasions and carried on a lengthy correspondence in English. To those closest to them, it seemed as if they were made for each other. Several of the family were sure that they would soon become betrothed, and the Duchess of Saxe-Coburg was happy to give her blessing to the marriage if it would ensure her daughter's happiness, but the Orthodox church in Russia would not permit the marriage of first cousins. Tsar Nicholas II refused to override this ruling, and for a while Beatrice seemed inconsolable. Michael was more ready than her to accept his brother's decision, and he soon lost his heart elsewhere.

It was not only Beatrice whose future greatly concerned the duchess. A marriage between the divorced Victoria Melita and Grand Duke Cyril, also first cousins, would likewise have been prohibited. Moreover, it would have been doubly unwelcome in Russia as in the eyes of Empress Alexandra she had tarnished the family name by divorcing her brother, to whom she had always been devoted. The duchess asked her sister-in-law the dowager tsarina to try and bring some influence on the tsar and allow them to marry, but she was equally opposed to the mere idea.

To her unending anxiety, matters in Russia went from bad to worse. In February 1904 the empire declared war on Japan, a conflict in which the former was confident of its numerical and organizational superiority and therefore quick victory. However, the Russo-Japanese war ended a little over a year later in humiliating defeat for the Romanov empire, and Tsar Nicholas was forced to sue for peace. It came at a time when imperial prestige was suffering one blow after another. In January 1905 a peaceful march and demonstration led by Father Gapon, a young radical Orthodox priest, to present a written petition to his sovereign at the Winter Palace demanding better working conditions, fairer wages, a reduction in the working day, an end to the increasingly ignominious conflict with Japan and the introduction of universal suffrage, ended in bloodshed when the police opened fire and charged. Over 200 men, women, and children were killed, with over twice as many injured, in what would go down in Russian history as 'Bloody Sunday'.

A few weeks later the Duchess of Saxe-Coburg was shocked, if not surprised, to learn that her brother Grand Duke Serge, Governor-General of Moscow, had suffered the same fate as their father and fallen victim to an assassin's bomb in the streets. She and Beatrice immediately went to Moscow to be with the family and attend the funeral, despite having been advised by the police to absent themselves for reasons of security. Grand Duke Cyril had served with distinction as an officer in the Russian navy and was seriously wounded in action when a Japanese mine exploded at the battle of Port Arthur in February 1904. After being sent home on sick leave he gradually recovered, and delivery from the jaws of death made him determined to seize his opportunity. Despite the disapproval of the tsar and tsarina, he and Victoria Melita decided they would marry and accept the consequences.

Determined that her second daughter should find happiness at last, regardless of what the higher powers might think, the duchess never wavered for a moment in her support of their plans. She had her doubts about Cyril, whom she thought irresolute, too passive in his attitude, and worst of all, seemed to be more interested in motoring than matrimony, having just bought himself a new and very expensive car in Paris that was his pride and joy: 'he was so jubilant that others might have thought he had just come from the altar.'[6] Nevertheless, as she was confident that it would be in the couple's best interests, she persuaded her chaplain, Father Smirnoff, to give them the official blessing. On 8 October 1905 the couple arrived at the home of her gentleman-in-waiting, Count Adlerberg, at Tegernsee, as he had offered them his Orthodox chapel for the ceremony. Apart from the bride and groom, the only ones present were the Duchess, Adlerberg, Mr Vigneau, her two ladies-in-waiting, and the count's housekeeper. The duchess's brother Grand Duke Alexis, who was in Munich, had been invited to Tegernsee but without being told that he was required as an official witness to the occasion, and he appeared half an hour after the start of the wedding breakfast. Father Smirnoff had feared the anger of the Holy Synod and above all that of the tsar, but the arrival of the jovial, good-humoured Alexis, who proved totally supportive, immediately reassured him.

The marriage created instant divisions among the Romanovs. Dowager Empress Marie had been just as shocked and angry as Empress Alexandra was in 1901 when Grand Duchess Victoria Melita obtained her divorce, and the young couple were destined to pay dearly for their effrontery. As soon as Cyril returned to Russia, the tsar deprived him of his imperial allowance and title of Imperial Highness, all his honours and decorations, and his position in the navy, and then banished him from Russia. Grand Duke Vladimir was so outraged by this treatment of his son that he immediately resigned all his army positions, then returned his medals and decorations in protest. The Duchess of Coburg was equally furious with her nephew, and immediately gave her daughter and son-in-law her full financial and emotional support when they came to settle in Paris during their period of banishment.

A few months earlier, upon coming of age on 19 July 1905, Charles, Duke of Saxe-Coburg Gotha, assumed full constitutional powers and that week the family attended his accession ceremony or 'enthronement', as the dowager duchess named it. She recorded her impressions in a latter to Missy, noting that her young nephew was 'nice, well-mannered and simple'. It was, however, hard for her to see the Duchess of Albany occupying the position that would have been hers had it not been for her son's self-inflicted death. Helen, she wrote angrily, was disporting herself in the rooms that had been theirs not long ago, revelling in having everybody of importance presented to her. Her appearance and behaviour were 'very disgusting, *soi-disant* very amiable and even sentimental with me but triumphant and proud to a degree! And her dress! A long white robe with an untidy look about it, the smallest bonnet with strings, a blue-red face and general fussiness!'[7]

Three months later, the duke married Princess Victoria Adelaide of Schleswig-Holstein, a niece of the German empress. Her predecessor as duchess praised her warmly, telling Missy in a letter that the young duchess was 'very nice indeed and seems *très bien elevée* and very ladylike … charming, fresh-looking and takes great pains to be amiable.' She was less complimentary about the duke, whom she believed was 'only occupied with the pomp and the vanity of his new position … wears always uniform and even his family dinners are extraordinarily pompous.' As before, she still found it difficult to say much in favour of the Duchess of Albany, who was 'most sweet at first,' but later 'became rather exhausted and looked grumpy … inconceivable, with a brick red face and stomach sticking miles out!'[8] The 'grumpy' duchess was probably worried about how her son was faring in Coburg at a time when Anglo-German relations were becoming ever more uncertain. One of his letters to her revealed how glad he was to have one possession of great sentimental value. 'Now I am finally getting round to being able to thank you by letter for Papa's cane. It is very kind of you to send me the very cane, which he had used as an invalid. I thank you for it from the bottom of my heart. I carry it every day.'[9]

* * *

In 1904 the Marquis de Villalobar, a Spanish diplomat who had always been close to Empress Eugenie, widow of Napoleon III, ex-emperor of the French, was sent to London as an attaché at the Spanish Embassy. One of his duties was to find out information on the British princesses, and report back to Don Alfonso de Aguilar, then private secretary of Maria Cristina, Queen Dowager of Spain, and Regent during the minority of her son King Alfonso XIII, who had been a reigning sovereign literally since birth. She had shown interest in a British bride for her son, and her first choice fell on Patsy of Connaught, whose mother thought it would be an excellent idea. She had perhaps been encouraged to some extent by the Infanta Eulalia, who thought that under Queen Patricia of Spain she would have some influence at court in Madrid.

Patsy had very different ideas. While she may not have been keen to renounce her faith and become a Roman Catholic, a more likely explanation for her refusal was that her father had told her all she needed to know about Spain and its young sovereign to decide for herself that she had no enthusiasm for any future in such a country and with such a husband. Once the Infanta knew her views, she decided to try and suggest her niece, Louise of Orleans, as King Alfonso's bride instead. It was rumoured that she did her best to give Patsy all manner of unattractive ideas about Spain to ensure that she did not change her mind.

The Duchess of Connaught was disappointed that her youngest child should decline the honour of a consort's crown. Not long afterwards, Empress Eugenie suggested the name of Ena, Princess Beatrice's daughter, to Villalobar for the first time. Bearing in mind Ena's sad subsequent history as queen consort, Patsy must have been relieved to escape such a fate.

The rivalry between Beatrice and her Prussian sister-in-law was to bring a certain amount of opinionated discussion in its wake. In December 1904 Villobar told Aguilar that Princess Henry of Battenberg had informed him that 'her brother the Duke of Connaught is a very kind man, much more so than the Duchess who is terrible and violent scaring everyone (so good we got rid of her!).'[10] He had made enquiries as to Ena's health, although it was uncertain whether anybody had brought up the possibility that she could be a carrier of haemophilia, the hereditary scourge that had afflicted one of her brothers. Beatrice, he continued in the same letter, had been at pains to advance the cause of her own daughter against that of her Connaught niece. She had firmly refused any possibility of Ena marrying a notoriously immoral Romanov bachelor, but considered the young bachelor King Alfonso of Spain infinitely better.

> You can see by yourself how well she looks in spite of what my sister-in-law the Duchess of Connaught keeps saying to the contrary to everybody ... I have absolutely refused the proposition of my daughter marrying Grand Duke Boris of Russia. This man is not

a good person and if my daughter marries a good man, which is so important, I do not want her to be away from me. On top, he is from a different religion. But if he were he a good man that would not matter.[11]

As for the views of Empress Eugenie, he pointed out that she liked and was on good terms with the Connaught family, but was closer to Beatrice, who was 'her true friend'. The duke and duchess, he stressed, were neighbours of the empress in Surrey and visited her regularly, 'but I believe that [Empress Eugenie] never forgets that the Duchess is the daughter of the victor of Metz.' The fact that Prince Frederick Charles had been in command of the Prussian army at the battle of Metz, which had helped to bring down the French Second Empire, still weighed heavily on France's imperial widow.[12]

* * *

The fraternal relationship between King Edward and the Duke of Connaught always remained uneasy at best, and the former was reluctant to let his brother and sister-in-law stay in England longer than absolutely necessary. Having little choice but to continue with their travels abroad, they went to Egypt and the Sudan in January 1905, taking their daughters. As they travelled across Europe, the king was hoping that any visits they made to the courts in Europe, no matter how brief, would aid the cause of royal friendships and therefore future alliances, to say nothing of potential marriages between his two very attractive nieces and European sovereigns, present or future. He was most insistent that the duke and duchess should stop in Lisbon, something the duke was reluctant to do on the grounds of expense, but he bowed to his brother's will.

During their few days in Portugal, King Carlos and his family gave them a warm welcome, and one evening he took them to the opera. The duke and duchess shared a box with the king and Queen Amelie, while Princesses Margaret and Patricia were in the next one with the two Portuguese princes. Many eyes in the audience were fixed on the latter pair, with rumours that one or the other might be the next queen of Portugal. The duchess was doubtless keen that their daughters should make as good an impression as possible on their host's sons. However, the double assassination three years later that claimed the lives of King Carlos and his elder son, Luis Felipe (who thus technically became king for a few minutes before succumbing to his wounds), and a bloodless revolution that heralded the birth of a Portuguese republic two years after that, made them eternally grateful that such an idea never progressed any further.

A less pleasant time awaited them when they went to Spain a few days afterwards. They were almost overwhelmed by the throngs of spectators at Cádiz and Seville, and when they visited the cathedral at Málaga, a mob prevented them from being able to see anything and then almost stopped them from getting into their carriage when they came out afterwards. The people were at heart being friendly, if over-enthusiastic, pressing their noses against the windows of the royal carriage when not calling out, '*Viva la futura Reina d'Espana!*' According to the duke's biographer the family were quite angry, especially the duchess, who apparently 'visited it all' on her husband (he was just as disgusted as she was by the want of reverence that everyone showed within the cathedral).[13] Patsy, who was quite shy and detested crowds, particularly ill-behaved and vociferous ones, was especially upset, while Daisy was equally annoyed but remained calm. In spite of this, the duchess gave Lady Leslie a very different impression of their feelings at what happened. The girls, she wrote, were 'the centre of attraction', while '"Pss. Victoria" is acclaimed future Queen by the crowds wh[ich] is most embarrassing! Patsy cross & grumpy but D[aisy] fortunately takes it as a huge joke!! –there is an amiable and admiring mood at every station we stop at!! It is really *very* funny.'[14]

Thankfully there were no recurrences of similar behaviour when they reached Africa a few days later. On the contrary, this stage of their travels through Algiers, Tunis and Egypt was to lead to abiding happiness. When they stopped at Luxor on their return journey they met Prince Gustav Adolf, the eldest son of Crown Prince Gustav. He accompanied them to Cairo, and it was noticed that Patsy took no notice of him, but he and Daisy seemed particularly taken with each other. All five of them went to Cairo together, the prince went riding with both sisters, and matters took their course. On 24 February he proposed to Daisy and she was delighted to accept. Not everybody shared her joy at first. Patsy, in floods of tears, complained that she would miss her sister deeply and declared that she would not marry the King of Spain.[15]

Yet at least one other member of the family saw it as something of a release for the future bride. Her aunt the Duchess of Saxe-Coburg was pleased for her, as she 'always looked so depressed of later years and [her] life at home was miserable.'[16] As Duchess Marie had seen very little of the Connaught family in the previous few years, she may have been relying rather too much on secondhand gossip from other members of the family who, with the exception of Arthur's favourite sister, Louise, Duchess of Argyll, were not particularly close to them. Daisy's own letter certainly gave no indication of any impatience to fly the nest, and on the contrary, felt deeply for her mother and siblings and how they would react to this first break in the family circle. 'The only cloud on my otherwise cloudless sky,' she wrote from on board HMS *Essex* to Leonie, 'is Mama being so sad at my going & Patsy & Arthur, I'm afraid they are very miserable & I don't know what to do but I know I can trust to you to try to cheer up Mama who feels it dreadfully.'[17] Sad she may have been, but her mother had no doubts about the suitability of the match. 'You will be pleased I know when you see her happy face, & you will also like her young man,' she wrote to Leonie a few days later, 'he is quite charming, plus they are both madly in love – it is too funny to see them.'[18]

On 5 June, less than a month after his nineteenth birthday, King Alfonso XIII of Spain arrived in England for a visit of five days. His ultimate aim, a rather poorly kept secret, was to find himself a wife, and being ever keen to extend British royal influence throughout Europe as much as possible, King Edward VII and the rest of the royal family were more than ready to assist. Despite the Connaughts' disagreeable experiences in Spain at the beginning of the year, the duchess was still prepared to welcome him to the family as a husband for her daughter Patsy. She sensed that her sister-in-law Beatrice had similar ideas for her daughter Ena, who would celebrate her eighteenth birthday later that year. Unwilling to let such a chance go by, the duchess continued to try and apply pressure on her daughter, and probably did not stop short of trying to disparage her niece Ena, but to no avail. It had already been rumoured that an engagement between the king of Spain and the princess was to be announced, and the matter had been discussed by King Edward and his prime minister, Arthur Balfour.

However, an obdurate Patsy stood her ground by refusing to give in to the combined weight of parental and sibling wishes. When the king and queen held a family dinner party at Buckingham Palace, King Alfonso had every opportunity to take a careful look at the assembled company. Although he already knew Patsy by sight, it was Ena, whom he did not yet know at all, who also caught his eye as he sat at table. At a subsequent luncheon at Clarence House later that week, he was seated next to Patsy, but she remained coldly immune to his charm. Despondently, he complained to the Duchess of Westminster, who was sitting on his left, that he must be very ugly because he did not please the lady on his right.[19] With this, all hopes that the Duke and Duchess of Connaught would acquire a son-in-law in royal Madrid were over. Yet they still had the consolation of an elder daughter marrying into the ranks of Scandinavian royalty. On 15 June, five days after King Alfonso left London, the family were at the Chapel Royal, St James's, attending the wedding of Princess Margaret and Prince Gustav Adolf.

At this time, very few people were aware that Patsy had as good as rejected Alfonso. As an ever-assiduous informant to Don Alfonso de Aguilar, the Marquis de Villalobar noted that 'It seems that prior to the arrival of our King [Alfonso] there took place such scenes (and so violent from the Duchess) that the princess [Patsy] decided not to talk and not to look at our King.'[20] Yet he was among those who had not completely given up hope. While it seemed that the Duke of Connaught was prepared to let his wife conduct any matchmaking exercises as she saw fit, he was eventually brought into the arena, although by then it was too late for anybody to alter the course of events.

Determined to involve all her immediate family, the duchess even enlisted the help of her newly married elder daughter. The duke and duchess, Villalobar wrote to Aguilar later that month, 'have forced her sister [Daisy], who has a great influence on her, to give her advice in writing. Most of all there are daily fights between the Duchess and her daughter and the former has even said to the latter that there would be no need to change her religion.'[21] The need never arose, for by this time the duchess had to accept that her younger daughter also had a will of her own.

In January 1906 Ena and King Alfonso became engaged. Whether Daisy was ever brought into the fray to support their mother is uncertain, but she thought it 'a mercy' that Patsy had stood her ground and said no. 'I hear there is a most awful row going on about Ena in connection with her marriage,' she wrote to Lady Leslie, 'people seem much more angry than one had expected about the forced change of religion. Ena wrote & told me she was very happy but didn't mention the religious question.'[22] Queen Alexandra had similar concerns, writing to the Prince of Wales to ask what he thought of the engagement. They certainly seemed very much in love with each other, she thought, but on the issue of changing her religion to do so, 'here people are furious and we are getting letters about it!! The archbishops were very much against it and were indignant but papa said he had nothing to do with it as she was not an English princess.'[23]

In the spring the Dowager Duchess of Saxe-Coburg and her daughter Beatrice were invited to the wedding in Madrid. The duchess was annoyed when she heard that Grand Duke Michael had been chosen to represent Tsar Nicholas II at the ceremony. Although he had hardly been to blame for the end of the thwarted romance between himself and Beatrice, she and her mother felt it was a rather insensitive gesture on the part of the Romanovs, especially as he was now said to be pursuing his sister Olga's lady-in-waiting, Alexandra Kossikovskaya, the thirty-year-old daughter of a lawyer. Although she was unmarried, any request on his part to marry her was unlikely to be greeted with approval by his brother. When the duchess asked her sister-in-law the dowager empress to intervene and make sure he did not attend, her wish was granted and Grand Duke Vladimir represented the family instead.

At the wedding on 31 May, the bride, groom and many of their guests had a narrow escape when a young anarchist, Mateo Morales, threw a bomb at the wedding procession. It exploded close to the coach, killing twenty people and wounding at least sixty others. None of the royal guests were injured, although the bride was deeply shocked when her white dress was spattered with blood. The duchess tried to reassure them by pointing out calmly that such matters were commonplace in Russia: *'Je suis tellement accoutumée a ces choses.'*[24]

It had been rumoured not long before that Beatrice, rather than her Battenberg cousin Ena, might have become the queen of Spain. During the years to come, Beatrice and her family would have good reason to be grateful for having been spared such a fate, as King Alfonso would prove a notoriously unfaithful husband to his long-suffering consort. Instead, while at the wedding Beatrice met her future husband, the king's exact contemporary and much more likeable cousin, Infante Alfonso ('Ali'). In September she and the Duchess of Saxe-Coburg were invited to Spain, where she met the infante again. She was now aged twenty-two, and her mother was increasingly anxious about her still being single. Much as she loved her daughter, she admitted that she could 'be so charming and friendly when she wants to be, and it troubles me; people try to approach her but she immediately rejects them all, or most of them.'[25]

Beatrice and Alfonso soon fell for each other. Unlike Ena, she was not immediately prepared to become a Roman Catholic, though she agreed that any children born of the marriage would be raised thus. The Spanish government objected, but the couple were prepared to wait. They were assured that the differences in religion need not be an obstacle, and became betrothed. The Duchess of Saxe-Coburg, who had liked Alfonso at once, assured her daughters that he was the kind of man who could manage a strong-willed wife with the right degree of firmness and kindness. During the Christmas holidays in December 1907 Alfonso visited Pope Pius X to obtain the necessary dispensation, generally given on condition that the children would be raised as Catholics. Yet the government had already intervened and he was denied this until he had the king's consent. He spent Christmas at Coburg, and as the duchess wanted to celebrate their engagement, Beatrice's sisters and their husbands joined them.

Chapter 3

The position of Inspector-General of the Army meant that the Duke of Connaught was regularly on the move, and the duchess always accompanied him. She did not always find living in England congenial, convinced that very few of the royal family really liked them, or more specifically her, and perhaps felt that in the death of Queen Victoria she had lost the relative who, next to her husband, was her greatest champion. Adding to her mood of general discomfort was her impression that the duke's annual reports for the Army Council were not taken seriously, and nobody seemed prepared to support him. Any improvements he suggested, such as making good the defects in soldiers' rifles, the general standard of their barracks, or the often degrading treatment of military prisoners, were usually fobbed off with bland responses that such matters were either outside their scope or else under consideration. Sometimes the duchess's anger boiled over. 'The Duke is very much bothered, worried and dismayed by those who are in power,' she wrote to Leonie Leslie, 'and I feel quite sickened by the way he is treated!!'[1]

In December 1905 both of them, and Patsy, visited South Africa, where he had been asked to report on the military situation throughout the country. All three returned home that spring, before resuming their travels. This time their destination was Stockholm, where a happy family occasion awaited them when they attended the christening in June 1906 of their first grandchild and nephew, Gustav Adolf. The duchess still enjoyed travelling, and was increasingly lonely at home, something that never ceased to worry her elder daughter in Sweden. 'I'm afraid tho' Bagshot may be good for Mama,' she wrote to Lady Leslie, 'it will be rather dull, with no one there it can be very quiet & she won't like papa having to me away so much. They all write me rather depressed letters, & I feel a perfect brute; but it can't be helped now!'[2]

In November 1906 King Edward began to press his brother to accept the Malta command as High Commissioner and Commander-in-Chief of all British garrisons in and bordering the Mediterranean, when his time as inspector general ended. Meanwhile, early in 1907 the duke and duchess embarked on an extensive tour of the Far East. Despite complaining that the scheme involving the command was 'academic and ill-conceived,' on 27 June the duke finally, and unwillingly, gave way to his brother's insistence. He and the duchess moved into San Antonio Palace, the governor's residence at Valletta, in February 1908.

It was the start of a difficult time for the duke and duchess. Neither of them liked living in Malta, while he complained to his brother that the Mediterranean command, a source of inefficiency in peace, 'would be a positive danger in war'. He likened his position to that of 'a fifth wheel on a coach,' and that he intended to resign so they could come home. When the king argued that his brother had taken so much home leave that he had not given the experiment a fair chance, the duke and duchess declared that because of their personal popularity in England, King Edward had wanted them to be based abroad. Although proud of the duke's professional prowess in the army, he was 'much annoyed by his Brother's persistent obstinacy', and wrote to Herbert Asquith, his prime minister, warning that he would have to consider his military career at an end. If he did not intend to return to Malta he should resign his appointment at once,[3] and he did so in July 1909.

After a period of reflection had allowed tempers to cool on both sides, the king realised that it would be to everyone's advantage if his brother was offered another post, and his initial solution was to make him Lord-Lieutenant of Ireland. The idea remained under active consideration until January 1910, when it was suggested instead that as the post of Governor-General of Canada would shortly fall vacant, the duke would be an ideal successor. To this the monarch readily agreed. It was still under active consideration when the duke and duchess, with their two younger children, set off on a prolonged safari in East Africa in February.

Despite her troublesome leg, the duchess was still able to ride. On one occasion her pony slipped while crossing a stream, but although she got very wet neither the duchess nor her horse were injured. She also tried her hand at shooting and even hairdressing, when it was decided that her husband needed a trim and there was nobody else around to assist. They were close to Nairobi at the beginning of April, when the duke received a letter from Asquith, offering him the Canadian post, which he accepted.

* * *

As the Dowager Duchess of Saxe-Coburg and her family celebrated Christmas 1907 at Coburg, nobody ever imagined that they would have to wait another twenty months, until July 1909, before the wedding of her daughter, Beatrice, and Alfonso took place. By the spring of 1908 the royal house of Spain had not issued any official statement, and as the foreign press had published the news of the engagement at Christmas, in May the Duchess of Saxe-Coburg wrote to the Crown Princess of Roumania for her opinion. She was anxious about the effect the uncertainty was having on Beatrice, and angry that they had 'to act faced with such dishonesty and deceitful tricks, we really do not know how and where to go to ask for help and advice.'[4] King Alfonso, the Spanish government and the Vatican, she believed, were working together to prevent the marriage. Alfonso's mother, the Infanta Eulalia, had been unenthusiastic about the wedding mainly because of the religious differences, but despite his insistence that Spain would not accept 'a Protestant princess', she did not think the king opposed it and was prepared to give it her support for her son's sake. When she visited the duchess at Coburg later that year, the latter was touched at her evident fondness for Beatrice and enthusiasm for the grandchildren that would surely follow in due course.

In July 1909 Spain and Morocco were at war, and the duchess's already sorely tried patience snapped. When she learnt that Infante Alfonso was being sent on active service to Africa she was furious, especially as King Alfonso had not had the courtesy to tell her himself. She sent him a telegram insisting on an explanation for Ali's sudden departure to Morocco, and why nobody had already mentioned it was likely. He replied unapologetically that, as head of the Spanish army, he was unable to tell her what he did with his officers. In his defence, he added that the Moroccans had not advised that they were going to attack his troops, that Ali had asked voluntarily to go to Melilla so he could join the expedition, and that he could not refuse such a request to an Infante of Spain.

The peremptory tone of his telegram reduced the duchess to tears. An equally incensed Bee replied to him in French the following day that she was less angry on the account of herself and her husband than on that of their mother. His missive was nothing short of an insult to an enquiry from an old, sick woman 'broken by the pain of seeing a boy who she loves like her own son, who she lost, going to war and she asks for news ... I found it, and everyone finds it, like me, to be unworthy conduct from a man and a king. May God forgive you.'⁵ The king did not reply to her or her mother, but later wrote to Ali of his annoyance at receiving what he called a very impertinent letter from Bee, saying that he could not let her treat him in such a manner: 'they amuse me when they insult me.' Beatrice was reassured to hear that her fiancé was leaving Spain, and on his way to Coburg. Nevertheless, the duchess was not easily appeased, and sent another angry telegram to the king, reproaching him for his 'nameless cruelty' in sending Ali to Morocco so suddenly, simply because he wanted to get rid of him in order to prevent the wedding. It would be a disgrace, she thundered, 'if his blood falls on your heads [sic].'⁶

Another, slightly more conciliatory response followed a day later, stressing that she had never put either the royal prerogative nor the veneration of His Majesty in doubt, but she still reserved every right as a German princess and a grand duchess of Russia, 'as well as being your aunt, my dear cousin, of posing all totally justified questions as well as discussing your decisions, knowing that there is not the slightest possibility of you changing them. I beg you to consider this telegram as the last which will refer to this sad episode.'⁷ He replied that he thought it better if she did not reply. When he took a decision, he warned her that it was final; she was not allowed to question it, and he was not obliged to give her an explanation.

The duchess and her daughter had ready allies in Charles, Duke of Saxe-Coburg Gotha, and his wife, Victoria Adelaide. They were keen to arrange the wedding quickly, and thought that as the fiancé was to leave to fight in Morocco, they should take advantage of the Catholic church's dispensation and have the wedding at once before he left for the front. The duke called his Minister of State in Gotha and promised to go with him the following morning to celebrate the civil marriage. A Roman Catholic and Lutheran ceremony was thus arranged at Coburg and took place on 15 July 1909. 'They are royally united forever!' the dowager duchess exclaimed triumphantly after the proceedings. The Duke of Saxe-Coburg telegraphed King Alfonso to confirm that the wedding had taken place and the latter sent back his congratulations, although adding that he would have preferred the news to remain secret.

Not all the family were so supportive. Sandra arrived in Coburg later that week, fearful that it would cause future problems for her sister. When Grand Duchess Vladimir met King Alfonso and Queen Ena (who was very fond of her cousin Beatrice and had always been in favour of such a union) at Biarritz a few weeks later, her views on the subject suggested that she held her sister-in-law, the duchess, responsible for what had happened. The young couple accepted the government's ruling that they would have to live in exile at first, and settled at Coburg, ready to wait until allowed to return.

* * *

Although Queen Alexandra naturally took a keen interest in politics, she respected the convention that it was not for her to do anything that might be construed as unconstitutional interference. As Princess of Wales, in 1890 she had made a rare move that might have been seen as trying to influence matters of state with regard to an Anglo-German agreement in which the British North Sea island of Heligoland was to be ceded to Germany in exchange for the German colony of Zanzibar in Africa. In a memorandum written by herself and distributed to senior British ministers and military personnel, she warned against the planned exchange, citing Heligoland's strategic significance and pointing out that it could be used either by Germany to launch an attack, or by Britain to contain German aggression. It was to no avail, and under the terms of an Anglo-German agreement later that year, Britain carried out the transfer, thus allowing the Germans to fortify the island, making it a keystone of Germany's maritime position for defence. The German press evidently had some knowledge of the matter, presumably through the indiscretion of some unnamed official in the British or German embassies, and at least one German journalist condemned the princess and her sister, the dowager empress of Russia, who they called 'the centre of an international anti-German conspiracy'.

Throughout Alexandra's nine years as queen, she never ceased to worry about the state of her husband's health. One particular incident particularly alarmed her, when they were on a three-day state visit to Berlin in February 1909. Rarely was a royal journey carried out more in the name of duty and less out of pleasure than this one. Neither of them was well at the time: she was suffering from neuralgia and had barely recovered from influenza, while the king had fever and a bronchial chill.

Their state drive through the streets of Berlin was marred when the coach in which Queen Alexandra and Empress Augusta Victoria were travelling suddenly stopped, as the horses refused to proceed any further, and they had to be asked to move into a less grand vehicle. When they failed to arrive at the palace on time, Emperor William and King Edward both feared at first that they might have been held up by an assassination attempt. Once the coach had brought them to journey's end, late but unharmed, the emperor was furious at having been made to look foolish in front of his British hosts.

Matters went from bad to worse. The king looked tired and unwell throughout the visit. After a luncheon the British Embassy, he was sitting on a sofa chatting to Princess Daisy of Pless, when he suddenly collapsed after a choking fit, and fainted. The princess immediately feared the worst. 'My God, he is dying; oh! why not in his own country?'[8] was her immediate despairing reaction. Everyone present was asked to withdraw for a few minutes while the queen unfastened his collar and he recovered. Their programme was accordingly modified for the rest of their time in Berlin, to spare him any unnecessary exertion.

Although the queen was now in better health, at every meal she was placed next to the emperor. Having always thoroughly disliked him, she could not resist gently teasing him. Surprised to see that he never seemed to do any more at dinner than touch his food without having any, she told him he ought to eat more, and offered to give him some of her lozenges as they would be good for his brain. When he asked coldly if she thought he was stupid, she assured him she certainly did, for 'making all this commotion about nothing and kidooodle [sic] about your navy.' Later, she laughingly told Margot Asquith, the prime minister's wife, that the emperor showed her lozenges to his doctor as he thought she was trying to poison him. She confessed she would certainly have liked the opportunity to do so.[9]

During the summer of 1909, when the weather improved, so did the king's health. However, that winter the queen and the whole family were again alarmed at his increasing lethargy, continual breathlessness and severe attacks of bronchitis. After Christmas the doctors recommended that as soon as convenient he ought to go and spend some time in the milder climate of Biarritz, where he arrived early in March 1910. A heavy cold and recurrence of bronchitis left his physician, Dr James Reid, fearing for his life at one point. Although he recovered, none of those close to him seemed to have any reason to disbelieve his despondent remark to one of his old friends that he did not have long to live.

During the spring of 1910 Queen Alexandra became the first queen consort to visit the House of Commons during a debate. In a notable departure from precedent, she sat in the Ladies' Gallery overlooking the chamber for two hours while the Parliament Bill, to remove the right of the House of Lords to veto legislation, was debated. Privately she disagreed with the bill, but felt it her duty to take a full interest. In view of her deafness, how much she actually heard of the debate was open to question. A few days later she paid a short visit to her brother, King George of Greece, at Corfu. She was aware that she could be summoned back at any time, and it came as no surprise to her to be warned early in May that King Edward, who had just left Sandringham and returned to Buckingham Palace, was gravely ill. On 5 May she arrived back in London, and it was noticed that for once he was not at the station to meet her. As soon as she entered the palace and saw him again, she saw that his strength was failing.

On the following day he tried to continue working as usual, receiving visitors in appropriate dress, but the effort was too much for him and he spent most of the day propped up in an armchair as he struggled for breath. After several heart attacks, he fell into a coma. The queen allowed his companion Alice Keppel to come and take her leave of him during the final hours, but the latter, who was normally calm and self-possessed, suddenly became hysterical. According to Dr Laking, one of the few who was present, the queen was so distressed that she had to take him aside at one stage and whisper to him, 'Get this woman away.'[10] At about 11.00 pm that evening King Edward was lifted from his armchair and removed to bed, and died at about a quarter to midnight.

Although he was fighting poor health for much of his reign, he had remained relatively active until the end, and the suddenness of his passing took many of those around him by surprise. As the Dowager Duchess of Saxe-Coburg wrote in a spirit of generous tribute to the Crown Princess of Roumania:

> who would have thought that the life-loving Uncle Bertie would depart so soon from this world he loved so much. Yes, he enjoyed life thoroughly, to the very last. His was a happy character and I believe a happy life ... And now he died in his full, manly glory and is regretted and missed by everybody in England. Of course the last

year was a very hard one to bear on account of the internal politics and I believe he suffered a great deal under it. It might even have hastened his death. Strange to say, this event did not upset me much. I think that is because I have had so many losses in my family these last years that I am immune to it.[11]

His body lay in the bedroom at Buckingham Palace for eight days. When Sir Frederick Ponsonby came to visit, Queen Alexandra told him that she felt as if she had been turned into stone, 'unable to cry, unable to grasp the meaning of it all, and incapable of doing anything.' Lord Esher saw a rather different queen, who seemed quietly content, almost happy in a way, that at long last 'she had got him there all to herself ... the womanly happiness of complete possession of the man who was the love of her youth and ... of all her life.'[12]

Part V

The Georgian Era 1910–25

Chapter 1

After their long-awaited sojourn in Africa, the Duke and Duchess of Connaught had set out on their way back to England, and they had just arrived at Port Said when they were told of King Edward's death. As their relations with him had not always been particularly amicable, the thought may have crossed their minds that England might now be a little more hospitable towards them, especially as the nephew they had known as the Prince of Wales for the last few years was more diffident than his father, younger than them and more inclined to treat them with respect. They prepared for the journey back to London as soon as possible in order to be ready for the funeral at Windsor and all the other functions where their presence would be required.

The ceremony was not held until 20 May, a fortnight after the king's passing. It was said that delay was unavoidable because the newly widowed queen was initially reluctant to be parted from his body. A more likely explanation was that the organization involved for so many family members and guests travelling from overseas to be suitably received, entertained and accommodated was a complicated process that involved two weeks' careful planning. On hearing that her brother-in-law had died, Marie, Dowager Empress of Russia, came to England as soon as she could to be with Alexandra. They spent a few days at Sandringham, as good as cut off from the rest of the family, where they could mourn and grieve together. By this time Alexandra was in deep shock, as if uncertain what had happened, murmuring repeatedly, 'they took him away from me.'[1] She was about to create problems for her son and daughter-in-law, now King George V and Queen Mary, by insisting on a precedence that was not hers by right as she was no longer the first lady in the land. It was a problem that would be exacerbated by the arrival of her sister.

Anxious not to put herself forward more than she had to, Queen Mary was keen to avoid any unpleasantness. At the funeral, she gave way unhesitatingly to Queen Alexandra, who behaved throughout with flawless dignity and composure, even though she took a more prominent role than anyone had expected. When the funeral ceremony took place and the procession of clergy and heralds moved up the aisle, followed by the coffin, the queen mother was walking behind the king's body. It had been assumed that she would be watching the service unobserved from the King's Closet above the north end of the altar; instead, deeply veiled, she took her place behind the coffin, her right hand clasping her stick, the left holding her son's hand.[2] As she came out of St George's Chapel following the burial, she held out her hand to various old friends she saw standing on the long flight of steps in a restrained greeting.

It was unfortunate for the rest of the family that the dowager empress chose to remain in England and stay with her sister for the next few weeks. In Russia, it had long been customary for the widowed empress to take precedence at court over the wife of her husband's successor, and she was doubtless unaware that there was no similar status for a queen dowager in Britain. She therefore thought nothing of urging Alexandra to assert herself boldly by claiming the position and privileges that were no longer hers but now those of her daughter-in-law. Queen Mary was tactful enough to hold her tongue, but her elderly aunt Grand Duchess Augusta was quite angry on her behalf, writing to her afterwards that she hoped 'that pernicious influence [would] soon depart, *then* I hope all will come right.'[3]

Towards the end of 1910 Queen Alexandra moved out of Buckingham Palace to Marlborough House, but retained possession of the 'Big House', Sandringham, in accordance with the provisions in King Edward's will that bequeathed it to her for the rest of her lifetime. King George, Queen Mary and their family, therefore, had to make do with the less regal accommodation at York Cottage. However, the king was so sentimentally attached to what had been his home at Norfolk ever since he had married that he was prepared to accept the situation. Nevertheless, he was concerned to discover that while she was moving house, his ever-generous mother was taking it upon herself to give certain royal heirlooms away to friends and what she considered deserving institutions. These were not hers to dispose of, and Lord Esher was given the unenviable task of retrieving them as diplomatically as possible.

Three of the sisters-in-law were present at the coronation of King George and Queen Mary at Westminster Abbey on 22 June 1911. The

Dowager Duchess of Saxe-Coburg, and the Duchesses of Connaught and Albany all rode in a carriage with four of the king and queen's sons, the Prince of Wales and his brothers, Albert, Henry and George, and their sister, Mary. Queen Alexandra was not there, largely as it was not customary for a crowned queen to attend the coronation of another sovereign. She could probably have done so had she really wished, as her daughter-in-law would do a quarter of a century later when she intended to demonstrate family solidarity with King George VI after the abdication of his elder brother Edward VIII. Instead she chose to absent herself and spend the day some distance away at Sandringham, with the unmarried Princess Victoria keeping her company and thus being denied a chance to see the most important state occasion at which her brother would take centre stage. Throughout the day the matriarch's thoughts went back to 'poor dear Eddy', the late Duke of Clarence, who, she maintained, should have been at the centre of the grand event instead. Much to the embarrassment of her entourage, she kept on saying, '*Eddy* should be King, not *Georgie*.'[4] The king was convinced that his elder brother's death had 'completely knocked her out', and she was never the same woman since.[5]

Despite her increasing deafness and lameness, Queen Alexandra continued to devote herself to her charities to the best of her ability. One good cause that bore her name was Alexandra Rose Day, launched in 1912 on the fiftieth anniversary of her arrival in England, after she had requested that the anniversary be marked by the sale of artificial roses made by young women and girls with disabilities, and sold by women volunteers in aid of hospitals and other favourite charities. It was an immediate success, and the first such event raised £32,000. Within eight years, £775,000 for London hospitals had been accumulated. Nevertheless, after a few years she found 'that tiresome Alexandra Day, *which I dread*'[6] had become something of a drudge.

Old habits would die hard for the woman who had had such a thrifty upbringing in Denmark with the maxim 'waste not, want not'. Throughout her life she had insisted her old stockings should be darned for reuse, and old dresses be recycled by being made into furniture covers. Yet she was kindness itself to others, much to the distress of Sir Dighton Probyn. He would protest that her funds were not unlimited, only for her to wave her hand as she pretended that she had not heard a word he was saying. Any letters asking for money were generally acknowledged with a cheque in the next post, without any enquiries being undertaken as to whether the writer was genuinely in need or not.[7]

Throughout her life she had always depended to a major extent upon her relationships with others who were closely involved with her personal domestic affairs. In widowhood, she came to rely even more on her two main trusted friends and servants. Probyn had been King Edward's Keeper of the Privy Purse and wanted to retire altogether, but he was begged to stay on as her comptroller and treasurer. It was a similar situation for Charlotte Knollys, her Woman of the Bedchamber. The queen was several years younger than both of them, but they had become devoted to her and realised how much she needed people she had known for many years, and with whom she felt comfortable.

Another person on whom she leaned on was 'poor Toria', her lifelong spinster daughter Victoria, whose relationship with her mother demonstrated one of the least praiseworthy aspects of the elder woman's character. While she was still Princess of Wales, and then during her husband's reign, Alexandra had kept a bell by her side to ring whenever she wanted to call her daughter. Her cousin Grand Duchess Olga knew what it was like to have a possessive mother (Empress Marie Feodorovna of Russia) but at least she managed to marry once, disastrously, and after divorce, a second time and more happily. She recalled in her memoirs that many a time a conversation or a simple game would be abruptly broken off by a message from her Aunt Alix, 'and Toria would run like lightning, often to discover that her mother could not remember why she had sent for her, and it puzzled me because Aunt Alix was so good.'[8]

To the general public, and to those who did not know her so well, the queen was always 'good', but towards members of her family she could often be inconsiderate if not a domestic tyrant. Even King George V once admitted that although he was always very fond of 'Motherdear', for all her good qualities she was still the most selfish person he knew. Unlike cousin Olga, Victoria never managed to escape from the maternal shadow until death intervened. It was hardly surprising that she became increasingly embittered and depressed over the years as she, like her mother, gradually entered a lonely old age. As for the younger generation, Queen Alexandra adored her grandchildren, and enjoyed having them with her when the king and queen went on a tour of India in November

1911. She was especially devoted to their youngest son, John, then aged six, who suffered from epilepsy and learning difficulties.

Foreign affairs and domestic politics continued to interest her passionately, and perhaps none more than matters in the Balkans where Greece was involved. The assassination at Salonika in March 1913 of King George I, who had always been her favourite brother, bitterly distressed and horrified her. Even so, a touching sense of realism did not desert her. One of her friends sent a huge laurel wreath to Marlborough House, asking her if she could send it to Greece so it could be laid on his grave. Realising that this would be an awkward task, she called for a butler and told him it would be far too much trouble. Her favourite Pekinese, Beauty, had recently died. Would he mind putting it on Beauty's grave in the garden instead?

At home the Parliament Act of 1911 was about to become law, following an undertaking that King George had given to use his prerogative to create the necessary number of peers to ensure its passage through the Upper House. Although she called it an 'odious, horrible bill', she assured the king that it was unavoidable and she was certain that 'Papa would have been obliged to act exactly in the same way.' It was not the only political issue that worried her deeply during her son's first years on the throne. She looked with dread on Irish dissension over the matter of Home Rule, urging him to speak out in order to save his country 'from such a calamity'.[9]

* * *

In Germany, the Dowager Duchess of Saxe-Coburg was experiencing anxiety as a result of the situations of all four daughters. After ten years or so of marriage, Sandra was finding the atmosphere at Berlin increasingly difficult, especially after the young Duke of Saxe-Coburg attained his majority and Ernest relinquished the regency. Soon after this, he was appointed head of the colonial office in Berlin, a post for which he was plainly unsuited. His reluctant involvement in imperial politics, and the atmosphere engendered by the subsequent backstabbing and political rivalries, made life increasingly difficult for husband and wife.

Matters worsened when the controversial memoirs of a distant relation of Ernest, a member of the Hohenlohe family, were published. Although he was completely innocent of any wrongdoing, it was guilt by association, and he and his wife found themselves unfairly criticised as a result. Sandra became unwell, suffering from neuralgia, and after giving birth to a son and three daughters, all healthy, in April 1911 she had a second son, her last child, who only lived for two days. Finding her homeland so uncongenial and her family lacking in sympathy, she took to spending more of her time in the more hospitable climate of the Riviera, where she was less likely to be disturbed by obtrusive relations. She learned to drive, and regular motoring expeditions with her chauffeur, with whom she may have been enjoying an affair, led to unsavoury gossip.

Yet at least the duchess could console herself with the knowledge that the situation of the youngest child was improving. Once Beatrice and her husband, Ali, were allowed back to Spain in 1912, their ranks as infante and infanta were restored to them, while the former had been raised to the rank of lieutenant in the army the previous year. A letter from the duchess from Chateau Fabron in Nice that April gave the first impressions of her youngest daughter a week after her arrival. Bee, she said, had written from Madrid, very satisfied with their reception and happy in her new house, although not accustomed to so many visitors, audiences and courtesies. With some relief she could say that the painful episode had drawn to a close, and now her daughter could put it all behind her, free to concentrate on using her tact and her *savoir-faire* in making a good position for herself and her husband in Spain.

In Spain, controversy had arisen in 1911 after publication of the memoirs of Beatrice's mother-in-law. Infanta Eulalia's *Au fil de la vie* ('The Thread of Life') appeared under the pseudonym of La Comtesse de Avila, but her identity was no secret. Her views on education, the independence of women, the equality of classes, socialism, religion, marriage, prejudices, and traditions were very much in advance of her time, and when her nephew King Alfonso XIII had been made aware that she was putting pen to paper, he ordered her to suspend publication until he had seen it and received his permission to do so. She ignored him and went ahead regardless. The Dowager Duchess of Saxe-Coburg was annoyed, on the grounds that its appearance would make the position of Beatrice and Ali difficult by irritating the notoriously thin-skinned king. Even so, the duchess had never liked the latter, and thought he was behaving 'like an ill-mannered schoolchild'. The whole episode, she said, 'was simply idiocy on both sides'. Beatrice, she noted, had been sent a copy of the book, and after seeing it the duchess thought Eulalia was mistaken in mentioning one or two matters, but conceded that the rest was 'absolutely inoffensive'.[10]

The duchess and her daughters were together at Coburg for Christmas 1911, never suspecting that it was the last festive season they would ever spend together. It was overshadowed that same week with reports of unrest in Morocco. Having anticipated a further period of military service, Ali was recalled to his regiment, arrived in Madrid on 1 January 1912, and took the train for northern Africa immediately. The Duchess of Coburg wrote to Crown Princess Marie of her sadness at this interruption and a time of worry ahead for them all, after a short time in which they had 'been able to breathe more easily' once more.

Beatrice had another son on 28 May 1912, named Alonso. The family spent the summer at Coburg with her mother before returning to Madrid for Christmas, intending to celebrate the festive season at her new home in her husband's country, much to her mother's surprise. 'What a strange life they lead in Spain!' the duchess commented. Throughout her marriage, and after some twelve years of widowhood, she had never reconciled herself to her husband's country or indeed his family. She could have told many a terrible story, she said, about her earliest experiences in England 'and the extreme desperation I had to overcome. But what for? You will not believe me and at least she has a good friend there in Ena, which is a consolation I lacked intensely because my sisters-in-law were strange, incomplete, and jealous.'[11]

* * *

The only surviving son of Queen Victoria, the Duke of Connaught, was now the senior male member of the British royal family. As he had perceived, King George V had always looked up to his uncle, and also had the utmost respect for his military and administrative abilities. Naturally there were none of the difficulties between uncle and nephew that there had been between two brothers, the senior one slightly jealous of the long-favoured younger sibling, and the duchess was likewise pleased to welcome the new reign as the beginning of a new, more favourable era for them. In October 1910 they went to Cape Town, where, on behalf of the king, the duke opened the first Union Parliament, and five months later the king appointed him as his representative in Canada. Four months after the coronation, husband and wife crossed the Atlantic, and when he took the oath on 13 October 1911 at Quebec, he became the first Governor-General who was a member of the British royal family.

The duchess embarked on a round of duties similar to those she had performed in India three decades earlier. She was as tireless as ever in visiting hospitals, attending state functions and supporting her husband as he toured the dominion, performing constitutional and ceremonial tasks such as opening parliament in 1911, at which he was attired in his field marshal's uniform and the duchess in the gown she had worn at the king's coronation.

Now in her early fifties, she was increasingly in pain, and inclined to be dissatisfied with their situation. Early in 1912 she and the duke visited America, but she disliked the country and was shocked by the opulent lifestyle of the wealthier families, who seemed over-eager to entertain them, and not necessarily for the right reasons. In her letters she complained that they were both doomed to see only the very rich people, never 'the more interesting ones'.[12] Like a number of other members of royalty from her generation, she considered the *nouveau riche* vulgar, keener to hobnob with the king of England's uncle and aunt in order to improve their social standing than from any genuine desire to meet them as people. She also seemed to find these people harder to assess, suspecting they were too ready to try and involve her and the duke as unwitting victims in their underhand business and property deals.

In May 1912 they both embarked on what was intended as a major tour of the Canadian provinces, so they could see more of the country and learn more about its people from first hand. They had left Ottawa and travelled nearly 300 miles east to Quebec when in June she came down with a painful, acute illness. The doctors immediately thought it was either peritonitis or appendicitis, and in June she was admitted to the Royal Victorian Hospital at Montreal with what turned out to be the former. She made a steady recovery, was discharged a few weeks later, and joined her husband and younger daughter at the beginning of July for their journey to Quebec.

The illness returned in January 1913, and she had to be readmitted to the hospital at Montreal. Despite the annoyance of some Canadians, who accused the duke of using his wife's illness as an excuse to return home to an easier life in Europe, he decided that he would have to take her back. They left Canada on 22 March, sailing from Ottawa on the *Empress of Britain* and arriving at Liverpool a week later. On 9 April she underwent a serious operation, at the outset of which the doctors feared she might not have peritonitis but cancer instead. Fortunately tests revealed no trace of malignancy, and they supposed the problem had been caused by her appendix. Nevertheless, she suffered a relapse and required a second operation, from which she recovered steadily but slowly.

During her convalescence, she was cheered at home by a visit from her brother Prince Frederick Leopold. His wife, Louise Sophie, was one of the younger sisters of German Empress Augusta Victoria, although there were regular disagreements between the couple (who took delight in sometimes unconventional behaviour and liberties with the strict Prussian court etiquette) on one hand, and the emperor and empress on the other. Frederick Leopold and his wife had always liked England, and paid regular visits to London incognito. The latter was highly amused when, after they had lunched with the Connaughts, a gentleman of the household was puzzled by seeing her at the station afterwards and immediately asked her husband's equerry who she was.[13] It was destined to be the last time that both couples ever met.

On 15 October 1913 the duke and duchess attended the wedding of their son Arthur – who had followed in his father's footsteps and become an officer in the army – in the Chapel Royal at St James's Palace. His bride was his cousin Alexandra, Duchess of Fife, a granddaughter of King Edward VII and Queen Alexandra. Two days later, the Connaughts sailed for Canada again on the *Empress of Britain*, reaching Quebec at midnight on 24 October. The duchess had not yet fully recovered from the medical treatment that followed her operation. Throughout the journey, she had a nurse in constant attendance and she remained apart from the suite, sitting out in daytime and taking her meals in privacy on a screened-off area of the deck.

* * *

In the final spring and summer before war broke out, the Dowager Duchess of Saxe-Coburg regularly visited Russia to stay with Grand Duchess Cyril and her two small daughters, Marie and Kira. Little did she know that she would be seeing these countries for the last time before the world in which they had been raised would be altered almost beyond recognition.

During May and June 1914 she was in England to see her relations in London. It proved a very hot and humid summer: 'I manage to get a free hour from time to time as I strike at taking morning walks with Aunt B[eatrice] which are a trial in the vast park where the sun is most powerful,' she wrote, adding that she hated 'having to dress and be dragged to dinners in the great heat,' where it changed so suddenly 'from unbearable high temperature to almost icy evenings and nights.' In a long letter from Kensington Palace to Missy describing her visit, she wrote kindly, albeit with occasional criticism of her feelings towards the English relations. At a luncheon at Buckingham Palace she 'was very pleased' to see King George V, 'but as there were 5 Majesties present I could not get a good talk with him but all were very gay and talkative.' The same could not be said of his eldest son Edward, and she admitted to being

> horribly shocked, even grieved at the appearance of the nice little Prince of Wales, whom I find looking very ill. He is tiny and so thin that if I was his mother I would fret away with anxiety ... He has not grown a bit since I saw him last but then he was jolly and looked healthy, now he looks feeble and depressed. The second boy [Prince Albert, later King George VI], the midshipman is small but looks healthy now, the girl [Princess Mary], small too and not a bit pretty but chubby and fresh looking. Aunt Alix who is 70 now is prettier than ever but so deaf that conversation is almost impossible. Aunt Minny very jolly and going about but of course not to parties, they mostly frequent the opera.[14]

Chapter 2

On 28 June 1914, Archduke Francis Ferdinand, heir to the throne of Austria-Hungary, and his morganatic wife, Sophie, Duchess of Hohenberg, paid an official visit to Sarajevo and fell victims to the bullets of Gavrilo Princip. Within six weeks most of Europe was at war. Spain was one of the few countries that remained neutral throughout the four years of warfare that ensued. Beatrice and Ali, whose family was now complete with three sons, were staying in Coburg at the time with her mother, and in common with so many others, they thought the conflict would be over within months if not weeks. Others were less sanguine. 'Austria has I think behaved abominably and has declared war on Servia,' King George V wrote to the Duke of Connaught at the end of July. 'We are doing all we can to prevent a general war. Please God we shall be able to keep out of it, but things look very bad.'[1] On 4 August Britain declared hostilities on Germany.

For the first two years of fighting the Duke and Duchess of Connaught continued to serve in Canada. Emphasising the need for military training and readiness for Canadian troops departing for war, he was active in working on behalf of auxiliary war services and charities and visiting hospitals. In his field marshal's uniform, without advice or guidance from his ministers, he visited training grounds and barracks to address the troops and to see them off before their voyage to Europe. It did not meet with the approval of Sir Robert Borden, the prime minister, who thought he was overstepping constitutional conventions, labouring under the handicap of his position as a member of the royal family and perhaps unaware of his limitations as governor general.

Meanwhile, the Duchess's strength gradually returned and she was able to undertake official duties again, though her travelling was still restricted. She worked diligently for the Red Cross and other organisations to support the war cause, and was Colonel-in-Chief of the Duchess of Connaught's Irish Canadian Rangers battalion, one of the regiments in the Canadian Expeditionary Force. Yet the division from her daughter's family in Sweden, and from her relations in Germany after the declaration of war, further distressed her and taxed her failing health.

There was, however, no doubt about her patriotism and sense of belonging wholeheartedly to her husband's country. 'Oh, the sadness of all this war!' she wrote wearily to Leonie Leslie in November 1914. 'I am every day more and more thankful that Germany was my home only *so few* years of my childhood!!'[2] She must have been even more thankful that, thanks largely to Queen Victoria's support, she and her husband had not had to take up the Coburg inheritance that they had resisted so fiercely, despite the wishes of so many of their other relations. In increasingly poor spirits, she confided in her old friend over the next several months how depressed she was, of her despair at the mounting horrors of the conflict, how she did nothing but sit at home and knit, how oppressive she found the bitter Canadian climate in winter, and of her longing to go home. Extracts from a letter written on 12 January 1915 to an unnamed friend published in *The Times* made her feelings against the Fatherland and wholehearted devotion to England and the empire even clearer:

> I feel that Germany is not the country nor Germans the people now which they were when I left as a mere child; some terrible influence, the greed and longing for more power, has become the ruling passion. The Germany of science, art and literature has disappeared ... I am intensely proud of our Army and the way they have fought, and are fighting, 'small and contemptible' though they were thought to be by our enemy and his people.[3]

After the Duchess of Saxe-Coburg's last journey to London, she had returned to Coburg, and was still there in August 1914 when hostilities began. For the remaining six years of her life she would find little peace of mind in a world of ever-deepening shadows. Like so many of her relations by marriage, her sympathies were cruelly divided, as were those of so many other members of the extended family. Yet despite her Russian birth, she had now become a passionate German and was convinced that the Fatherland would ultimately emerge victorious. Of her daughters only Sandra, the one who had become German by marriage and ironically the one who had always enjoyed the least satisfactory relationship with her mother, was on her side. Crown Princess Marie of Roumania was thoroughly British in her sympathies, while her new home remained neutral at first and only declared war on Germany in October 1916, despite the misgivings of her husband, who had become King Ferdinand on the death of his pro-German father two years earlier. Russia was an ally of Britain and France, and Victoria Melita, Grand Duchess Cyril, was likewise on the same side as her elder sister – and against their mother.

The Saxe-Coburg family faced bitter hostility during the war for their British and Russian connections, and her position in Coburg became untenable as Russophobia took over the German Empire. In order to spare them all unpleasantness, she made the decision to stay away from Coburg, retiring to her home at Tegernsee. Once while she was returning home with her two younger daughters, their car was stopped by an angry mob who recognised her and harassed her for her Russian heritage. It took the police over an hour to extricate them from the painful situation without any harm coming to them.

Increasingly embittered against the world, she found her children, all of whom had problems of their own, were the only people to whom she could pour out her sorrows. She still nursed a grievance at having to marry, as she saw it, almost beneath her, and how it had scarred her inside. Shortly after her eldest daughter, Marie, became queen, she wrote to her, stating that she had been born at the grandest of courts, and how she was 'pleased to marry into a second-rate position but for an Emperor's daughter it has been a sad experience and I felt it only as I was growing older. The world is terribly snobbish on the whole and I was only "someone" because I was rich.'[4]

Her unwavering devotion to Germany took some of her Romanov relations by surprise. Grand Duchess Vladimir, who had, naturally, always been passionately pro-German until the outbreak of war and found it as hard to adjust her loyalties as many of the family, wrote to Missy that the Duchess of Saxe-Coburg had returned to Coburg again because she disliked having to live or stay in hotels. 'I believe that she simply loves Germany so much that she cannot live in another country.'[5]

* * *

During the war, the long-established custom of hanging the banners of foreign princes invested with Britain's highest order of knighthood, the Order of the Garter, in St George's Chapel at Windsor, came under fierce criticism as the German members of the Order were fighting against Britain. The enemy nation had few more bitter enemies than Queen Alexandra, who lost no time in joining calls to 'have down those hateful German banners in our sacred Church'.[6] Driven by public opinion, somewhat against his own inclinations, the king bowed to their wishes and in 1915 he ordered their removal. Yet to his mother's dismay it was not only 'those vile Prussian banners' that were removed, but also those of her Hessian relations, also on the enemy side but who, in her opinion, were 'simply *soldiers* or *vassals* under that brutal German Emperor's orders.'

Although she was now too deaf to take part in conversations about the details of hospital management with the staff whom she met on her visits, the queen dowager was a regular visitor to wounded soldiers and sailors as they lay in their beds. When she was called to see a man who had been wounded in the leg and warned that his knee would be permanently stiff and useless, she went straight to his bed to comfort him by talking about her own disability, 'and look what I can do'. By way of demonstration, she lifted up her skirt, and to his astonishment she swept her leg easily over the seat of an adjacent chair.[7]

For the first few months of the war, the dowager empress of Russia corresponded with Queen Alexandra. Thanks to Hans Niels Andersen, founder of the East Asiatic Company, based in Denmark, letters were carried between the two, some of them containing privileged intelligence. The authorities in Denmark were aware of his connections with the Danish royal family and in particular his friendship and close association with the tsar's formidable mother. In February 1915 Queen Alexandra informed her sister that the Germans were planning to attack Warsaw and hoped that her son was aware of the fact. 'Her information has usually been correct,' the empress told him. 'God grant that they do not succeed.'[8]

When Zeppelin raiders appeared over Sandringham in the early months of the war, all her fighting instincts were aroused. She promptly wrote to Admiral John Fisher, who had recently returned to his old post at the Admiralty as First Sea Lord, to ask for some rockets with spikes or hooks on to defend the Norfolk coast, adding that she was sure he 'could invent something of the sort which would bring down a few of those rascals.'⁹ During a Zeppelin raid over Sandringham in September 1916, along with her daughter Victoria and members of the household, she watched in the darkness from the windows. Next day, she went to see for herself the damage the bombs had wrought at Dodhill village nearby, and was deeply shocked by the loss of life and destruction to their cottages.

At the beginning of the war, in August 1914, the Duchess of Albany still lived at Claremont. Within a few weeks she had made part of Claremont available as an officers' convalescent home, taking full charge herself. Having worked tirelessly for good causes during the previous thirty years, she continued to help on various projects with Princess Beatrice and their niece Princess Marie Louise at the former's War Hospital Supply Depot in Cavendish Square. This supplied military, naval and civil hospitals, aided by volunteers who made frostbite socks, mosquito nets, gas masks and other items for those on active service. In October 1914 she became one of the first of the British royal family to experience the sadness of losing a close relation fighting for the other side when her half-brother, Wolrad, a Lieutenant in the Royal Prussian Dragoon Guards, was killed on patrol duty. She was delighted two years later when HMS *Neptune*, which she had launched, flew, at the battle of Jutland, the silk ensign she had made with her own hands and presented to the ship.

Still living at Claremont, she had thrown her energies into running a hospital for officers with the help of a nursing sister. In 1917, for financial reasons, she decided she would have to part with the house. She therefore leased it, and when it was sold she moved into the Clock House, Kensington Palace, which had been offered to her by the king. Her parting gift to Esher was a magnificent Bible that she presented to St. George's Church, where she had worshipped regularly.

Her daughter Alice always missed the Albanys' childhood home of Claremont, with its wonderful park and garden. After the war, she decided they needed a country place with a garden. Brantridge Park in Sussex was chosen; while it was larger than they really wanted or needed, they required somewhere relatively spacious to accommodate the duchess and her household. She intended to live there in the summer, while her daughter and son-in-law would stay there every winter.

Every member of the royal family in England had cousins fighting for Germany during the war, and it was the misfortune of the Duchess of Albany and her daughter to have their son and brother in the enemy camp. As Duke of Saxe-Coburg, Charles was obliged with a heavy heart to break off relations with his family over the North Sea. For some months he served on the staff of a German infantry division, taking up arms against the Russian troops. Although he had escaped the taint of his father's haemophilia, as a young man he suffered from rheumatism and had to relinquish active service before long. He never held a command, and was perhaps not offered one because of his status as first cousin of King George V, who had ordered the removal of his name alongside many others on the German side from the register of the Order of the Garter. Nevertheless, he visited the western and eastern fronts on several occasions. 'Charlie has been touring to see his subjects who are scattered in various regiments,' the duchess wrote to Alice in April 1915, 'his people are devoted and grateful to him for sharing all with them. Thank God! Charlie has turned this evil to some good.'[10]

* * *

The Dowager Duchess of Saxe-Coburg still saw each of her daughters from time to time during their ever rising and falling fortunes. Sandra managed to lead a relatively peaceful existence, but Bee and Ali were expelled from Spain for several years and had to settle in Switzerland. The official reason was that Beatrice had been very tactless and uttered mischievous remarks about the allies. In fact, she had always been the soul of circumspection, and only those closest to her were aware that the campaign of character assassination was purely a smokescreen for the unpleasant conduct of her cousin King Alfonso XIII, whose word in Spain was law.

The king, who had grown apart from his English wife, Ena, and blamed her for the haemophiliac condition of all but one of their sons, had attempted to make advances to Beatrice, his attractive cousin. Such behaviour did much to explain the contempt in which he was held by King George V and his other relations in England. As a scrupulously faithful wife who was devoted to her husband, Beatrice firmly kept him at arm's length. He also had dalliances with several 'loose women', resulting in illegitimate children whose existence remained a closely guarded secret to anyone who did not need to know, and he was unaccustomed to rejection from anybody who crossed his path. He therefore sent Ali to Switzerland, ostensibly on a diplomatic mission, but one that turned out to be a subtle disguise for exile for him and his wife. When Roumania was in danger of being defeated by Germany in the war, there was a risk that King Ferdinand and Queen Marie would be compelled to abdicate and go into exile, before their fortunes changed and the Germans were defeated instead. Grand Duchess Cyril, her husband and children managed to escape from Russia shortly after revolution had toppled the empire and stayed in Finland for a while, before settling in northern France.

Of all the Duchess of Saxe-Coburg's daughters, Beatrice was probably the one whose situation gave her the most worry, especially as she was blameless and had been grossly maligned by the king and his sycophants. She knew there was never any good reason for the infanta to antagonise the Spanish court by taking a pro-German stance during the war, but she was also aware that this youngest daughter had taken after her in not suffering fools gladly, and knew her self-assertiveness could lead her into trouble if not checked. She acknowledged in a letter to Queen Marie of Roumania that there was 'no doubt that Bee has a very difficult character and a sharp tongue which has made her many enemies.' Nevertheless, it did not excuse the 'outrageous' conduct of King Alfonso, who was 'ten times worse than any of us can believe. Morally he is a coward, but he is in no way stupid, although he never says a truthful word, and is under the influence of the worst clique imaginable, and the marriage [to Queen Ena] is on the rocks.'[11]

Thanks to the King of Spain's associates, malicious reports of the infanta and her supposedly indiscreet if not treacherous comments and bad behaviour, none of which had been specified, had been circulating around Europe, and he had made no effort whatsoever to refute them. It evidently never crossed his mind that uncontrolled gossip, which it was in his power to curtail, could seriously tarnish the image of the Spanish monarchy throughout the rest of the continent. Beatrice had always got on very well with the foreign ambassadors in Madrid, and they respected her good character. Yet after what they described to others, it was evident that life had become increasingly difficult, if not impossible, for them in Spain and there was no alternative but to go elsewhere for an indefinite period.

In August 1917 the Dowager Duchess of Saxe-Coburg wrote that at the age of sixty-three, she still felt 'very fresh in mind, if not in body, and

I can support with patience and resignation a sad and perhaps miserable end of life which is in store for my old age ... Sometimes I also seem to despair, but not about myself, but about the state of things in general.'[12] The previous autumn, Roumania had entered the war on the side of the Entente powers, much to her anger. A fierce eight-page letter to Queen Marie of Roumania was devoid of tact or sympathy, telling her angrily that 'they specially accuse "you" of having been the chief element of bringing it [Roumania's participation on the side of Britain and her allies] about! ... I can hardly believe that a daughter of mine is at the head of such a movement, my former little beloved, peaceful, fair Missy, the sunshine in the house ... But all Germany says it was you, you who pushed on towards the war from insane, blind confidence in the Entente.'[13]

Ironically, her letter was written the same week that the queen was grieving for her youngest child, her son Mircea who had just died from typhoid at the age of three. It sometimes seemed that she stood accused of having wanted the conflict, the queen wrote in her diary a month later. She felt that in Germany above all she was being held responsible, and that her own mother never meant to write to or communicate with her as long as the war lasted: 'it was only the death of Mircea which made her break though her silence to send me a word of sympathy, then to return to her silence! Can she really believe that I am responsible for this war?'[14] The passionately pro-German duchess was sure that Germany would emerge triumphant from the conflict. Bee was equally distressed, commenting, 'It all seems to be eating at her heart and one feels for her; it is very, very, difficult.'[15]

The duchess's anger was tempered somewhat by the fact that three of her daughters were still going through severe problems. In 1917, just over two months after the hated Russian self-proclaimed 'holy man', Rasputin, had been murdered – ironically, as part of a conspiracy that included the close involvement of Grand Duke Dmitri, son of the Duchess of Coburg's only surviving brother, Grand Duke Paul – the doomed monarchy was no more. Her forebodings that the coronation of 1896 would probably have been the last one were proved correct. In March 1917 Tsar Nicholas II abdicated in favour of his brother, Grand Duke Michael, who declined the poisoned chalice. One month later Grand Duchess Cyril wrote to Queen Marie of Roumania that she had been abandoned in her hour of need and refused all help, her worries exacerbated by her expecting another child at the age of forty. Beatrice received another letter from her in May, and from Lausanne she told the queen everything she knew. Their sister's communication, written 'in her curious and brusque manner,' was full of bitter reproaches against her in particular and their mother, 'and you have no idea what this meant for Mama. Not to mention me. Our hearts were consumed writing and telegraphing to get news of her. Even Ali was trying to arrange everything so that I, risking everything and leaving him and the children here, could be with Ducky when she gave birth.'[16]

Having been interned in Switzerland, Beatrice and Ali were still thoroughly miserable. It upset Beatrice that their mother never took into consideration that it was the Russian revolution that had prevented her and her husband from being able to help, but she was persistently lashing out in her anger, accusing her and the others, saying that she detested and despised them. It also hurt her deeply that 'in this horrible war' it seemed that the family's love was 'being thrown to the winds'. They were in deep financial trouble, with their once wealthy mother now finding herself probably the worst off of them all as her most valuable jewellery was still somewhere in Russia, and her finances were in Russian investments. There was little chance that she would ever regain her rightful property once it had been seized by the Bolsheviks.

It saddened Beatrice even more that their mother had apparently 'thrown away her best jewels' behind her back and, after realizing what she had done, was so ashamed that she asked her not to mention the matter to anybody else. In order to pacify the ever-complaining Sandra, she had made her a gift of her complete ruby parure. The 'grasping and envious conduct on one hand' of this sister annoyed her, 'but on the other the frightful anxiety I feel for you two devours my anger.' Sandra, she insisted, had taken advantage so often in the last few years that she was now in a far more comfortable position and certainly the best off financially of the four sisters, but she never thought to help their mother, who was now in worse circumstances than all of them. 'Ali and I are trying to save the little that remains for Mama, in order to see if much later, if nothing is settled in Russia, it might be possible to raise a little capital for her ... It is too tiresome to enter into details but it is heart-breaking.'[17]

Towards the end of summer 1917 the Queen of Roumania had a letter from her mother, having at last changed her previously unforgiving attitude towards her eldest daughter for the better, and assuring her that she was thinking of her and her 'terrible trials' all the time. She appreciated and saluted her eldest daughter's bravery, as she faced the dangers of war and sickness in her beleaguered kingdom. Dressed in her Red Cross uniform, the queen was always ready to help the wounded, eagerly kissing the faces of those who were plainly dying, and without hesitation giving assistance to a doctor who tried to cure a wounded soldier whose face had been so hideously damaged that few people around could even bear to watch the operation.

* * *

The Duke of Connaught's term of office as Governor-General in Canada was coming to an end. King George V had been unfailingly appreciative of the work he and the duchess had undertaken, but he was glad to lay down his burden. Although he did not suffer from the rigours of the bitter North American weather as much as his wife, he was sometimes unwell, and the strain of his duties was at last telling on him. In December 1915 the duchess reported of a cough that he was unable to shake off, and 'an irritable throat wh[ich] always worries me – he works very hard & has many difficult nuts to crack – politicians are terrible people!!!'[18] They bade farewell to the Canadian nation at Ottawa in October 1916, and he and the duchess returned to London ten days later.

Their homecoming was just in time, for her fragile health might not have stood another winter in the harsh climate. Years of physical suffering had taken their toll, and she could no longer conceal how weak and weary she had become. After a severe bout of bronchitis several weeks later, added to complications from measles and influenza, she gradually lost ground. By Christmas and the new year she was increasingly exhausted and weary, and by the time of their thirty-eighth wedding anniversary, 13 March 1917, the bulletins on her condition gave more cause for concern. This time there was no way back, and shortly after 8.00 the following evening at Clarence House, with the duke by her side, she died, aged fifty-six.

Tributes to the shy German princess, who had never regretted leaving the land of her birth to become thoroughly Anglicised, were heartfelt. In *The Times* it was observed that very few women could have travelled so far within the British Empire, and it was probable that nobody in her position had ever known personally so many of the leaders in its work.[19] Yet she had not always been popular with her husband's family. Her eldest surviving sister-in-law, Helena, wrote to her old friend Emily Baird how saddened they were by her death, and how desolate her brother was as they had always been so happy. 'But God knows what is best, and for *her* we cannot grieve.'[20]

A private service was held on 18 March, and the main funeral was held the following morning, both at St George's Chapel, Windsor. At the duke's request, because of wartime economic shortages, no large floral tributes were sent. With his son and daughter-in-law, he followed the coffin as chief mourners, but neither of their daughters were able to attend. To her abiding sorrow, Margaret, Crown Princess of Sweden, could not make the journey across the North Sea. 'I feel so dreadfully not being there to help Papa,' she wrote to Leonie Leslie. 'He must want *all* he can get. The blow is an overwhelming one for him & I can see so well how helpless & forlorn & lost, almost like a child, he must be without Mama.' When she next came back to Clarence House, she said, home would never be the same again, but she was thankful to know that the end was so peaceful. 'I somehow feel that Mama is so near, she sees us all & understands better than ever all we are striving to be, I almost feel her smiling at which she would approve of!'[21] Her sister Patsy was confined to her bed with an attack of measles.

King George, Queen Mary and most other members of the royal family were in attendance, with ambassadors representing the royal families of friendly and neutral powers, including Spain and the Scandinavian countries. Only one European cousin, Grand Duchess George of Russia, a sister of King Constantine of Greece, was present. She and her daughters had been on holiday in England at the outbreak of war and decided not to return to Russia, where she was never happy, choosing to stay in England where she became a patron of three military hospitals in Harrogate and generously helped to finance their upkeep. Two inevitable absentees were Louise's brother, Prince Frederick Leopold, and his wife, Louise Sophie. To the end of their lives, it remained a source of sadness that the war had prevented them from being able to visit her during her illness, or join the rest of her family in paying their final respects.

In death the duchess made history in becoming the first member of the royal family to be cremated, at Golders Green Crematorium. As the procedure of burying ashes in an urn was uncommon at the time, the vessel was taken in an ordinary coffin during the funeral ceremonies. Her ashes were later buried at the royal burial ground at Frogmore. Though she had not lived to a great age, in some ways she had been the most fortunate of the daughters-in-law. She had left an unhappy childhood home to spend the rest of her life with a faithful husband who had always supported her throughout almost forty years together, and while their responsibilities in India and Canada may have affected her never very robust health, she and her family had been able to refuse the poisoned chalice of the Coburg succession that would have made them the wartime enemies of their cousins.

The Duke of Connaught survived his wife by nearly twenty-five years. In his long life he had the sorrows of outliving not only his wife but also two of their three children. Their elder daughter, Margaret, Crown Princess of Sweden, died suddenly from sepsis while she was eight months pregnant with a sixth child, on 1 May 1920, which was, in a cruel twist of fate, her father's seventieth birthday. Arthur, their son who would have succeeded to his father's title, succumbed to stomach cancer on 12 September 1938. The duke himself died on 16 January 1942, aged ninety-one, at that time a record age for a male member of the British royal family. His grandson Alastair succeeded him as duke, but failed to emulate his grandfather's life of service. Sir Alan Lascelles, private secretary to King George VI, referred to him as 'the wretched young Duke of Connaught, whom his regiment have had to get rid of, as he is wholly incompetent.'[22] A heavy drinker, he died at the age of twenty-eight, allegedly from hypothermia after being found on the floor of his room at Ottawa early one morning in April 1943.[23]

* * *

Since the abdication of Nicholas II in March 1917, the Duchess of Coburg had never stopped thinking of Russia or the loved ones whom she had had to leave behind. Like the rest of the family, she was horrified when told that the former ruler and his family had been taken to Tobolsk in Siberia. In November 1917 the Russian provisional government ceded power to the Bolsheviks, who intended to make peace with Germany and Austria and ordered the Roumanians to do likewise, planning to imprison the royal family and government.

Next month, Queen Marie received a telegram from King George V, informing her that she and her children would be welcome in England if they had to leave Roumania. As German defeat became increasingly apparent the following summer, this never happened. Meanwhile, they were all fearful for the fate of the former tsar and his family. In August 1918 the Queen of Roumania received a letter from the duchess, telling her that they had been 'bundled off in the night to some unknown destination'.[24] They were as yet unaware that the former ruler, his wife, children and last remaining servants had been removed to squalid captivity in Ekaterinburg and put to death the previous month. Some of the Romanovs, notably Grand Duke and Duchess Cyril and their children, had left Russia just in time, but the tsar's brother, Grand Duke Michael, his sister-in-law, the widowed Grand Duchess Serge and several others were also imprisoned and killed by the Bolsheviks during that fateful year.

Earlier in 1919 her sole surviving brother, Grand Duke Paul, the youngest and her favourite, had been shot in the Peter and Paul Fortress in Petrograd. After the war it became clear that she had lost her large fortune, as much of it had been held in trust in Russia. Circumstances had changed irrevocably for the worse since less than fifty years ago when the young soon-to-be-married Grand Duchess Marie Alexandrovna of Russia could be called one of the most well-off unmarried royalties in Europe, if not the world. She had to sell much of what jewellery she had left, and was left with no alternative but to return to the hotel life that she apparently disliked so much. She went to live in Switzerland at the Walhaus, an annexe of the Dolder Grand Hotel in Zurich. Queen Marie's daughter Ileana pitied her grandmother, who had been brought up in the splendours of Romanov Russia, reduced to having to make do with 'an awful little *pension* – very refugee-like.'[25]

In March 1919 Queen Marie was attending a peace conference in Paris when she received a letter from her mother which she opened 'with trembling fingers'. Every word, she said, 'was a fiery dart of pain, every sentence a cry of smothered anguish.' She had lost everything, not merely her fortune, 'but all her old beliefs, traditions, ideas and ideals had been shattered, desecrated. A new world had grown up around her in which she could find no footing, in which the grand old autocrat she was no longer had a place.'[26]

At length the duchess was reunited with her eldest and youngest daughters for the first time since the outbreak of war. The queen left Paris in April 1919, arriving at Bucharest five days later, leaving Beatrice to prepare the meeting with her mother. As Marie was 'on the side of the victors and she among the vanquished,' she knew it would be a delicate time. The Russia and Germany she had loved and believed in had vanished. At Lausanne, Bee was waiting for her so she could discuss with her the best way to meet and approach the matriarch.

The Duchess of Coburg seemed keen to postpone the meeting in order to be in Lucerne. For the queen, 'the tragic meeting was as cruel as [she] predicted,' and she was thankful that Bee and Ali were able to join them. Ali's presence helped to relieve the tension between mother and daughter. Missy was shocked by the change in her mother. No longer the proud, autocratic, domineering, awe-inspiring matriarch of previous years,[27] a thinner, bent woman, whose once plump fingers were now thin and trembling, had taken her place. 'The dominant look in her eyes, formerly one of her characteristics, had been tarnished, today they were anxious eyes, almost haunted.'[28]

As one who had been on the side of the victors, Queen Marie only spoke of her own experiences and tried as far as possible to talk only about what happened to them. The tension between them lessened, but there could be no heart-to-heart chat between mother and daughter. For beneath the former's changed exterior 'burned the same proud spirit, unbending, refusing to admit defeat.' They had been in different camps during the war, Roumania having entered on the side of the Allies and helping to overthrow Germany had evidently rankled deeply, and 'the thought was with us both, all the time, underlying our every conversation.'

The duchess 'still stuck to her old tradition of separating the generations.' Once Bee and Ali had left, the queen persuaded her mother to let her take her to Florence. It proved an emotional time for them both. The queen later recalled that as she was leaving, 'Mama's defences broke down and in hurried words she confessed to me something of her grief: she suddenly became soft and motherly, allowing, for once, her oppressed heart to speak.' She seemed unexpectedly frail as her daughter took her, for what would be the last time, in her arms. 'Mama's tear-stained face, with its sunken cheeks and with those eyes out of which all fire had died, kept rising up before me ... It was unbearable to know that I could do nothing for her, and that Fate had so irrevocably parted our ways.'[29]

Perhaps realizing that she had little time left, in the last winter of her life, the dowager duchess went about trying to make amends for having behaved with such bitterness to the daughters who were to a large extent victims of circumstance beyond their control. Above all, she was grateful to see Ducky again. After three years of exile with her family in Finland, Grand Duchess Cyril reached Berlin where Sandra met them. Preoccupied with the end of the civil war and the triumph of the Soviets, King Gustav V of Sweden helped the family to leave Finland and they departed from their temporary home at Borgo in May 1920. They spent two days in Berlin where they met Sandra, then the duchess in Munich, and went with her to Zurich. Missy visited her mother again, and found her suffering from a weak heart, even thinner and more tired. She was relieved that her mother was surrounded by her four daughters and her grandchildren to whom she was very close.

In July the aged matriarch bewailed her utter disgust with the state of the world, and mankind in general, for having 'destroyed and ruined my beloved Russia, my much-loved Germany.' Now a broken woman, her once plump figure was thin, she was a martyr to gastric troubles, and her hands trembled. Bee tried to prevent her from reading the newspapers, full of distressing reports of events in Russia. She still received her post and, it was said, was infuriated to receive a letter one day addressed to 'Frau Coburg'. In Roumania, Queen Marie was still upset by her mother's apparently unforgiving attitude towards her, and the world, writing to her old friend, Joseph Boyle, that she did not feel such a complete failure, but that her mother 'continues to bicker, bicker about quite forgotten things I did or left undone. She never admitted that I had any intelligence, only a certain smiling good nature & a sunny face that bamboozled the world. Poor dear, stormy old Mama!'[30]

Eight days after her sixty-seventh birthday, on 25 October 1920, the duchess died in her sleep after a heart attack. She had lived too long into a strange, new world that had changed so much for the worse. Beatrice was with her at the end, and it fell to her to inform her sisters: Ducky came from France, Sandra from Germany and Missy from Roumania.

Once they were reunited in a modest bedroom in the Hotel Dolder Waldhaus, the sisters planned to take her to Coburg and so that they could lay her to rest in the mausoleum at Glockenburg next to her loved ones. Much to her sadness, the Queen of Roumania was denied the chance to join the cortege as she was still greatly disliked in Germany for her actions during the war, and she had to remain in Switzerland. The body of the duchess was placed in the ducal mausoleum in Coburg next to her husband and their son. She had always been a profoundly religious woman whose faith had never wavered throughout an often-trying existence. Her eldest daughter – the only one who could not be there at the final farewell – wrote to her cousin King George V how their mother's death had been 'a terrible, cruel shock to us all, we were in no wise prepared for it. I had been with her hardly two months before. She was certainly thin, weak & very changed, but nothing made us imagine that her end could be so near.' She prayed fervently that 'God will not disappoint her as most things and beings did in this life'.[31]

Despite its revolutionary, even republican atmosphere since the end of the war, Coburg had received its old ruler's widow with respect and devotion. Notwithstanding her brusque character and lack of tact, she had been much loved and respected in the duchy, and the people remembered her fondly. The letter in which Ducky replied to her cousin Xenia in November 1920, three weeks after the death of her mother, was full of bitterness, her lack of any hope for the future, and what she perceived as the 'atrocious manner' of most members of her family. 'You really understand the hopeless sorrow that Mama's death has caused us,' she wrote.

> All those years have been like a long period of difficulties in order to catch up again and, when she had caught up, it was for her to leave forever. Nothing has any importance for me now, only to live for my children, educate them well, and give them a happy life if that is possible. Most of the members of our family act in an atrocious manner, giving an ugly picture to the world of what remains of the Romanovs. Our own brothers and sisters give the worst example of all. I am completely heartbroken and upset. I have no hope nor desire for anything.[32]

Chapter 3

After the end of the war in November 1918, the Duchess of Albany carried on with her charitable work as diligently as ever. The partnership that she had established with Princess Beatrice continued in their patronage and support of the newly established League of Remembrance, honouring the memory of those who had given their lives for their country by looking after some of their widows and families. By June 1920 the League had a membership of 1200 whose subscriptions augmented the pensions of the widows and other dependents of officers who had been killed or incapacitated in war. Among other causes to which she gave her support was a home in Lingfield, Surrey, on whose behalf she attended a special matinee at the Whitehall Theatre to raise funds that would provide for sufferers from epilepsy to enjoy days out at the seaside, the Waterloo Hospital for Children and Women, and the International Bureau for the Suppression of the White Slave Traffic. Yet it was the now well-established Deptford Fund that remained the primary beneficiary of her fund-raising efforts. These included an annual fete in the grounds at Claremont, her sale in 1916 of a rope of 258 pearls presented to her by Queen Victoria, and a fancy dress ball and children's party in April 1920 at Devonshire House. Both these functions raised over £3,700 between them.

The elder surviving members of the family had increasingly drifted apart over the previous twenty-or-so years, and the duchess's remaining contacts with her in-laws and their families were few and far between. During the winter of 1920–21, she spent a few days holidaying in Cannes with her daughter Alice and son-in-law Alexander, created Earl and Countess of Athlone three years earlier. Her niece Ducky was also there at the time and they met briefly, but the grand duchess found her strangely uncommunicative on the subject of her son Charles, who, like the rest of the German sovereigns and dukes, had been deprived of his titles at the end of the war after Germany's defeat. She wrote succinctly to Queen Marie of Roumania that she had seen 'Aunt Helen Albany, fat and vulgar but amiable. I could not get her to talk or listen to anything concerning Charly.'[1]

The Duchess of Albany also paid regular visits to Charles and his family in Germany. Although she suffered from mild heart trouble in later years, she refused to let it curtail her plans for travelling abroad. Each time she did, she used to write to Alice in detail about her journeys, the weather, and perhaps characteristically, the splendid food, but always seemingly at pains to avoid commenting on any political issues of the time. One such letter, written on arrival at the Hotel Tyrol, Innsbruck, in midsummer 1921, recounts some of her impressions:

> Here be we safe and sound and very hot but pure air! The journey was perfect, quite pre war, the courier, an Italian, was a great success and all as comfortable as could be – rain to start with and a bit fresher. Boat new and clean and good – sharp wind, the sea looked rough but wind in light quarters the crossing was perfect, sat in the shade and enjoyed myself but glad of my fur cloak. ... I had to be the good Samaritan to an invalid Lady who was lame and dragged up and down the train to find a seat, and finally dropped on the wooden seat in the corridor – so I helped her in and she drank our tea as she had not been able to get any lunch and any drink since London. She was not English, her French was perfect. ... the route is glorious all round – up those hills, the valleys so fertile, and all fresh and green ... the heat was terrific ... at last we got the tail end of a thunderstorm ... I am astonished at myself; I am a wee bit tired...but most flourishing no aches and pains ... Food good but portions *much* smaller. I revelled in a dish of wild strawberries!! only crowned with cream, a Devonshire cream.[2]

During the summer of 1922 she made similar arrangements to be with her son and family at their shooting property in the Tyrol. While she was not one to complain about her state of health, she might have had a presentiment that time was not on her side, and was aware that the next journey overseas to see her relations might be her last. On her departure at the end of July she left Kensington Palace and seemed in good spirits, and everyone expected her to return at the end of September. She was aged only sixty-one, and although she had put on considerable weight over the years, nobody apparently had any indication that she was unwell. Her wish regarding the family was fulfilled, for they enjoyed a happy reunion at Hinterriss in Tyrol, Austria, just in time.

At the end of August she was taken ill with respiratory trouble, which led to a diagnosis of coronary problems, and after a heart attack she died suddenly on 1 September. As she had expressed a wish to be buried where she died, the funeral took place there seven days later in the presence of her children, and of three of her siblings: Queen Emma of the Netherlands; Elizabeth, Princess Erbach-Schönberg; and Frederick, Prince of Waldeck-Pyrmont.

The tributes that were paid to her in the press were appropriately respectful, although an obituary in *The Times* found it necessary to defend her loyalties and patriotism to her adopted country. The anonymous contributor admitted that she was German by birth, but wholeheartedly English by marriage, by adoption, and by affection. 'She was never a Prussian. She was devoted to the British cause.' It added that she had always detested the Prussian government and that it had been a sore trial to her that her son 'became of necessity the enemy of this country during the war.'[3] That the last Duke of Saxe-Coburg had done his best to ameliorate conditions for British war prisoners in Germany under his control during the war had gone largely unnoticed by those who were quick to condemn him.

* * *

Of Queen Victoria's four daughters-in-law, Queen Alexandra, the eldest by several years as well as the first to marry into the family, was to be the longest-lived and the last survivor. Her parents and siblings had always been healthy, and apart from two of her brothers, King Frederick VIII of Denmark and King George of Greece (whose life was shortened by assassination), they all reached their eightieth year.

One of her last major public appearances was at one of the first official victory celebrations after the end of the war and the armistice. On 23 November a review of disabled ex-servicemen was held in Hyde Park at which the king rode down the lines on horseback, followed by Queen Mary and her mother-in-law in an open landau. In the excitement, the king briefly disappeared in a group of over-enthusiastic soldiers, and was almost pulled off his mount. The queens were surrounded by a similarly excitable group, and some men forgot themselves sufficiently to try and climb into the carriage with them. In order to stop them, the officer of the escort forced his animal close up against the vehicle so its head was in Queen Alexandra's lap. Noticing that it was becoming nervous, she gently took its nose in her gloved hands, stroking and soothing it while she smiled and bowed calmly to the crowds. Her instinctive, quick-witted reaction to a difficult situation had helped to avert what could have been an unpleasant accident. She was always devoted to horses, and if she ever saw one that was lame, or pulling a particularly heavy load in the street, she would invariably go up to its owner and scold him for his thoughtlessness.

Two months later there was further sadness for the family when the king's youngest son, John, aged thirteen, died at Sandringham. Perhaps Queen Alexandra, who had always loved his company, missed him more than the rest of the family. After his funeral service, when he was buried next to her own youngest son who had lived but a day almost fifty years earlier, she observed sorrowfully to Queen Mary that 'now our darling Johnnies lie side by side'.[4]

What was perhaps the last great joy of her life was a reunion several months later with her favourite sister, the Dowager Empress of Russia. She and her daughter, Grand Duchess Xenia, managed to escape the vengeance of the Bolsheviks and return to England in May 1919, when the ship HMS *Lord Nelson* docked at Portsmouth. For several months she was able to enjoy the hospitality of her English relations, living at Frogmore and regularly visiting her sister at Sandringham. However, despite occasional visits to England thereafter, at length she decided it would be better for all concerned if she went to spend the rest of her life in her homeland in Denmark. The two widows, both in their seventies and in failing health, were now forced to recognise that they found each other's company less congenial than they had in the past. Due to her almost total deafness, increasing vagueness, loss of memory and eccentricity, Queen Alexandra was not the easiest of company, and she soon came to find her more sprightly, sometimes impatient younger sister's long visits increasingly exhausting.

The queen had retained a relatively youthful appearance into her later years, but by her early seventies the ageing process was taking its toll and she took to wearing elaborate veils and heavy make-up, which some observers said gave her an enamelled appearance. One of the last people outside the family to be granted an audience with her at Marlborough House was T.E. Lawrence, 'Lawrence of Arabia'. Afterwards, he left a less than kindly description of his short meeting with 'the mummied thing, the bird-like head cocked on one side', as her bony fingers fiddled with albums, penholders, photographs and other items on the table in front of her. It was surely a relief to them both when the ordeal came to an end.[5]

In 1920 a blood vessel burst in one eye and left her with temporary partial blindness. During her remaining five years, her memory and speech became increasingly impaired. With worsening dementia, her friends and relatives were distressed to see how advancing years had taken their toll of her mental and physical health. When Queen Olga of Greece came to visit, and went to London for the day, Alexandra would weep as she bid her farewell, presenting her with jewels and photographs. Next day they would dine together quite normally, as if the previous meeting had never happened.[6]

It was now too much of an effort for her to go and stay at Marlborough House, let alone travel abroad to see her sister or indeed any other relatives. She retired from the public gaze to the seclusion of Sandringham, and now rarely ventured outside the familiar comforts of her home environment except to attend family weddings in London, with those of her grandchildren bringing her particular pleasure. Writing letters to her family and friends became more and more difficult, and she had little to say, except to lament her ever-worsening frailty, while assuring them that they and the younger generation were always in her thoughts. King George remained as devoted to her as ever. At Sandringham Church they would sit together, while he would find the hymns, psalms and prayers for her in their books.

The death of Sir Dighton Probyn, aged eighty-seven, in June 1924, saddened her further, although she would be spared what would have been the penance of reaching a similar age. Only the ever-faithful Charlotte Knollys, now aged almost ninety, was left. From the younger generation, the ever-querulous spinster Princess Victoria remained constantly at her beck and call.

By the time of her eightieth birthday that December the decline was well advanced, though she lingered for nearly another year. A heart attack on the morning of 19 November 1925 presaged the approaching end, and the family were warned that she was slipping away. King George went to see her for a while, and after she rallied a little he returned to his shooting, though he and Queen Mary returned in the evening. She breathed her last later the following day.

Her body lay in state in the church at Sandringham until its removal to the Chapel Royal in St James' Palace. King Edward VII had been buried on a glorious summer day some fifteen years earlier. In contrast, snow was falling beneath grey skies on 27 November as members of royalty from all over Europe took part in the funeral procession to Westminster Abbey. Four kings, namely her son George V, her nephew Christian X of Denmark, her son-in-law and also nephew Haakon VII of Norway, and Albert of the Belgians, plus several English and European princes, were among those who followed the coffin. Many members of the public filed through the abbey to pay their respects. That evening, her body was removed to Windsor for a smaller family service, with her banner before the altar in the Albert Memorial Chapel.

An elaborate tomb next to that of her husband at St George's Chapel would be the final resting place for the first and last of Queen Victoria's daughters-in-law. Six years after her death, an ornate bronze memorial by the sculptor Sir Alfred Gilbert, set into the garden wall at Marlborough House, was unveiled to commemorate the princess who for almost thirty-eight years had been a much-loved Princess of Wales, and subsequently for nine years an exemplary queen consort.

For seventy-one years after the accession of King George V and Queen Mary, there would be no Princess of Wales until the marriage of Charles, Prince of Wales, and Lady Diana Spencer, on 29 July 1981. It was said that at the time of their wedding well-wishers personally handed her a copy of Georgina Battiscombe's biography of Queen Alexandra, believing it would be a helpful guide for her in her new role.[7]

* * *

For the three princesses and the grand duchess who married into Queen Victoria's family and became her daughters-in-law, it was a demanding role that they all filled with varying degrees of success. The two elder women were daughters of crowned heads themselves, and the two younger of slightly less exalted rank but with close family connections to European royalty. While the queen was always a demanding mother-in-law, sometimes difficult and occasionally selfish, all of them came to respect and appreciate her love of and solicitude for her large family, realizing that as a matriarch she had their best interests at heart. They all played a worthy role in supporting their husbands, though the two elders were neither the most faithful of spouses nor the easiest people to live with, and the married life of the youngest was sadly cut very short. As supportive wives and devoted mothers, they fulfilled the family roles expected of them, while also devoting much effort as tireless workers on behalf of charitable causes, some of which they had themselves helped to found.

Like all families, they sometimes had their differences, their rivalries and petty jealousies, with the occasional bitter argument. They were strong characters; they could be as obstinate as their mother-in-law when the occasion demanded, and knew how to get their own way if necessary. Yet each one contributed in no small measure to the British monarchy, helping it to withstand the waves of republicanism that swept throughout parts of British society during several years of the nineteenth and twentieth centuries, and brought an end to some of their relatives' kingdoms and empires in Europe at the same time.

Notes

Abbreviations:
A – Queen Alexandra, formerly Princess of Wales
DA – Duchess of Albany
DC – Duchess of Connaught
DE – Duchess of Edinburgh, later of Saxe-Coburg Gotha
E – King Edward VII, formerly Prince of Wales
LL – Lady Leslie
M – Marie Feodorovna, Empress of Russia
MR – Queen Marie of Roumania, formerly Crown Princess
QV – Queen Victoria
RA – Royal Archives (Windsor unless stated otherwise)
V – Victoria, Princess Royal and German Empress

Part I: The Early Victorian Years 1840–74

Chapter 1
1. Victoria, Queen, *Dearest Child*, p.186, QV to V, 27 April 1859
2. Bennett, p.110
3. McClintock, p.25, QV to Prince Albert, 7 October 1857
4. Corti, *English Empress*, p.63, QV to V, 31 October 1860

Chapter 2
1. Trowbridge, p.53
2. Madol, p.100
3. *The Times*, 5 July 1858
4. Paget, p.139
5. Battiscombe, p.19
6. Victoria, Queen, *Dearest Child*, p.289, V to QV, 7 December 1860; p.291, QV to V, 11 December 1860
7. Victoria, Queen, *Dearest Child*, p.350, V to QV, 26 September 1861
8. Battiscombe, p.28
9. Victoria, Queen, *Dearest Child*, p.353, QV to V, 1 October 1861
10. Battiscombe, p.2
11. Battiscombe, p.38
12. *The Times*, 5 November 1862
13. Corti, *English Empress*, p.97, QV to V, 12 November 1862
14. Trowbridge, p.76
15. Battiscombe, p.43
16. *Punch*, 31 January 1863

17. Trowbridge, p.92
18. Kennedy, p.214, Lord Clarendon to Duchess of Manchester, 10 March 1863
19. Trowbridge, p.99
20. Victoria, Queen, *Dearest Mama*, p.226, QV to V, 8 June 1863; p. 236, 24 June 1863
21. Battiscombe, p.60, E to Caroline, Dowager Queen of Denmark, 9 June 1863
22. Corti, *English Empress*, p. 118, V to QV, n.d.
23. Victoria, Queen, *Dearest Mama*, p.289, QV to V, 11 January 1864
24. Battiscombe p.80, QV to V, 31 March 1866; p.81, QV to V, 14 November 1866
25. Victoria, Queen, *Your Dear Letter*, pp.200–1, QV to V, 10 July 1868
26. Magnus, p.100, E to QV, 26 February 1869
27. Ridley, *Bertie*, p.127, A to M, 21 February 1870
28. Ramm, *Political Correspondence*, p.133, Gladstone to Granville, 26 September 1870
29. Ridley, *Bertie*, p.141, A to M, 27 May 1871; and E to QV, 10 April 1871
30. Battiscombe, p.118, A to Lady Macclesfield, 31 January 1872
31. Trowbridge, p.124
32. Ridley, *George V*, p.41

Chapter 3
1. Gelardi, p.10
2. Victoria, Queen, *Your Dear Letter*, p.147, QV to V, 7 August 1867
3. Abrash, 'Curious Royal Romance'
4. Victoria, Queen, *Darling Child*, pp.74–5, QV to V, 22 January 1873
5. Victoria, Queen, *Darling Child*, p.101, QV to V, 12 July 1873
6. Victoria, Queen, *Further Letters*, p.195, QV to Empress Augusta, 25 May 1873
7. Longford, p.394, QV to Princess Alice, 26 July 1873
8. Hall, *Queen Victoria and the Romanovs*, pp.106–7
9. Victoria, Queen, Letters, II, ii, p.310, Queen Victoria's Journal, 23 January 1874
10. Vovk, p.49
11. Gelardi, pp.41–2
12. *The Graphic*, 24 January 1874
13. Stanley, p.205
14. Victoria, Queen, *Darling Child*, p.132, QV to V, 9 March 1874; QV to V, 14 March 1874
15. Pakula, p.31
16. Monypenny & Buckle, VI, p.320, Disraeli to Anne, Lady Chesterfield, 17 March 1878; p.344, 9 September 1878
17. Corti, *Downfall of Three Dynasties*, p.216
18. Pope-Hennessy, p.76
19. Queen Victoria's Journal, 18 April 1874
20. Derby, p.371, Queen Sophie to Countess of Derby, 14 April 1873, 22 December 1873
21. Leeds Russian Archive, DE to Tsar Alexander II, 27 March 1874
22. Longford, *Victoria*, p.404
23. Buchanan, p.115
24. Victoria, Queen, *Darling Child*, pp.153–4, QV to V, 23 September 1874
25. Corti, *Downfall*, Empress Marie Alexandrovna to Prince Alexander of Hesse, 25 April/7 May 1878
26. Gelardi, pp.112–3

27. Victoria, Queen, *Further Letters*, p.202, QV to Empress Augusta, 25 November 1874
28. Victoria, Queen, *Darling Child*, p.159, QV to V, 27 October 1874
29. Ridley, *Bertie*, p.168, A to M, 22 November 1874
30. Mandache, *Dearest Missy*, p.129, DE to MR, 17 July 1893
31. Churchill, p.238
32. Leslie, *Jennie*, p.127
33. Goliczov, 'Grand Duchess Marie Alexandrovna'
34. John Wimbles Papers, DE to MR, May 1910
35. Marie, Queen of Roumania, I, p.47
36. Corti, *Downfall*, p.216, Empress Marie Alexandrovna to Prince Alexander of Hesse, 26 March/7 April 1874
37. Gelardi, p.73
38. Queen Victoria's Journal, 21 September 1874
39. Corti, *Downfall*, p.216, Empress Marie Alexandrovna to Prince Alexander of Hesse, 26 March/7 April 1874

Part II: The Mid-Victorian Years 1874–87

Chapter 1
1. Battiscombe, pp.122–3
2. Ridley, *George V*, p. 39, A to Prince George, 22 May 1890
3. Ridley, *George V*, p. 130
4. Battiscombe, p.141
5. *New York Times*, 23 May 1886
6. Victoria, Queen, *Dearest Child*, p.98, QV to V, 28 April 1858
7. Victoria, Queen, *Darling Child*, p.255, QV to V, 7 July 1877
8. Frankland, p.62, Duke of Connaught to QV, 14 February 1878
9. Frankland, p.63, Sir Howard Elphinstone to QV, 3 March 1878
10. RA VIC/MAIN/ADDA15/2724 Draft of proceeding, QV to Emperor William, 3 March 1878
11. Ponsonby, p.88, QV to Sir Henry Ponsonby, 2 May 1878
12. RA VIC/MAIN/ADDA15/2806 Prince Frederick Charles to QV, 12 May 1878
13. RA VIC/MAIN/ADDA15/2819 Lord Odo Russell to QV, 13 May 1878
14. RA VIC/MAIN/ADDA15/2833 DC to QV 16 May 1878
15. McClintock, p.191, Sir Howard Elphinstone to Lady Elphinstone, 12 May 1878
16. McClintock, p.157
17. Frankland, p.64, Duke of Connaught to DC, 12 July 1878
18. Longford, *Darling Loosy*, p.210, Princess Louise to DC, 3 May 1878
19. Monypenny & Buckle, VI, p.320, Disraeli to QV, 17 June 1878
20. Frankland, p.68
21. Aston, p.100
22. RA VIC/MAIN/ADDA15/3014 Lady Adela Larking to QV, 13 March 1879
23. RA VIC/ADDA30/1347 DC to A, 22 November 1879
24. Zeepvat, 'Mrs Arthur', I
25. Friedrich Leopold, p.156
26. Zeepvat, *From Cradle*, p.160, Mary Egerton to QV, 20 March 1882
27. Alice, p.42

28. Dennison, p.118, Princess Beatrice to DA, 23 November 1881
29. RA VIC/ADDA30/1347 Princess Louise to DA, 18 December 1881
30. Alice, p.39
31. Victoria, Queen, *Beloved Mama*, p.117, QV to V, 11 April 1882
32. Victoria, Queen, *Letters*, II, iii, p.270, Queen Victoria's Journal, 27 April 1882
33. Victoria, Queen, *Beloved Mama*, p.118, QV to V, 29 April 1882
34. Hough, p.39, QV to Princess Victoria of Hesse, 16 August 1882
35. Ponsonby, p.90
36. Aronson, *Alice*, pp.44–5
37. Zeepvat, *Leopold*, p.181
38. Wright, 'Helena Frederica Augusta'
39. Zeepvat, *Leopold*, p.186
40. Zeepvat, 'Worth telling' 1
41. Victoria, Queen, *Letters*, II, iii, p.493, 29 March 1884
42. RA VIC/MAIN/R/14 Duke of Connaught and DC to QV, 30 March 1884
43. Battiscombe, p.170
44. Victoria, Queen, *Letters*, II, iii, p.493, 29 March 1884
45. Alice, p.52
46. RA VIC/ADDA30/1250 Robert Collins, report to QV, 27 November 1884
47. Hough, p.71, QV to Princess Victoria of Hesse, 8 December 1884
48. Aronson, *Alice*, p.28
49. Victoria, Queen, *Beloved Mama*, p.172, QV to V, 27 November 1884
50. Battiscombe, pp.171–250
51. Victoria, Queen, *Letters*, II, iii, p.586, Queen Victoria's Journal, 29 December 1884
52. Victoria, Queen, *Beloved Mama*, p.173, QV to V, 16 December 1884
53. Mallet, p.12, 27 December 1887

Chapter 2
1. Victoria, Queen, *Darling Child*, p.163, QV to V, 25 November 1874
2. Millar, p.233
3. Monypenny & Buckle, VI, p.217, QV to Disraeli, 10 January 1878
4. Corti, *Downfall*, p.244, Tsarina to Prince Alexander Of Hesse, 27 February/11 March 1878
5. Gelardi, p.89, Lord Dufferin to QV, 18 February 1880
6. Belyakova, p.72
7. Khorvatova, p.61
8. Barkhatova & Burkova, p.50
9. Hamilton, p.168
10. Victoria, Queen, *Beloved Mama*, p.97, QV to V, 16 March 1881
11. Vorres, p.54
12. Duff, *Alexandra*, p.146
13. Battiscombe, p.171
14. Zeepvat, *From Cradle*, p.160, QV to Duke of Connaught, 18 January 1884
15. McClintock, p.224
16. RA VIC/MAIN/Z/182/3 DC to QV, 18 January 1887
17. Longford, *Darling Loosy*, p.229, Princess Louise to DC, 3 May 1878
18. RA VIC/MAIN/Z/182/12 DC to QV, 10 February 1887
19. RA VIC/MAIN/Z/182/14 DC to QV, 18 February 1887

20. Wimbles, *Daughter*, p.47
21. Warwick, pp.82–3

Part III: The Later Victorian Years 1887–1901

Chapter 1
1. Battiscombe, p.174
2. Frankland, p.147
3. McClintock, p.248–9, Sir Howard Elphinstone to QV, 17 February 1888
4. RA VIC/MAIN/Z/185/13 DC to QV, 20 August 1888
5. Longford, *Darling Loosy*, p.234, Duke of Connaught to Princess Louise, 14 November 1888
6. RA VIC/MAIN/Z/185/31 DC to QV, 29 November 1888
7. RA VIC/MAIN/Z/185/17 DC to QV, 10 September 1888
8. Victoria, Queen, *Beloved Mama*, p.190, QV to V, 17 June 1885
9. Ridley, *George V*, p.40
10. Röhl, p.800, DC to QV, 25 April 1888
11. Battiscombe, p.174
12. RA VIC/MAIN/Z/185/3 DC to QV, 9 July 1888
13. RA VIC/MAIN/Z/185/5 DC to QV, 16 July 1888
14. RA VIC/MAIN/Z/185/8 DC to QV, 30 July 1888
15. RA VIC/MAIN/ADDA5/479/27 DC to V, 30 July 1888
16. Battiscombe, p.182
17. Magnus, p.239, QV to V, 16 January 1892
18. Battiscombe, p.196
19. Bing, 260
20. Mandache, *Dearest Missy*, p.126, DE to MR, 3 July 1893
21. Ridley, *George V*, p.40
22. Gill, 'Duchess [of Edinburgh]'
23. Mandache, *Dearest Missy*, p.62, DE to MR, 30 January 1891
24. Mandache, *Dearest Missy*, p.136, DE to MR, 3 July 1893
25. Marie, Queen of Roumania, I, p.156
26. Victoria, *Empress Frederick Writes to Sophie*, p.150
27. Fontenoy, p.99
28. Mandache, *Dearest Missy*, p.282, DE to MR, 10 March 1897
29. Pakula, p.33
30. Mandache, *Dearest Missy*, p.169, DE to MR, 18 March 1894
31. Duff, *Hessian Tapestry*, p.233
32. St Aubyn, 296
33. Wimbles, 'Forgotten princess', Part I
34. Frankland, p.202

Chapter 2
1. Dennison, pp.201–2, Princess Beatrice to Bishop Taylor Smith, 14 October 1897
2. Battiscombe, p.211
3. Mallet, p.155, 16 March 1899
4. Kehoe, p.191
5. Leslie, *Edwardians*, p.204
6. Leslie, *Edwardians*, p.205

Notes 211

7. Mallet, p.159, 21 March 1899
8. Alice, pp.39–40
9. Longford, p.447
10. Zeepvat, p.163, *From Cradle*, DA to QV, 23 July 1886
11. Zeepvat, p.163, *From Cradle*, DA to QV, 28 July 1886
12. Alice, p.117

Chapter 3
1. RA VIC/ADDA30/1256 Robert Collins to QV, March 1899
2. *The Times*, 10 April 1899
3. John Wimbles Papers, DE to MR, 24 April 1899
4. John Wimbles Papers, DE to MR, 23 May 1899
5. RA VIC/ADDA30/1259 Notes on interview between QV and Robert Collins, 13 May 1899
6. RA VIC/ADDA30/1264 Emma, Queen of the Netherlands to DA, 1 June 1899
7. RA VIC/ADDA30/1267 DA to QV, June 1899
8. RA VIC/ADDA30/1275 DA to QV, 27 June 1899
9. Frankland, p.209
10. RA VIC/ADDA30/1266 DA to QV, June 1899
11. Mandache, p.381, DE to MR, 21 June 1899
12. Alice, p.90
13. Mandache, *Dearest Missy*, p.336, DE to MR, 11 April 1898
14. Zeepvat, p.171, *From Cradle*, DE to Elizabeth Winter, n.d.
15. Ridley, *Bertie*, p.340; Hall, *Victoria*, p.256; Mandache, *Dearest Missy*, p.393, DE to MR, 10 October 1899
16. John Wimbles Papers, DE to MR, 27 June 1900
17. Mandache, *Dearest Missy*, p.438, DE to MR, 16 July 1900
18. John Wimbles Papers, DE to MR, 16 July 1900
19. Queen Victoria's Journal, 28 July 1900
20. Queen Victoria's Journal, 31 July 1900
21. Gelardi, p.171, Princess Beatrice to Rev. W. Boyd-Carpenter, 8 August 1900
22. RA VIC/MAIN/ADDA15/6408, Duke of Connaught to QV, 29 July 1900
23. Frankland, 215
24. Victoria, *Empress Frederick Writes to Sophie*, p.341
25. John Wimbles Papers, DE to MR, 13 December 1900
26. John Wimbles Papers, DE to MR, 25 December 1900
27. John Wimbles Papers, DE to MR, 16 January 1901
28. Gelardi, pp.172–3, DE to MR, 26 January 1901
29. John Wimbles Papers, DE to MR, 26 January 1901

Part IV: The Edwardian Era 1901–10

Chapter 1
1. Esher, I, p.279
2. Lutyens, pp.151–2, Sir Frederick Ponsonby to Lady Lytton, 26 January 1901
3. John Wimbles Papers, DE to MR, 26 January 1901
4. Frankland, p.217
5. Duff, *Whisper Louise*, p.126
6. Battiscombe, pp.143–4

7. Battiscombe, p.216
8. Airlie, 106
9. Magnus, p. 290, A to V, 14 May 1901
10. *New York Times*, 'Lord Rosebery to marry a Princess?' 11 July 1901
11. Zeepvat, 'Worth telling', Part 2
12. Lady Leonie Leslie Papers, DC to LL, 20 June 1902, Box 1, Folder 3
13. Frankland, p.218
14. Zeepvat, *From Cradle*, p.159, Duke of Connaught to FK, 17 April 1902
15. Lady Leonie Leslie Papers, DC to LL, 30 May 1904, Box 1, Folder 3
16. Lady Leonie Leslie Papers, DC to LL, 4 September 1904, Box 1, Folder 3
17. John Wimbles Papers, DE to MR, 25 July 1905
18. Trowbridge, pp.223–4

Chapter 2
1. Marie, Grand Duchess, *Things I Remember*, p.56
2. Quinlan, p.17
3. Gelardi, p.175
4. Mandache, *Dearest Missy*, p.283, DE to MR, 21 March 1897
5. Zeepvat, *From Cradle*, p.167, 12 February 1902, DE to MR
6. John Wimbles Papers, DE to MR, 4 October 1905
7. John Wimbles Papers, DE to MR, 25 July 1905
8. John Wimbles Papers, DE to MR, 10 November 1905
9. RA VIC/ADDA30/1212 Charles, Duke of Saxe-Coburg to DA, 22 November 1908
10, 11, 12. RA, Madrid, Alfonso XIII, Secretaría particular Reina Cristina, box 25.024, exp. 1, 12 December 1904
13. Frankland, p.236
14. Lady Leonie Leslie Papers, DC to LL, 17 January 1905, Box 1, Folder 4
15. Frankland, p.238
16. John Wimbles Papers, DE to MR, 2 March 1905
17. Lady Leonie Leslie Papers, Princess Margaret of Connaught to LL, 10 March 1905, Box 1, Folder 7
18. Lady Leonie Leslie Papers, DC to LL, 15 March 1905, Box 1, Folder 4
19. Noel, p.47
20. RA Madrid, Alfonso XIII, Secretaría particular Reina Cristina, box 25.024, exp. 1, 6 July 1905
21. RA Madrid, Alfonso XIII, Secretaría particular Reina Cristina, box 25.024, exp. 1, 23 July 1905
22. Lady Leonie Leslie Papers, Princess Margaret of Connaught to LL, 25 January 1906, Box 1, Folder 7
23. RA GV/PRIV/AA33/28, Queen Alexandra to Prince of Wales, 15 March 1906
24. Marie zu Erbach-Schonberg, *Reminiscences*, p.321
25. Sagrera, p.147, DE to MR, n.d

Chapter 3
1. Lady Leonie Leslie Papers, DC to LL, 25 June 1905, Box 1, Folder 4
2. Lady Leonie Leslie Papers, Princess Margaret of Connaught to LL, undated (probably 1906), Box 1, Folder 4

Notes   213

3. Magnus, p.427–8, E to Asquith, 15 July 1909
4. Sagrera, p.156, DE to MR, 11 May 1908
5. Sagrera, p.169, Infanta Beatrice to Alfonso XIII, 12 July 1909
6. Sagrera, p.169, DE to Alfonso XIII, 13 July 1909
7. Sagrera, p.169, DE to Alfonso XIII, 14 July 1909
8. Daisy, Princess of Pless, pp.176–7
9. Ridley, *Bertie*, pp.431–2, Margot Asquith diary, 1 April 1909
10. Ridley, *Bertie*, p.458
11. John Wimbles Papers, DE to MR, May 1910
12. Esher, III, 1

Part V: The Georgian Era 1910–25

Chapter 1
1. Edwards, p.81
2. Fitzroy, *Memoirs*, II, p.409
3. Pope-Hennessy, QM, p.422; Battiscombe, p.273, Grand Duchess Augusta to Queen Mary, 24 May 1910
4. Pope-Hennessy, QM, p.441
5. Ridley, *George V*, p.336
6. Battiscombe, p.287
7. Windsor, p.83
8. Vorres, p.53
9. Battiscombe, pp. 278, 282
10. Sagrera, p.191, DE to Infanta Beatrice, 12 December 1911
11. Sagrera, p.201, DE to Infanta Beatrice, 6 December 1912
12. Frankland, p.283
13. Friedrich Leopold, p.212
14. John Wimbles Papers, DE to MR, 24–5 June 1914

Chapter 2
1. RA VIC/MAIN/ADDA15/6509 George V to Duke of Connaught, 29 July 1914
2. Lady Leonie Leslie Papers, Box 1, Folder 5, DC to LL, 20 November 1914
3. *The Times*, 16 March 1917
4. Harwood, p.55, DE to MR, 27 October 1914
5. Sagrera, p.245, Grand Duchess Vladimir to MR, 14 October 1916
6. Battiscombe, p.285; Rose, p.173
7. Windsor, p.83
8. Bing, p.292, 1/15 February 1915
9. Battiscombe, p.284, A to Admiral Fisher, 21 January 1915
10. RA VIC/ADDA30/990 DA to Princess Alice 17 April 1915
11. Sagrera, p.244, DE to MR
12. Mandache, 'Always Imperial'
13. Sullivan, p.290, DE to MR, 4 November 1916
14. Marie, Queen of Roumania, III, p.107, 7 December 1916
15. Sagrera, p.248, Infanta Beatrice to MR, p.248
16. Sagrera, p.254, Infanta Beatrice to MR, 15 May 1917
17. Sagrera, p.257, Infanta Beatrice to MR, p.257

18. Lady Leonie Leslie Papers, DC to LL, 30 December 1915, Box 1, Folder 5
19. *The Times*, 15 March 1917
20. Baird, p.134, Princess Helena to Emily Baird, 19 March 1917
21. Lady Leonie Leslie Papers, Princess Margaret of Connaught to LL, 23 March 1917, Box 1, Folder 5
22. Hart-Davis, p. 39
23. Aronson, *Alice*, p.211
24. Pakula, p.223, DE to MR, 16 August 1917
25. Pakula, p.301
26. Mandache, *Later Chapters*, pp.76–7, MR diary, 11 April 1919
27. Buchanan, p.119
28. Mandache, *Later Chapters*, p.116
29. Mandache, *Later Chapters*, pp. 116–7
30. Pakula, pp.301–2, MR to Joseph Boyle, 21 August 1920
31. RA GV AA43/314 MR to George V, 29 November 1920
32. Sagrera, p.278, Grand Duchess Cyril to Grand Duchess Xenia, December 1920

Chapter 3
1. John Wimbles Papers, Grand Duchess Cyril to MR, 12 February 1921
2. RA VIC/ADDA30/1050 DA to Princess Alice, 2 July 1921
3. *The Times*, 4 September 1922
4. Batttiscombe, p.280
5. Aronson, *Family of Kings*, 216
6. Ridley, *George V*, p.336
7. Warnes, 'Queen Alexandra'

Bibliography

Correspondence

Hanna Holborn Gray Special Collections Research Center, University of Chicago Library. Papers of Lady Leonie Leslie, including letters of Louise, Duchess of Connaught, and Princess Margaret of Connaught, later Crown Princess of Sweden

John Wimbles Papers, Archivo Orleans-Borbón, Sanlúcar de Barrameda, Spain. Letters of Marie, Duchess of Saxe-Coburg Gotha, and Grand Duchess Cyril of Russia

Leeds Russian Archive, University of Leeds Special Collections. Letters of Marie, Duchess of Edinburgh, later Duchess of Saxe-Coburg Gotha

Royal Archives, Madrid. Letters of Marquis de Villalobar to Don Alfonso de Aguilar

Royal Archives, Windsor. Letters of Louise, Duchess of Connaught, Helen, Duchess of Albany, and Queen Marie of Roumania

Books

Airlie, Mabel, Countess of, *Thatched with Gold: The Memoirs of Mabel, Countess of Airlie* (London: Hutchinson, 1962)

Alexandra, Queen, *Queen Alexandra's Christmas Gift Book: Photographs From my Camera* (London: Daily Telegraph, 1908)

Alice, Princess, Countess of Athlone, *For my Grandchildren: Some Reminiscences of HRH Princess Alice* (London: Evans Bros, 1966)

Aronson, Theo, *A Family of Kings: The Descendants of Christian IX of Denmark* (London: Cassell, 1976)

—— *Princess Alice, Countess of Athlone* (London: Cassell, 1981)

Aston, Sir George, H.R.H. *The Duke of Connaught and Strathearn: A Life and Intimate Study* (London: Harrap, 1929)

Baird, Diana, arr., *Victorian days and a Royal Friendship* (Worcester: Littlebury, 1968)

Barkhatova, A.D. & Burkova, T.V. ed., *The Danish Princess Marie Sophie Friederike Dagmar – the Russian Empress Maria Feodorovna* (St Petersburg: Alibris, 2006)

Battiscombe, Georgina, *Queen Alexandra* (London: Constable, 1969)

Belyakova, Zoya, *Grand Duke Alexei Alexandrovitch: Pros and Cons* (St Petersburg: Logos, 2004)

Bennett, Daphne, *Queen Victoria's Children* (London: Victor Gollancz, 1980)

Bing, Edward J. ed., *Letters of Tsar Nicholas and Empress Marie: Being the Confidential Correspondence Between Nicholas II, Last of the Tsars, and His Mother, Dowager Empress Maria Feodorovna* (London: Nicolson & Watson, 1938)

Buchanan, Meriel, *Queen Victoria's Relations* (London: Cassell, 1954)

Cadbury, Deborah, *Queen Victoria's Matchmaking: The Royal Marriages that Shaped Europe* (London: Bloomsbury, 2017)

Churchill, Lady Randolph (Mrs. George Cornwallis-West), *The Reminiscences of Lady Randolph Churchill* (London: Edward Arnold, 1908)

Corti, Egon Caesar Conte, *The Downfall of Three Dynasties* (London: Methuen, 1934)
—— *The English Empress: A Study in the Relations Between Queen Victoria and her Eldest Daughter, Empress Frederick of Germany* (London: Cassell, 1957)
Daisy, Princess of Pless, *Daisy, Princess of Pless by Herself* (London: John Murray, 1929)
Dennison, Matthew, *The Last Princess: The Devoted Life of Queen Victoria's Youngest Daughter* (London: Weidenfeld & Nicolson, 2007)
Derby, Lady Catherine, Countess of, *A Great Lady's Friendships: Letters to Mary, Marchioness of Salisbury, Countess of Derby, 1862–1890* (London: Macmillan, 1933)
Duff, David, *Alexandra: Princess and Queen* (London: Collins, 1980)
—— *Hessian Tapestry* (London: Frederick Muller, 1967)
—— *Whisper Louise: Edward VII and Mrs Cresswell* (London: Frederick Muller, 1974)
Edwards, Anne, *Matriarch: Queen Mary and the House of Windsor* (London: Hodder & Stoughton, 1984)
Esher, Viscount, *Journals and Letters of Reginald, Viscount Esher*, 4 vols. (London: Ivor Nicholson & Watson, 1934)
Fitzroy, Sir Almeric, *Memoirs*, 2 vols. (London: Hutchinson, 1920)
Fontenoy, Marquise de (Margaret Cunliffe-Owen), *The Marquise de Fontenoy's Revelation of High Life Within Royal Palaces* (Philadelphia: Edgewood, 1892)
Frankland, Noble, *Witness of a Century: The Life and Times of Prince Arthur, Duke of Connaught, 1850–1942* (London: Shepheard-Walwyn, 1993)
Friedrich Leopold of Prussia, Princess, *Behind the Scenes at the Prussian Court* (London: John Murray, 1939)
Gelardi, Julia P., *From Splendor to Revolution: The Romanov Women 1847–1928* (New York: St Martin's Griffin, 2011)
Hall, Coryne, *Little Mother of Russia: A Biography of the Empress Marie Feodorovna* (London: Shepheard-Walwyn, 1999)
—— *Queen Victoria and the Romanovs: Sixty Years of Mutual Distrust* (Stroud: Amberley, 2020)
Hamilton, Lord Frederick, *The Vanished Pomps of Yesterday: Being Some Random Reminiscences of a British Diplomat* (London: Hodder & Stoughton, 1919)
Harwood, Maria, ed., *The Last Romanovs: Archival and Museum Discoveries in Great Britain and Russia* (London: Pindar, 2018)
Hough, Richard, sel., *Advice to a Granddaughter: Letters from Queen Victoria to Princess Victoria of Hesse* (London: Heinemann, 1975)
Kennedy, A.L., ed., *My Dear Duchess: Social and Political Letters to the Duchess of Manchester, 1858–1869* (London: John Murray, 1956)
Kehoe, Elisabeth, *Fortune's Daughters: The Extravagant Lives of the Jerome Sisters* (London: Atlantic, 2004)
Khorvatova, F.V., *Marie Feodorovna: The Fate of the Empress* (Moscow: Ast-Press, 2006)
Leslie, Anita, *Edwardians in Love* (London: Hutchinson, 1972)
—— *Jennie: The Life of Lady Randolph Churchill* (London: Hutchinson, 1969)
Longford, Elizabeth, *Victoria R.I.* (London: Weidenfeld & Nicolson, 1964)
—— ed. *Darling Loosy: Letters to Princess Louise 1856–1939* (London: Weidenfeld & Nicolson, 1991)
Lutyens, Mary, ed., *Lady Lytton's Court Diary, 1895–1899* (London: Rupert Hart-Davis, 1961)
Madol, Hans Roger, *Christian IX* (London: Collins, 1939)
Magnus, Philip, *King Edward the Seventh* (London: John Murray, 1964)

Mallet, Victor, ed., *Life with Queen Victoria: Marie Mallet's Letters from Court, 1887–1901* (London: John Murray, 1968)

Mandache, Diana, *Later Chapters of my Life: The Lost Memoir of Queen Marie of Roumania* (Stroud: Sutton, 2004)

—— ed. *Dearest Missy: The Correspondence between Marie, Grand Duchess of Russia, Duchess of Edinburgh and of Saxe-Coburg and Gotha and her Daughter, Marie, Crown Princess of Roumania, 1879–1900* (Falkoping, Sweden: Rosvall, 2011)

Marie, Grand Duchess of Russia, *Things I Remember* (London: Cassell, 1930)

Marie zu Erbach-Schonberg, Princess of Battenberg, *Reminiscences* (London: Allen & Unwin, 1925)

Marie, Queen of Roumania, *The Story of my Life*, 3 vols. (London: Cassell, 1934–5)

Millar, Oliver, *The Victorian Paintings in the Collection of Her Majesty the Queen* (Cambridge: Cambridge University Press, 1992)

Monypenny, W.F. & Buckle, G.E., *The Life of Benjamin Disraeli, Earl of Beaconsfield*, 6 vols. (London: John Murray, 1910–20)

Newsome, David, *On the Edge of Paradise: A.C. Benson the Diarist* (London: John Murray, 1980)

Noel, Gerard, *Ena, Spain's English Queen* (London: Constable, 1984)

Packard, Jerrold M.: *Farewell in Splendour: The Death of Queen Victoria and her Age* (Stroud: Sutton, 2000)

—— *Victoria's Daughters* (Stroud: Sutton, 1999)

Paget, Walburga, *Embassies of Other Days* (London: Hutchinson, 1923)

Pakula, Hannah, *The Last Romantic: A Biography of Queen Marie of Roumania* (London: Weidenfeld & Nicolson, 1984)

Ponsonby, Arthur, *Henry Ponsonby: His Life from His Letters* (London: Macmillan, 1942)

Pope-Hennessy, James, *Queen Mary, 1867–1953* (London: Allen & Unwin, 1959)

Quinlan, Paul D., *Playboy King: Carol II of Roumania* (Westport, CT: Praeger, 1995)

Ramm, Agatha, ed., *Political Correspondence of Mr Gladstone and Lord Granville, 1868–1876* (London: Royal Historical Society, 1952)

Rennell, Tony, *Days of Glory: The Death of Queen Victoria* (London: Viking, 2000)

Ridley, Jane, *Bertie: A Life of Edward VII* (London: Chatto & Windus, 2012)

—— *George V: Never a Dull Moment* (London: Chatto & Windus, 2021)

Röhl, John C.G., *Young Wilhelm: The Kaiser's Early Life, 1859–1888* (Cambridge University Press, 1998)

Rose, Kenneth, *King George V* (London: Weidenfeld & Nicolson, 1983)

Sagrera, Ana de, *Ena y Bee: En defensa de una Amistad (Ena and Bee: In defence of a royal friendship)* (Madrid: Velecio Editores, 2006) – English draft translation

St Aubyn, Giles, *Edward VII, Prince and King* (London: Collins, 1979)

Stanley, Lady Augusta, *Later Letters of Lady Augusta Stanley, 1864–1876*, ed., Dean of Windsor & Hector Bolitho (London: Jonathan Cape, 1929)

Sullivan, Michael John, *A Fatal Passion: The Story of Victoria Melita, the Uncrowned last Empress of Russia* (New York: Random House, 1997)

Trowbridge, W.R.H., *Queen Alexandra: A Study of Royalty* (London: T. Fisher Unwin, 1921)

Van der Kiste, John, *Alfred: Queen Victoria's Second Son* (Stroud: Fonthill Media, 2013)

—— *Edward VII's Children* (Gloucester: Alan Sutton, 1989)

—— *Queen Victoria's Children* (Gloucester: Alan Sutton, 1986)

—— *The Romanovs: Tsar Alexander II of Russia and his Family, 1818–1959* (Gloucester: Sutton, 1998)

—— *Princess Victoria Melita: Grand Duchess Cyril of Russia, 1876–1936* (Gloucester: Alan Sutton, 1991)

Victoria, Queen, *The Letters of Queen Victoria: a Selection from Her Majesty's Correspondence between the years 1837 and 1861*, ed. A.C. Benson & Viscount Esher, 3 vols (London: John Murray, 1907)

—— *The Letters of Queen Victoria, 2nd Series: A Selection from Her Majesty's Correspondence and Journal between the years 1862 and 1885*, ed. G. E. Buckle, 3 vols. (London: John Murray, 1926–8)

—— *The Letters of Queen Victoria, 3rd Series: a Selection from Her Majesty's Correspondence and Journal between the years 1886 and 1901*; ed. G.E. Buckle, 3 vols. (London: John Murray, 1930–2)

—— *Further Letters of Queen Victoria, From the Archives of the House of Brandenburg-Prussia*; ed. Hector Bolitho (London: Thornton Butterworth, 1938)

—— *Dearest Child: Letters between Queen Victoria and the Princess Royal, 1858–1861*; ed. Roger Fulford (London: Evans Bros, 1964)

—— *Dearest Mama: Private Correspondence of Queen Victoria and the Crown Princess of Prussia, 1861–1864*; ed. Roger Fulford (London: Evans Bros, 1968)

—— *Your Dear Letter: Private Correspondence of Queen Victoria and the Crown Princess of Prussia, 1865–1871*, ed. Roger Fulford, Evans Bros, 1971

—— *Darling Child: Private Correspondence of Queen Victoria and the Crown Princess of Prussia, 1871–1878*; ed. Roger Fulford (London: Evans Bros, 1976)

—— *Beloved Mama: Private Correspondence of Queen Victoria and the German Crown Princess of Prussia, 1878–1885*; ed. Roger Fulford (London: Evans Bros, 1981)

Victoria, Consort of Frederick III, Emperor, *The Empress Frederick Writes to Sophie, her Daughter, Crown Princess and later Queen of the Hellenes: Letters 1889–1901*, ed. Arthur Gould Lee (Faber, 1955)

—— *Letters of the Empress Frederick*, ed. Sir Frederick Ponsonby (London: Macmillan, 1928)

Vorres, Ian, *The last Grand Duchess: Her Imperial Highness Grand Duchess Olga Alexandrovna* (London: Hutchinson, 1964)

Vovk, Justin C., *Imperial Requiem: Four Royal Women and the Fall of the Age of Empires* (Bloomington, IN: iUniverse, 2012)

Warwick, Christopher, *Ella: Princess, Saint and Martyr* (Chichester: John Wiley, 2006)

Wimbles, John, 'The Daughter of Tsar Alexander II: Grand Duchess Marie Alexandrovna.' In *The Grand Duchesses: Daughters and Granddaughters of Russia's Tsars* (Oakland, CA: Eurohistory, 2004)

Windsor, Edward, Duke of, formerly King Edward VIII, *A King's Story: Memoirs* (London: Cassell, 1951)

Zeepvat, Charlotte, *From Cradle to Crown: British Nannies and Governesses at the World's Royal Courts* (Stroud: Sutton, 2006)

—— *Prince Leopold: The Untold Story of Queen Victoria's Youngest Son* (Stroud: Sutton, 1998)

Journals
European Royalty History Journal
The Graphic
Punch
Royalty Digest

The New York Times
The Times

Journal articles
Abrash, Merritt, 'A Curious Royal Romance: The Queen's Son and the Tsar's Daughter', *Slavonic and East European Review*, July 1969 (No 109)
Anon., 'The Prince of Wales and his Destined Bride', *The Times*, 5 July 1858
Fotescu, Diana, 'The Marriage of Princess Marie of Edinburgh and Ferdinand Crown Prince of Roumania', *Royalty Digest*, May 2001 (No 119)
Gill, Crispin. 'Duchess [of Edinburgh] was "too grand for Plymouth"', *Western Morning News*, 8 April 1985
Goliczov, Roman Ilmar, 'Grand Duchess Marie Alexandrovna and Music', *Royalty Digest*, August 2004 (No 153)
Mandache, Diana, 'Always Imperial', *Majesty*, October 2010 (Vol 31, No 10)
Wimbles, John, 'Death and the Duchess [of Edinburgh and Saxe-Coburg Gotha], *Royalty Digest*, January 2001 (No 115)
—— 'A forgotten princess: Alexandra of Hohenlohe-Langenburg', 3 parts, *Royalty Digest*, March-May 2005 (Nos 165–7)
Zeepvat, Charlotte, '"Mrs Arthur"', 2 parts, *Royalty Digest*, July-August 2004 (Nos 157–8)
—— 'Worth telling: Louisa, Lady Knightley of Fawsley and the royal family', 2 parts, *Royalty Digest*, April-May 2005 (Nos 166–7)

Internet (accessed January 2019–November 2021)
Alexander Palace Time Machine:
http://forum.alexanderpalace.org/index.php?topic=4567.240

Queen Victoria's Journals
http://www.queenvictoriasjournals.org

Royal Collection Trust
https://www.rct.uk

Warnes, Kathy, 'Queen Alexandra of Great Britain - Queen Victoria's daughter-in-law, Bertie's patient wife, and her own person'
https://windowstoworldhistory.weebly.com

Wright, Anne, 'Helena Frederica Augusta of Waldeck-Pyrmont'
https://people.elmbridgehundred.org.uk/biographies/helena-frederica-augusta/

Index

Adlerberg, Count Nicholas (1848-1916), 154
Aguilar, Don Alfonso de, 155-6, 160
Alastair, Duke of Connaught (1914-43), 194
Albert Edward, Prince of Wales *see* Edward VII
Albert I, King of the Belgians (1875-1934), 204
Albert of Saxe-Altenburg, Prince (1843-1902), 95
Albert Victor, Duke of Clarence (1864-92), 175
    birth, 18
    character, 53, 97
    betrothal and death, 99-100
Albert, Prince Consort (1819-61), ix, 5, 29, 59, 63, 69, 101
    wedding, 3
    and question of bride for Prince of Wales, 10
    death, 11
Alexander II, Tsar of Russia (1818-81), 30
    and Marie's betrothal and wedding, 31-3, 36-7
    visit to England, 41-2
    declares war on Turkey, 74
    and Catherine Dolgorouky, 75-7
    assassinated, 77
Alexander III, Tsar of Russia (1845-94), 31, 100
    wedding, 20, 78
    dislike of Queen Victoria, 78
    death, 109
Alexander John of Wales, Prince (b. & d.1871), 25
Alexander of Hesse, Prince (1823-88), 34, 76
Alexander of Teck, Prince, Earl of Athlone (1874-1957), 104
Alexander, Duke of Fife (1849-1912), 98
Alexander, Earl of Athlone (1874-1957), 187, 199
Alexandra of Edinburgh, Princess ('Sandra') (1878-1942), 191
    birth, 75
    childhood, 101-2
    engagement and wedding, 109-10
    and Beatrice's wedding, 166
    political anxieties and ill-health, 177-8
    and mother's death, 197
Alexandra, Duchess of Fife (1891-1959), 98, 181
Alexandra, Empress of Russia (1872-1918), 108, 150, 153, and Nicholas II's accession, 109, coronation, 111
Alexandra, Grand Duchess of Russia (1870-91), 150
Alexandra, Queen (1844-1925), 131, 181, 182
    birth, 7
    childhood, 8
    considered as bride for Prince of Wales, 8-11
    betrothal and wedding, 12-5
    and first year of married life, 16
    and Schleswig-Holstein disputes, 17, 19
    and birth of Albert Victor, 18
    visit to Denmark (1864), 19
    and birth of children, 19-20, 23, 25-6
    lameness and deafness, 20-1, 26-7, 141, 169, 175, 202
    character and popularity, 21, 25, 73-4
    visit to Ireland (1868), 23
    upbringing of and devotion to family, 24, 51, 53-4, 97, 148-9, 176
    and Prince of Wales's typhoid, 26-7
    and relations with Queen Victoria, 28, 91
    and question of precedence over Duchess of Edinburgh, 40-2, 46
    at Alfred of Edinburgh's christening, 44
    and Prince of Wales' visit to India, 52
    and Russo-Turkish war, 75
    at Alexander II's funeral, 77-8
    and Merrick, 79
    and reform bill demonstration, 79-80

visit to Dublin, 80
and Egyptian crisis, 80-1
nursing, welfare, charity work and hospital visits, 81, 112, 116, 175, 186
and silver wedding, 96
and Frederick III's funeral, 96
and death of Duke of Clarence, 98
and Edinburgh nieces, 102
at deathbed of Alexander III, 109
and attempt on Prince of Wales' life, 117-8
at Queen Victoria's deathbed, 135
and husband's accession, 139
and changed family relationships, 141
moves to Windsor, 142
at Empress Frederick's funeral, 143
relations with Duchess of Connaught, 146-8
and death of Christian IX, 149
at Hvidøre, and painting and photography, 149
and Ena's engagement and marriage, 161
and Heligoland affair, 167
and state visit to Berlin, 167-8
attends House of Commons debate, 169
at Edward VII's death and funeral, 170, 173-4
moves to Marlborough House and retains Sandringham as main home, 174
absent from George V's coronation, 175
and Parliament Act, 177
demands removal of banners in St George's Chapel, 186
at Hyde Park review, and John's death, 202
last years and death, 203-4
Alexandrine, Duchess of Saxe-Coburg Gotha (1820-1904), 4, 29
Alexis, Grand Duke of Russia (1850-1908), 31, 44, 76, 154
Alfonso XIII, King of Spain (1886-1941), 155-6, 159-61, 178
arguments with Duchess of Coburg, 165-6
estrangement from Ena, 188-9
sends Ali and Beatrice to Switzerland, 188
Alfonso, Infante of Spain ('Ali') (1886-1975), 162, 178, 183, 191, 196
military service in Africa, 165-6, 179
exiled to Switzerland, 188-9

Alfred of Edinburgh, Prince (1874-99), 101
birth, 43
christening, 53
military studies, 103
dissolute life and death, 122-3, 133
Alfred, Duke of Edinburgh, later Duke of Saxe-Coburg Gotha (1844-1900), 13, 28, 62, 145, 150
birth, 3
character, 4, 103, 106-7
elected King of Greece, 17, 29
attempt on life of, 23, 29-30
joins navy, and created Duke of Edinburgh, 29
betrothal and wedding, 30-8
at Clarence House, 39
at Eastwell Park, 43
and love of music, 44-5
at Balmoral, 47
and Mediterranean Fleet, 74, 87
and Queen Victoria's attitude to Russia, 75
at Coburg, 75, 101, 106
at Alexander III's coronation, 86
relinquishes command of Mediterranean Fleet, 91
and golden jubilee, 92
Commander-in-Chief at Devonport, 102, 105
heavy drinking, 103
accession to duchy of Saxe-Coburg, 105
at deathbed of Alexander III, 109
at diamond jubilee, 112
ill-health, 123
and Coburg succession, 124-8
final days and death, 130-2
Alice, Countess of Athlone (1883-1981), 63, 64, 67, 118, 120, 200
birth, 66
childhood activities and interests, 71-2, 120
at Coburg, 126-7
love of Claremont, 187
in Cannes, 199
Alice, Grand Duchess of Hesse and the Rhine (1843-78), 24, 71, 81, 86
birth, 3
wedding, 13
and Marie's betrothal, 32, 35
death, 59
Alonso, Infante of Spain (1912-36), 179
Amelie, Queen of Portugal (1865-1951), 157

Andersen, Hans Christian (1805-75), 7
Andersen, Hans Niels (1852-1937), 186
Anna of Prussia, Princess (b. & d. 1858), 54
Arthur of Connaught, Prince (1883-1938), 62, 93-4, 159, 194
  birth, 62, 82, 84-5
  at Empress Frederick's funeral, 143
  wedding, 181
Arthur, Duke of Connaught (1850-1942), 43
  birth, 3
  character, 4-5, 54, 156
  engagement and marriage, 54-9
  army career, 82
  in India, 83, 94-5
  and golden jubilee, 92
  visits far east, 94
  at Nicholas II's coronation, 111
  in Egypt, 114, 164
  and friendship with Leonie Leslie, 115-6
  and Coburg succession, 123-7, 132, 134
  ill-health, 133
  in Dublin, 140
  at Empress Frederick's funeral, 143
  relations with Edward VII, 146-8, 157
  in Portugal, Spain, and Africa, 157-8
  Inspector-General of Army, 163
  and Malta command, 163-4
  and Governor-Generalship of Canada, 164, 180, 183-4
  told of Edward VII's death, 173
  good relations with George V, 179
  and wife's death and funeral, 192-3
  death, 194
Asquith, Herbert (1852-1928), 164
Asquith, Margot (1864-1945), 168
Augusta of Mecklenburg-Strelitz, Grand Duchess (1822-1916), 9
Augusta Victoria, German Empress (1858-1921), 167, 181
Augusta, German Empress (1811-90), 35, 58
Augusta, Grand Duchess of Mecklenburg-Strelitz (1822-1916), 174

Baird, Emily (1846-1926), 193
Balfour, Arthur (1848-1930), 159
Battiscombe, Georgina (1905-2006), 142, 204
Beatrice of Edinburgh, Princess, later Infanta of Spain ('Bee') (1884-1966), 107
  birth, 86
  childhood, 101-2, 110
  at Nicholas II's coronation, 111
  travels as mother's companion, 112, 131, 133-4, 140, 150
  and Grand Duke Michael, 152, 161
  betrothal and wedding, 161-2, 165-6
  in Coburg at outbreak of First World War, 183
  returns to Spain after exile, 178
  exiled to Switzerland, 188-9
  accused by Victoria Melita of abandoning her, 191
  reunited with mother, 196
  and mother's death, 197
Beatrice, Princess Henry of Battenberg (1857-1944), 35, 78, 94
  birth, 3
  and Duchess of Edinburgh (later Duchess of Coburg), 46, 132, 182
  betrothal and marriage, 70-1
  and Connaught children, 86, 93
  comforted by Duchess of Albany in widowhood, 113
  and possibility of Ena's marriage to Alfonso XIII, 156-7, 159
  charity work, 187, 199
Benson, Arthur (1862-1925), 113
Beresford, Lord Charles (1846-1919), 97
Bernhard of Saxe-Meiningen, Prince (1851-1928), 55
Bismarck, Otto von (1815-98), 55, 74
Blagge, Mr, 26-8
Borden, Robert (1854-1937), 183
Boris, Grand Duke of Russia (1877-1943), 129, 156
Boyle, Joseph (1867-1923), 197
Brotherstone, Mrs, 61
Brown, John, 48
Brunov, Baron de, 36
Buchanan, Sir Andrew (1807-82), 32
Bülow, Bernhard von, father (1815-79), 8
Bülow, Bernhard von, son (1849-1929), 8

Cantacuzino, Zizi, 129
Carlos, King of Portugal (1863-1908), 157-8
Carol I, King of Roumania (1839-1914), 103, 129
Carol II, King of Roumania (1893-1953), 107
Carrington, Charles Wynn-Carington, Baron (1843-1928), 84-5
Carroll, Lewis (1832-98), 72
Chapman, Sarah, 147
Chapman, Susan, 61-2

Charles, Duke of Albany, later Duke of
    Saxe-Coburg Gotha (1884-1954), 166
  birth, 69
  childhood, 71, 118
  and Coburg succession, 124-8
  becomes Duke of Coburg, 132, 146
  education in Coburg, 145
  comes of age and assumes full powers,
    154-5, 177
  wedding, 155
  during First World War, 188
  deprived of titles after First World War,
    199
  and mother's last visits to Germany, 200
Charles III, King (b.1948), 204
Charlotte of Wales, Princess (1796-1817),
    13, 64, 66
Charlotte, Princess of Saxe-Meiningen
    (1860-1919), 55, 104
Chesterfield, George Stanhope, Earl of
    (1831-71), 26-7
Christian IX, King of Denmark, formerly
    Prince Christian of Schleswig-Holstein-
    Sonderburg-Glucksburg (1818-1906), 7,
    10, 24
  accession, and and war over Schleswig-
    Holstein, 17-8
  disapproved of by Queen Victoria, 53
  death, 149
Christian X, King of Denmark
    (1870-1947), 204
Christian Victor of Schleswig-Holstein,
    Prince (1867-1900), 134
Churchill, Lady Randolph (1854-1925),
    45, 115
Churchill, Lord Randolph (1849-95), 45
Churchill, Winston (1874-1965), 115
Clarendon, George Villiers, Earl of
    (1800-70), 15
Clifden, Nellie, 11
Collins, Robert (1841-1908), 66, 70, 124-6
Conroy, Sir John (1786-1854), viii, 16
Constantine I, King of Greece (1868-1923),
    193
Creak, Eliza, 118-9
Cyril, Grand Duke of Russia (1876-1938),
    152-4, 195

Daisy of Pless, Princess (1873-1943), 168
Derby, Edward Stanley, Earl of
    (1799-1869), 22
Diana, Princess of Wales (1961-97), 204
Dickens, Charles (1812-70), 15, 72

Dickum, Carl van (1804-93), 9
Disraeli, Benjamin, Earl of Beaconsfield
    (1804-81), 23, 39, 59, 75
Dmitri, Grand Duke of Russia (1891-1942),
    150, 190
Dolgorouky, Princess Catherine (1847-1922),
    32-3, 75-7
Dufferin and Ava, Frederick Blackwood,
    Marquis of (1826-1902), 76

Edberg, Nancy (1832-92), 7
Edward VII, King (1841-1910), 36, 104,
    131, 181, 204
  birth, 3
  character, 3-4
  tour of North America, 6
  Alexandra sought as bride for, 8-11
  betrothal and wedding, 12, 14-5
  and first year of married life, 16
  infidelity and lack of attention to wife,
    20-2
  unpopularity, 21, 25
  visit to Ireland (1868), 23
  and upbringing of children, 24
  and birth of Maud, 25
  and Alexander John, 25-6
  and typhoid, 26-7
  and Duchess of Edinburgh, 46
  and visit to India, 52
  at Alexander II's funeral, 78
  and reform bill demonstration, 79-80
  visit to Dublin, 80
  silver wedding, and at Frederick III's
    funeral, 96
  and Tranby Croft affair, 98
  and death of Duke of Clarence, 99-100
  at Alexander III's deathbed, 109
  and Alice Keppel, 114
  and attempt on life of husband, 116-7
  and Coburg succession, 126
  and death of Alfred, 131-3
  accession, 139
  and family changes, 141-2
  at Empress Frederick's funeral, 143
  coronation postponed, 144
  relations as King with Duke and
    Duchess of Connaught, 146-8, 157
  and Ena's engagement and marriage,
    159, 161
  offers Duke of Connaught Malta
    command, 163-4
  state visit to Berlin, 167-8
  death, 169
  funeral, 173

Edward, Duke of Kent and Strathearn (1767-1820), 3
Edward, Prince of Wales, later Edward VIII (1894-1972), 175, 182
Egerton, Mary, 61
Elizabeth (Ella), Princess of Hesse and the Rhine, Grand Duchess of Russia (1864-1918), 86, 134, 150, 193, killed, 195
Elizabeth of Hesse and the Rhine, Princess (1895-1903), 151, 152
Elizabeth, Grand Duchess of Oldenburg (1857-95), 55, 94, 95
Elizabeth, Princess of Erbach-Schönberg (1873-1961), 201
Elizabeth, Queen of Roumania (Carmen Sylva) (1843-1916), 8
Elphinstone, Annie, Lady (1856-1938), 84, 92
Elphinstone, Sir Howard (1830-90), 56-7, 62, 92
Emich Charles, Prince of Leiningen (1763-1814), 3
Emma, Queen of the Netherlands (1858-1934), 55, 69, 126, 201
Ena, Queen of Spain (1887-1969), 156, 166, 179
  engagement and marriage, 159-62, 188-9
Ernest I, Duke of Saxe-Coburg Gotha (1784-1844), 3
Ernest II, Duke of Saxe-Coburg Gotha (1818-93), 4, 126, 130, 145, 150
  at Prince and Princess of Wales's wedding, 14
  character, 101
  death, 105
Ernest of Hohenlohe-Langenburg, Prince (1863-1950), 124
  betrothal and wedding, 109-10
  regent at Coburg, 132, 145, 177
Ernest, Grand Duke of Hesse (1868-1937), 107-8
  and problems in first marriage, 128-9, 134, 151
Esher, Reginald Brett, Viscount (1852-1930), 139, 170, 174
Eugenie, Empress of the French (1826-1920), 155-7
Eulalia, Infanta of Spain (1864-1958), 156, 165, 178-9

Feodora of Leiningen, Princess (1807-72), 17, 109

Ferdinand, King of Roumania (1865-1927), 103-4, 129-30, 144, 185
  unable to attend diamond jubilee, 112
  and threat of Roumanian defeat, 189
Ffoliott, Anne, 130
Fisher, Sir John, Baron (1841-1920), 186
Francis Ferdinand, Archduke of Austria (1863-1914), 183
Francis, Duke of Saxe-Coburg-Saalfeld (1750-1806), 3
Francis, Duke of Teck (1837-1900), 98
Frederica of Hanover, Princess (1848-1926), 63
Frederick Augustus, Grand Duke of Oldenburg (1852-1931), 55, 94
Frederick Charles of Prussia, Prince (1828-85), 54-5, 57, 157
  death, 95
Frederick III, German Emperor (1831-88), 12
  at Prince and Princess of Wales's wedding, 14
  on Alfred and Marie's betrothal, 35
  at Connaughts' wedding, 60
  reign and death, 96, 123
Frederick Leopold of Prussia, Prince (1865-1931), 54, 95, 181, 193
Frederick VII, King of Denmark (1808-63), 17
Frederick VIII, King of Denmark (1843-1912), 7, 201
Frederick, Count of Hohenau (1857-1914), 94
Frederick, Duke of Schleswig-Holstein (1829-80), 17
Frederick, Prince of Waldeck-Pyrmont (1865-1946), 201
Frith, William Powell (1819-1909), 15

Galitzin, Prince, 34
Gapon, Georgy ('Father') (1870-1906), 153
George I, King of Greece, formerly Prince William of Denmark (1845-1913), 7, 14, 75, 169, 201
  elected King of Greece, 17
  assassination, 177
George III, King (1738-1820), 3
George Michaelovich, Grand Duke of Russia (1863-1919), 103
George V, King (1865-1936), 21, 161, 182, 198
  birth, 19
  and naval service, 52-4

Index   225

created Duke of York, and wedding, 100
and possibility of betrothal to cousin
    Marie, 103-4
allowed to see official papers, 141
imperial tour (1901), 142
created Prince of Wales, 149
accession, 173
coronation, 174-5
and 'Motherdear's' selfishness, 176
and Parliament Act, 177
relations with Duke of Connaught, 179
on approach of World War I, 183
and removal of banners and princes'
    names from Order of Garter, 186, 188
and dislike of Alfonso XIII, 188
at Duchess of Connaught's funeral, 193
invites Queen Marie of Roumania to
    bring family to England, 195
devotion to Queen Alexandra in last
    years, and her funeral, 203-4
George V, King of Hanover (1819-78), 31
George VI, King (1895-1952), 175, 182, 194
George Victor, Prince of Waldeck-Pyrmont
    (1831-93), 75
George, Duke of Cambridge (1819-1904),
    9, 62, 133
George, Duke of Kent (1902-42), 175
Gilbert, Sir Alfred (1854-1934), 204
Gladstone, William Ewart (1809-98), 23,
    36, 113-4
and Egyptian crisis, 81
Gordon-Cumming, Sir Arthur (1848-1930),
    98
Gordon, Charles (1833-85), 80-1
Granville, Granville George Leveson-
    Gower, Earl (1815-91), 31, 33-4, 36
Gustav Adolf of Sweden, Prince (1906-47),
    163
Gustav Adolf of Sweden, Prince, later King
    Gustav VI Adolf (1882-1973), 158, 160
Gustav V, King of Sweden (1858-1950),
    158

Haakon VII, King of Norway, formerly
    Prince Charles of Denmark (1872-1957),
    101, 204
Harrison, Sir Richard (1837-1931), 102
Hartington, Spencer, Marquis of
    (1833-1908), 80
Helen, Duchess of Albany (1861-1922), 140
betrothal and wedding, 64-5
character, 64, 66
birth of Alice 66

charity work, 68, 118-20, 145, 187, 199
death of Leopold, 69
birth of Charles, 70
at service for anniversary of Leopold's
    death, 71
devotion to family, 72, 118-20
comforts Beatrice in widowhood, 113
religious views, 117
and Coburg succession, 124-8
rumours of betrothal to Lord Rosebery,
    and at Edward VII's coronation, 144
criticized by Duchess of Coburg, 154-5
at George V's coronation, 175
moves from Claremont to Kensington
    Palace, 187
visits Charles in Germany, 200
death and funeral, 201
Helena Victoria ('Thora') of Schleswig-
    Holstein, Princess (1870-1948), 110
Helena, Princess Christian of Schleswig-
    Holstein (1846-1923), 134
birth, 3
drug addiction, 67
and nursing work, 81
on Duchess of Connaught's death, 193
Helena, Princess of Waldeck-Pyrmont
    (1831-88), 63
Henry of Battenberg, Prince (1858-96), 93,
    94, 132
betrothal and wedding, 71
death, 113
Henry of Orange-Nassau, Prince
    (1820-79), 59
Henry, Duke of Gloucester (1900-74), 175
Herman VI, Prince of Hohenlohe-
    Langenburg (1832-1913), 109-10
Hohenthal, Walburga, later Lady Paget
    (1839-1929), 8, 9

Ileana of Roumania, Princess (1909-91),
    195

John, Prince (1905-19), 176, 202

Keppel, Alice (1868-1947), 114, 169
Keppel, George (1865-1947), 114
Kira, Grand Duchess of Russia (1909-67),
    182
Kitchener, Herbert Horatio (1850-1916),
    114
Knightley, Lady Louisa (1842-1913), 68,
    145
Knollys, Charlotte (1835-1930), 176, 203

226 Queen Victoria's Daughters-in-Law

Knollys, Sir Francis, Viscount (1837-1924), 22, 147
Kossikovskaya, Alexandra (1875-1923), 161

Laking, Dr Francis (1847-1914), 169
Larking, Adela, 60
Lascelles, Sir Alan (1887-1981), 194
Lawrence, T.E. (1888-1935), 203
Leopold I, King of the Belgians (1790-1865), 3, 12-4, 17, 64
Leopold II, King of the Belgians (1831-1909), 59
Leopold, Duke of Albany (1853-84), 72, 98, 118
 birth, 3
 ill-health, 5
 intellectual character 5-6
 and Duchess of Edinburgh, 46-7
 absent from Connaughts' wedding, 60
 academic achievements and hopes of employment, 62
 relations with Duchess of Edinburgh, 62-3
 betrothal and wedding, 63-5
 public engagements and birth of daughter, 66
 Queen Victoria's confidence in, 67
 visit to Cannes, death and funeral, 68-70, 78
Leopold, Prince of Hohenzollern-Sigmaringen (1835-1905), 104, 129
Leopoldine of Hohenlohe-Langenburg, Princess (1837-1903), 109
Leslie, Leonie (1859-1943), 115, 146-8, 158, 161, 163, 184, 193
Leslie, Sir John (1857-1944), 115, 147
Lipton, Thomas (1848-1931), 112
Loftus, Augustus, Lord (1817-1904), 33
Londesborough, William Denison, Earl of (1834-1900), 26
Lorne, John Campbell, Marquis of, later Duke of Argyll (1845-1914), 58, 144
Louis IV, Grand Duke of Hesse and the Rhine (1837-92), 13, 81
Louis of Battenberg, Prince, later Marquis of Milford Haven (1854-1921), 71
Louisa, Duchess of Manchester (1832-1911), 59
Louise of Orleans, Princess (1882-1958), 156
Louise Sophie of Schleswig-Holstein, Princess, later Princess Frederick

Leopold of Prussia (1866-1952), 61, 71, 95, 181, 193
Louise, Duchess of Argyll (1848-1939), 140
 birth, 3
 wedding, 25
 and Duke and Duchess of Connaught, 58, 85, 93, 159
 at Edward VII's coronation, 144
Louise, Duchess of Connaught (1860-1917), 132, 134, 140, 141
 early life, 54
 engagement and wedding, 56, 58-60
 and Duchess of Albany, 64
 character, 82, 120-1
 in India, 83-4
 and children, 85, 92-3
 visits far east, 94
 ill-health, 95, 180-1, 133
 at Balmoral, 95
 angry with William II, and sympathises with Empress Frederick, 96-7
 at Nicholas II's coronation, 111
 in Africa, 114-5, 164
 and Leonie Leslie, 115-6
 and Coburg succession, 123-8
 at Empress Frederick's funeral, 143
 relations with Edward VII and Alexandra, 146-8
 and possibility of Patricia as bride for Alfonso XIII, 156
 in Portugal, Spain, and Africa, 157-8
 finds England less congenial after Queen Victoria's death, 163
 at George V's coronation, 175
 in Canada, 180-1, 183, 192
 views on Germany, 184
 return to England, death and funeral, 192
Louise, Duchess of Fife (1867-1931), 24, 98
 birth, 20
 christening, 22
 and children's birthday party, 52
 shyness, 53
Louise, Queen of Denmark (1817-98), 7-10, 24
 disapproved of by Queen Victoria, 53
 death, 114
Luis Felipe, King of Portugal (1887-1908), 158
Lyttelton, Sarah, Lady (1787-1870), 4

Macclesfield, Mary, Countess of (1821-1912), 18, 24, 27

Index 227

Mallet, Marie (1862-1934), 72, 114, 117
Manning, Henry, Cardinal (1808-92), 69
Margaret of Connaught, Princess, later Crown Princess of Sweden (1882-1920), 82, 84-5, 93
  birth, 61
  'frightened of mother', 125
  in Portugal, Spain, and Africa, 157-8
  unable to attend mother's funeral, 193
  death, 194
Maria Cristina, Queen Dowager of Spain (1858-1929), 155
Maria of Greece, Princess, later Grand Duchess George of Russia (1876-1940), 193
Marianne of Prussia, Princess (1837-1906), 54-5
Marie Alexandrovna, Empress of Russia (1824-80), 35, 43, 76-7
Marie Feodorovna, Empress of Russia, formerly Dagmar of Denmark, Princess ('Minnie') (1847-1928), 8, 26, 100, 141
  birth, 7
  marriage, 20, 31
  at Alexander II's funeral, 78
  purchases Hvidøre with sister, 149
  angered by Victoria Melita's divorce, 154
  and Heligoland affair, 167
  urges Alexandra to claim precedence over Mary, 173-4
  possessiveness, 176
  and Duchess of Coburg, 182
  visits Queen Alexandra in last years, 202
Marie, Princess of Leiningen (1907-51), 182
Marie Louise, Princess (1872-1957), 187
Marie of Greece, Princess, later Grand Duchess George of Russia (1876-1940), 193
Marie of Saxe-Altenburg, Princess (1855-88), 95
Marie of Württemberg, Princess (1857-82), 65
Marie Pavlovna, Grand Duchess Vladimir of Russia (1854-1920), 166, 185
Marie-Henriette, Queen of the Belgians (1836-1902), 59
Marie, Duchess of Edinburgh, later Duchess of Saxe-Coburg Gotha, Grand Duchess of Russia (1853-1920), viii, 100, 111, 141
  early life, 30
  character, 30, 41, 74, 102, 150

  betrothal and marriage, 32-7
  at Clarence House and Osborne, 39-40
  musical interests, 41, 44-5
  question of precedence in England, 41-2, 46
  and birth of Alfred, 43
  at Eastwell Park, 43-4
  and Prince of Wales, 46
  at Balmoral, 47-8
  and Leopold (later Duke of Albany), 62-3
  unpopularity, 73
  at Coburg, 75, 101, 105-6
  and birth of Alexandra, 75
  escapes assassination (1880), 76
  and Alexander II's assassination and funeral, 77-8
  and birth of Beatrice, 78, 86
  at Alexander III's coronation, 86
  at Malta, 87
  and children, 91
  at Devonport, 102
  and Marie's betrothal and wedding, 103
  and Victoria Melita's betrothal and wedding, 107-8
  at deathbed of Alexander III, 109
  at diamond jubilee, 112
  family problems, and silver wedding, 122-3
  and Coburg succession, 123-8
  anxiety over daughters, 128-9, 151-2, 177-9, 189
  financial worries, 130
  invited by Queen Victoria to England, 131, 134
  returns briefly to Germany, 133-4
  and Queen's death, 135
  and lack of organization after Queen's death, 139-40
  returns to Germany after Queen's funeral, 140
  and Connaughts, 148, 159
  lays foundation stone of Nice Orthodox Church, 151
  and Victoria Melita's second marriage, 153-4
  at Ena's marriage, 161
  and Beatrice's betrothal and wedding, 165
  anger with Alfonso XIII, 165-6
  pays tribute to Edward VII, 169-70
  at George V's coronation, 175
  last visits to England and Russia, 182
  position in Germany during First World War, 185

228 Queen Victoria's Daughters-in-Law

anger at Roumania's entry into war on side of Entente, 190
fury against daughters, 191
sells jewellery and settles in Switzerland, 195
reunited with daughters, 196
last months, death and funeral, 197-8
Marie, Grand Duchess of Russia (1890-1958), 150
Marie, Princess of Orange-Nassau (1855-88), 59
Marie, Queen of Roumania ('Missy') (1875-1938), 200
  birth, 44
  Duchess of Edinburgh's letters to, 46
  childhood, 101-2
  and possibility of betrothal with cousin George, 103
  betrothal and wedding, 104
  birth of Carol, 107
  and Victoria Melita's betrothal and wedding, 107-8
  nurses Ferdinand through illness, 112
  and mother's letters to, 127, 131-2, 139, 165, 169, 182
  affair with Cantacuzino and marital crisis, 129
  at Edward VII's coronation, 144
  supports Britain in First World War, 185
  and Roumania in First World War, 189, 190
  invited by George V to bring family to England, 195
  attends peace conference in Paris, 195
  reunited with mother, and mother's death, 196-7
  barred from returning to Germany for mother's funeral, 198
Marie, Queen of Yugoslavia (1900-61), 130
Mary Adelaide of Cambridge, Princess, later Duchess of Teck (1833-97), 9, 13, 98, 113
Mary, Princess Royal (1897-1965), 175, 182
Mary, Queen (1867-1953), 23, 98, 201, 204
  betrothal to Duke of Clarence, 99
  and wedding to Duke of York, 100
  imperial tour (1901), 142
  created Princess of Wales, 149
  becomes queen, 173
  coronation, 174-5
  at Duchess of Connaught's funeral, 193
Massy, Martha, 149
Maud, Queen of Norway (1869-1938), 53

  birth, 25
  wedding, 101
Meiji, Emperor of Japan (1852-1912), 94
Merrick, Joseph (1862-90), 79
Michael, Grand Duke of Russia (1878-1918), 152, 161
  declines Russian throne, 190
  killed, 195
Mircea of Roumania, Prince (1913-7), 190
Morales, Mateo (1880-1906), 161

Napoleon III, Emperor of the French (1808-73), 155
Nicholas I, Tsar of Russia (1796-1855), 30
Nicholas II, Tsar of Russia (1868-1918), 152, 161
  at Duke and Duchess of York's wedding, 100
  betrothal, 108
  accession, 109
  coronation, 111
  converts Villa Bermond into cathedral, 151
  abdication, 190, 194
Nicholas, Grand Duke of Russia (1843-65), 30-1, 100, 151
Nicholls, Victoria, 119

O'Farrell, James (d.1868), 29
Olga, Grand Duchess (1882-1960), 176
Olga, Queen of Greece (1851-1926), 204
Olga, Queen of Württemberg (1822-92), 101
Otto, King of Greece (1815-67), 17

Paget, Sir Augustus (1823-96), 9
Paget, Sir James (1814-99), 24
Palmerston, Emily, Viscountess (1787-1869), 13
Patricia of Connaught, Princess (1886-1972), 93, 142, 159, 163, 193
  birth, 85
  'frightened of mother', 125
  considered as bride for Alfonso XIII, 156, 159-60
  in Portugal, Spain, and Africa, 157-8
Paul, Grand Duke of Russia (1860-1919), 31, 150, 190
  killed, 195
Picken, Hilda, 102
Pius X, Pope (1835-1914), 162
Ponsonby, Mary, Lady (1832-1916), 45
Ponsonby, Sir Frederick (1867-1935), 139, 170

Ponsonby, Sir Henry (1825-95), 53, 56, 80, 81
  and Alfred's betrothal, 34-5
  and Marie of Edinburgh's precedence, 41
Princip, Gavrilo (1894-1918), 183
Probyn, Sir Dighton (1833-1924), 79, 175-6, 203

Rama VI, King of Siam (1881-1925), 140
Rasputin, Grigori (c.1872-1916), 190
Reid, Dr James (1849-1923), 168
Rosebery, Archibald Primrose, Earl of (1847-1929), 144
Rubenstein, Anton (1829-94), 45
Rudolf, Crown Prince of Austria (1858-89), 63
Ruskin, John (1819-1900), 68-9
Russell, Lord Odo (1829-84), 57

Serge, Grand Duke of Russia (1857-1905), 31, 76, 86, 91, 150, 151
  assassination and funeral, 153
Shuvalov, Count Peter (1827-89), 33
Sipido, Jean-Baptiste (1884-1959), 117
Smirnoff, Eugene (1846-1923), 154
Smith, John Taylor, 113
Sohn, Carl (1845-1928), 73-4
Sophie, Duchess of Hohenberg (1868-1914), 183
Sophie, Queen of Greece (1870-1932), 106, 133
Sophie, Queen of the Netherlands (1818-77), 40
Stanley, Arthur, Dean of Westminster (1815-81), 36
Stanley, Lady Augusta (1821-76), 36
Stephanie of Belgium, Princess (1863-1945), 63
Stockmar, Baron Christian von (1787-1863), 4
Sullivan, Sir Arthur (1842-1900), 45

Taylor, Ella, 67
Tennyson, Alfred, Lord (1809-92), 69
Thyra, Duchess of Cumberland (1853-1933), 7, 54
Tuxen, Lauritz (1853-1927), 91

Vacarescu, Helene (1864-1922), 104
Victoria Adelaide, Duchess of Saxe-Coburg Gotha (1885-1970), 155, 166
Victoria Melita of Edinburgh, Princess, later Grand Duchess of Hesse and the Rhine, later Grand Duchess Cyril of Russia ('Ducky') (1876-1936), 134
  birth, 74, 87
  childhood, 101-2
  first betrothal and wedding, 107-8
  and problems in first marriage, 128-9
  depression, temper, and stillborn child, 130-1, 133, 152
  divorced, 151
  second betrothal and wedding, 152-4
  and mother's visits to Russia, 182
  loyalties during First World War, 185
  escapes from Russia with family during revolution, 189, 195
  accuses relations of abandoning her, 190
  reunited with mother and her death, 197
  letter to Xenia, 198
  and Duchess of Albany, 199
Victoria of Baden, Princess, later Queen of Sweden (1862-1930), 63
Victoria of Hesse and the Rhine, Princess, later Marchioness of Milford Haven (1863-1950), 71
Victoria, Duchess of Kent (1786-1861), viii, 3, 16, 18
Victoria of Wales, Princess (1868-1935), 24, 175, 176, 187, 204
  birth, 23
  shyness, 53
Victoria, Princess Royal, later German Empress (1840-1901), 6, 35, 78
  birth, 3
  and question of bride for Prince of Wales, 8-10, 13-4, 17, 22-4
  and birth of Albert Victor, 18
  and Queen Victoria's annoyances over Princess of Wales's children, 19, 21
  suggests Louise as bride for Duke of Connaught, 55
  at Connaughts' wedding, 60
  and death of husband, 96-7
  on Duchess of Edinburgh, 106
  recommends school in Germany for Charles, 128
  suffers from cancer, 133, 135
  death and funeral, 143
Victoria, Queen (1819-1901), 98, 109, 117, 146, 204
  character, viii-ix
  wedding and birth of children, 3, 123
  praises Arthur during boyhood, and over-protective of Leopold, 5

and Prince of Wales' visit to North America, 6
and question of wife for Prince of Wales, 8-11
and betrothal and wedding of Prince and Princess of Wales, 12-4
and Schleswig-Holstein disputes, 17
and birth of Albert Victor of Wales, 18
and relations with Princess of Wales, 19, 22, 24, 62
and birth of Victoria of Wales, 23
suggests Prince and Princess of Wales should retire into mourning for Alexander John, 26
at Sandringham and Prince of Wales's typhoid, 27
and Edinburghs' betrothal and wedding, 30-2, 34-6
and Duchess of Edinburgh, 38-43, 47-8
and Connaughts' betrothal and wedding, 55
on Prince and Princess of Wales' children, 61
and Albanys' betrothal and wedding, 65
relations with Duchess of Albany, 66-7, 70, 72
and Leopold's death and funeral, 67-9
and Beatrice and Henry's betrothal and wedding, 71
and Duchess of Edinburgh, 73-4, 87
and Russo-Turkish war, 75
lets sons and daughters-in-law attend Alexander II's funeral, 77
disliked by Alexander III, 78
and Egyptian crisis, 81
and Duke of Connaught's army career and promotion, 84
and golden jubilee, 86
and 1887 jubilee, 91
and Connaughts in India, 92-3
and Duke of Clarence's death, 99-100
and Marie Duchess of Edinburgh, 101
and Victoria Melita's marriage, 107-8
and Sandra of Coburg's betrothal, 110
diamond jubilee, 112

close relationship with Albanys, 120
supports Connaughts in Coburg succession, 125-6, 184
helps pay off Coburg debts, 130
invites Duchess of Coburg to England, 131
and Duke of Coburg's death, 132
death, 135, 139, 163
funeral, 140
and family unity, 141
Vigneau, Mr, 154
Villalobar, Rodrigo de Saavedra y Vinent, Marquis de (1864-1926), 155-6, 160
Vladimir, Grand Duke of Russia (1847-1909), 31, 154, 161

Waldemar of Denmark, Prince (1858-1939), 7
Warwick, Frances, Countess of, formerly Maynard, Frances (1861-1938), 63, 98
Wellington, Arthur Wellesley, Duke of (1769-1852), 4
Westminster, Beatrice, Duchess of (1858-1911), 160
Willem III, King of the Netherlands (1817-90), 59. 65
William I, German Emperor (1797-1888), 22, 43, 55, 56
death, 96
William II, Emperor (1859-1941), 96, 103, 108, 123, 168
and Coburg succession, 125-8
at Empress Frederick's funeral, 143
and Charles' education in Germany, 145
William II, King of Württemberg (1848-1921), 127
Wilson, Lilian, 152
Winter, Elizabeth Saxton, 129-30, 151
Wolrad of Waldeck and Pyrmont, Prince (1892-1914), 187
Wolseley, Garnet, Viscount (1833-1913), 115

Xenia, Grand Duchess of Russia (1875-1960), 198, 202